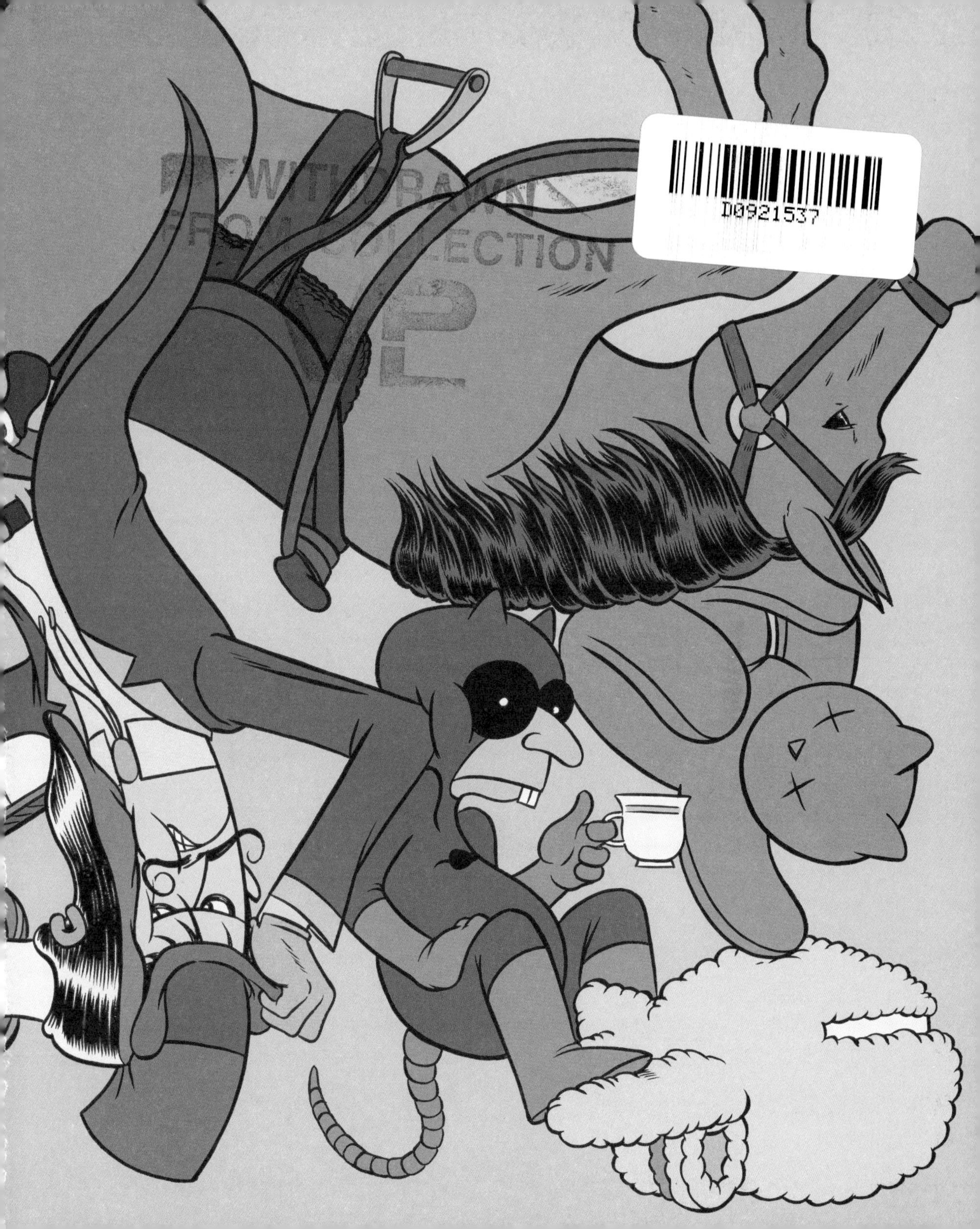

FOR MY MOTHER
WHO GAVE ME GAHAN WILSON

WRITTEN AND DRAWN BY PAUL HORNSCHEMEIER
PUBLISHED BY GARY GROTH AND KIM THOMPSON
PROMOTED BY ERIC REYNOLDS
BOOK DESIGN BY THE AUTHOR

ISBN-10: 1-56097-752-3
ISBN-13: 978-1-56097-752-0

PRINTED IN SINGAPORE

FIRST EDITION: SEPTEMBER 2006

LET US BE PERFECTLY CLEAR PUBLISHED BY FANTAGRAPHICS BOOKS, 7563 LAKE CITY WAY
NE, SEATTLE, WA 98115. WWW.FANTAGRAPHICS.COM. FORLORN FUNNIES, ALL RELATED STORIES,
ART, AND CHARACTERS ARE © COPYRIGHT 2002, 2003, 2004, 2005, AND 2006 PAUL
HORNSCHEMEIER. ALL RIGHTS RESERVED. NO PORTION OF THIS PUBLICATION MAY BE REPRODUCED
(EXCEPT FOR SHORT EXCERPTS FOR PURPOSE OF REVIEW) WITHOUT THE WRITTEN PERMISSION
OF PAUL HORNSCHEMEIER OR FANTAGRAPHICS BOOKS.

PORTIONS OF THIS COLLECTION WERE PUBLISHED PREVIOUSLY IN THE CHICAGO READER,
CHUNKLET MAGAZINE, AND FORLORN FUNNIES.

PERFECTLY CLEAR

CONTENTS

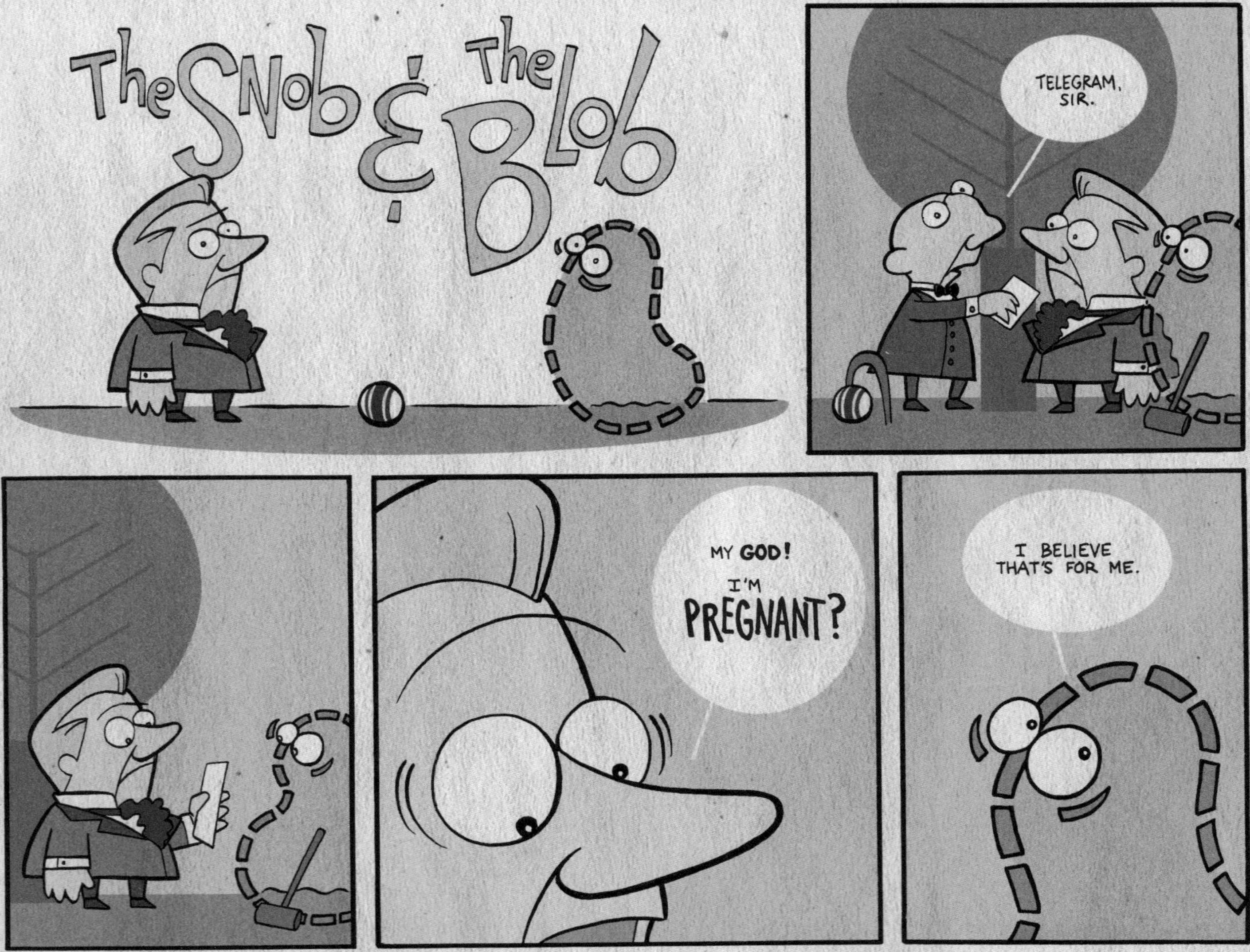
The Snob & The Blob
TELEGRAM, SIR.
MY GOD! I'M PREGNANT?
I BELIEVE THAT'S FOR ME.

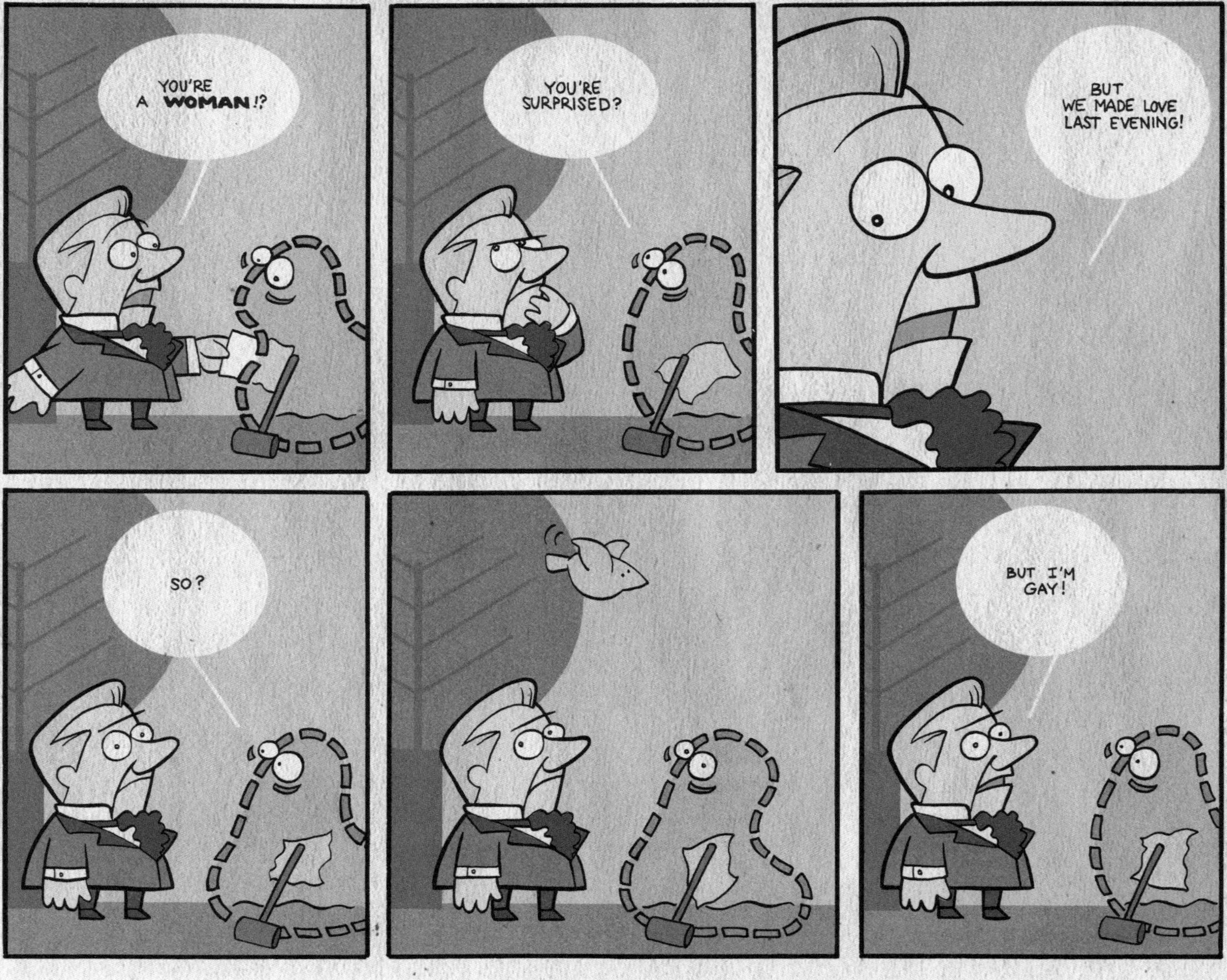
YOU'RE A **WOMAN**!?
YOU'RE SURPRISED?
BUT WE MADE LOVE LAST EVENING!
SO?
BUT I'M GAY!

EVERYONE FELT IT

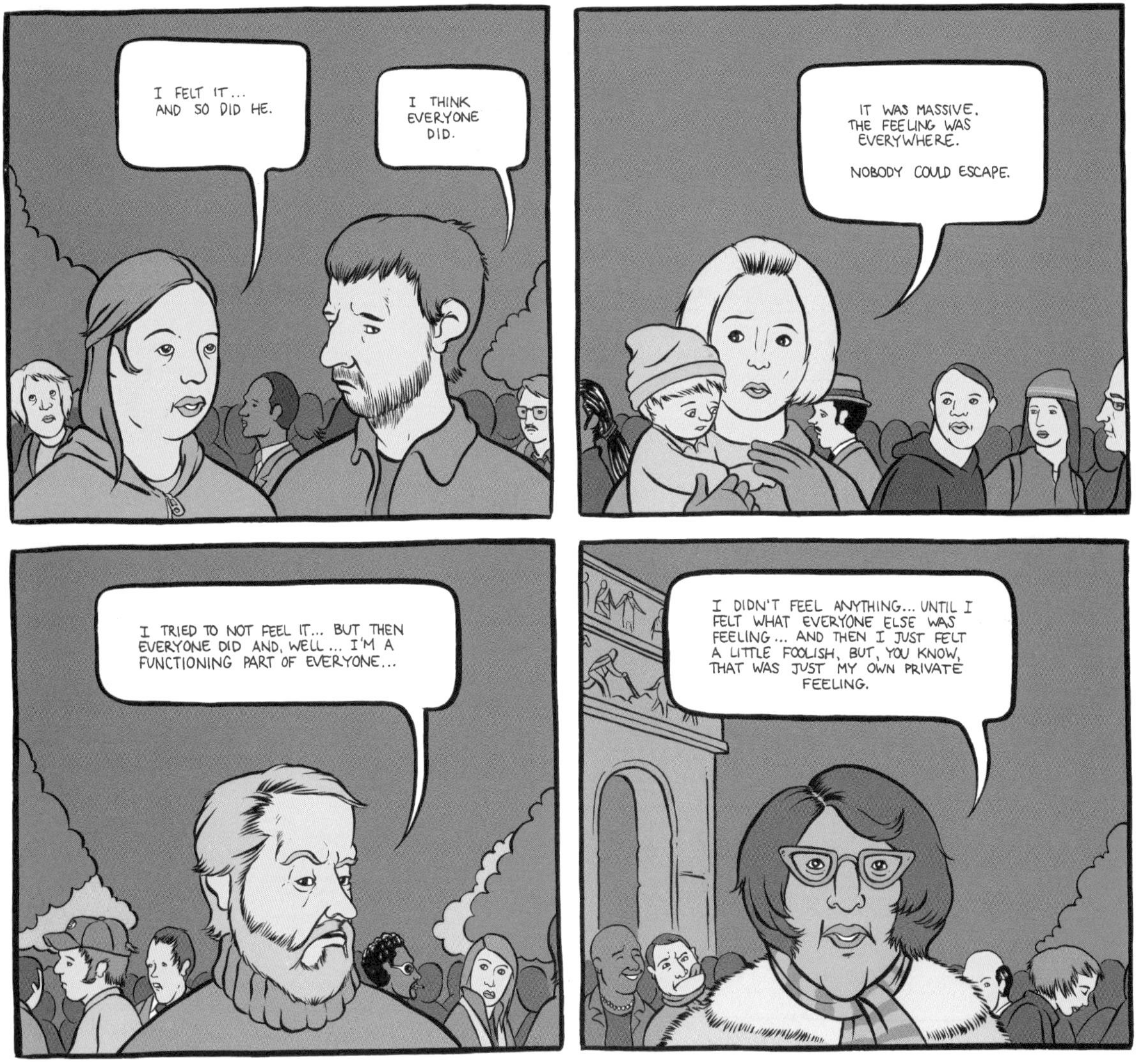
I FELT IT... AND SO DID HE.
I THINK EVERYONE DID.
IT WAS MASSIVE. THE FEELING WAS EVERYWHERE.
NOBODY COULD ESCAPE.
I TRIED TO NOT FEEL IT... BUT THEN EVERYONE DID AND, WELL... I'M A FUNCTIONING PART OF EVERYONE...
I DIDN'T FEEL ANYTHING... UNTIL I FELT WHAT EVERYONE ELSE WAS FEELING... AND THEN I JUST FELT A LITTLE FOOLISH, BUT, YOU KNOW, THAT WAS JUST MY OWN PRIVATE FEELING.

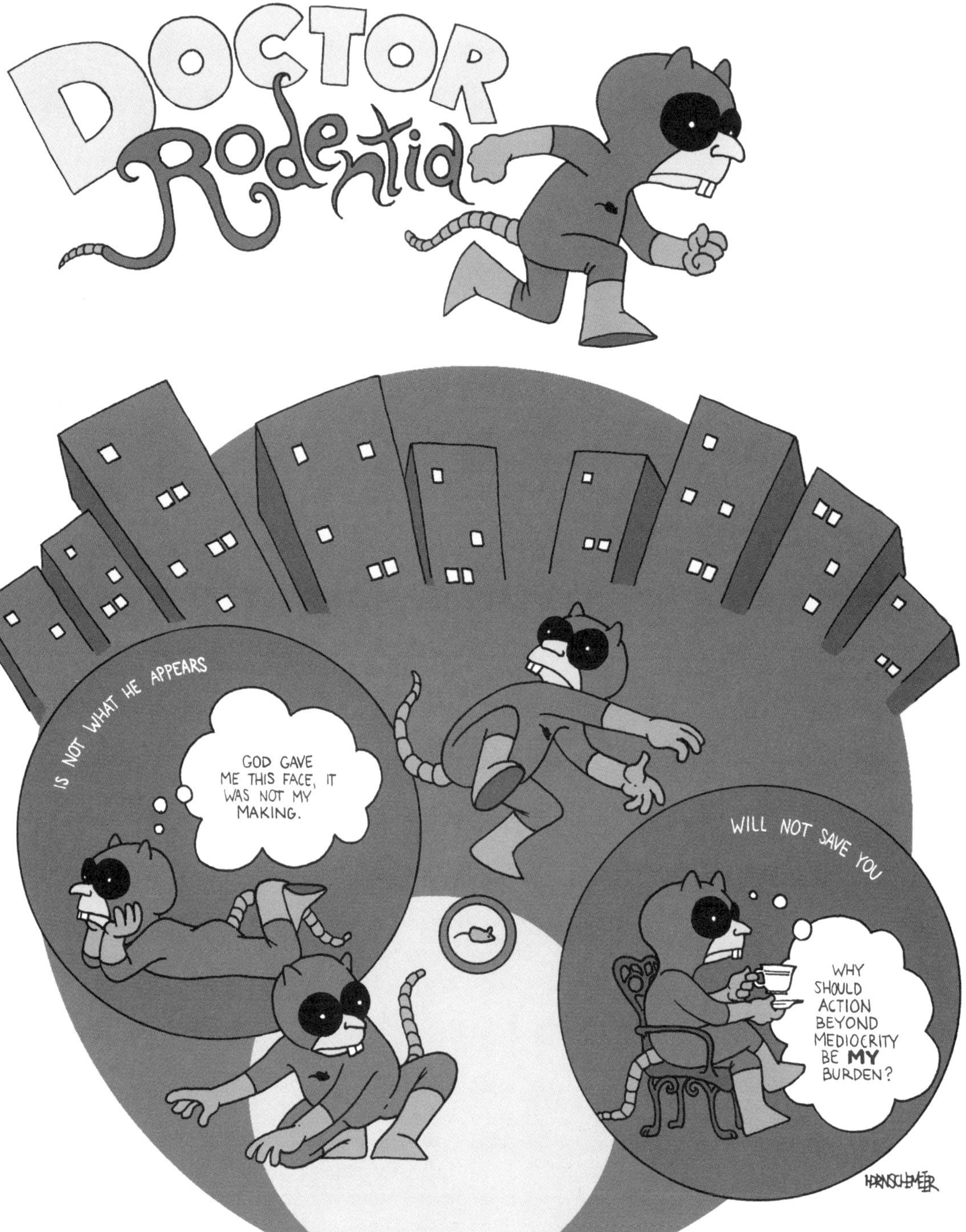
DOCTOR Rodentia
IS NOT WHAT HE APPEARS
GOD GAVE ME THIS FACE, IT WAS NOT MY MAKING.
WILL NOT SAVE YOU
WHY SHOULD ACTION BEYOND MEDIOCRITY BE **MY** BURDEN?
HORNSCHEMEIER

FEELINGS CHECK

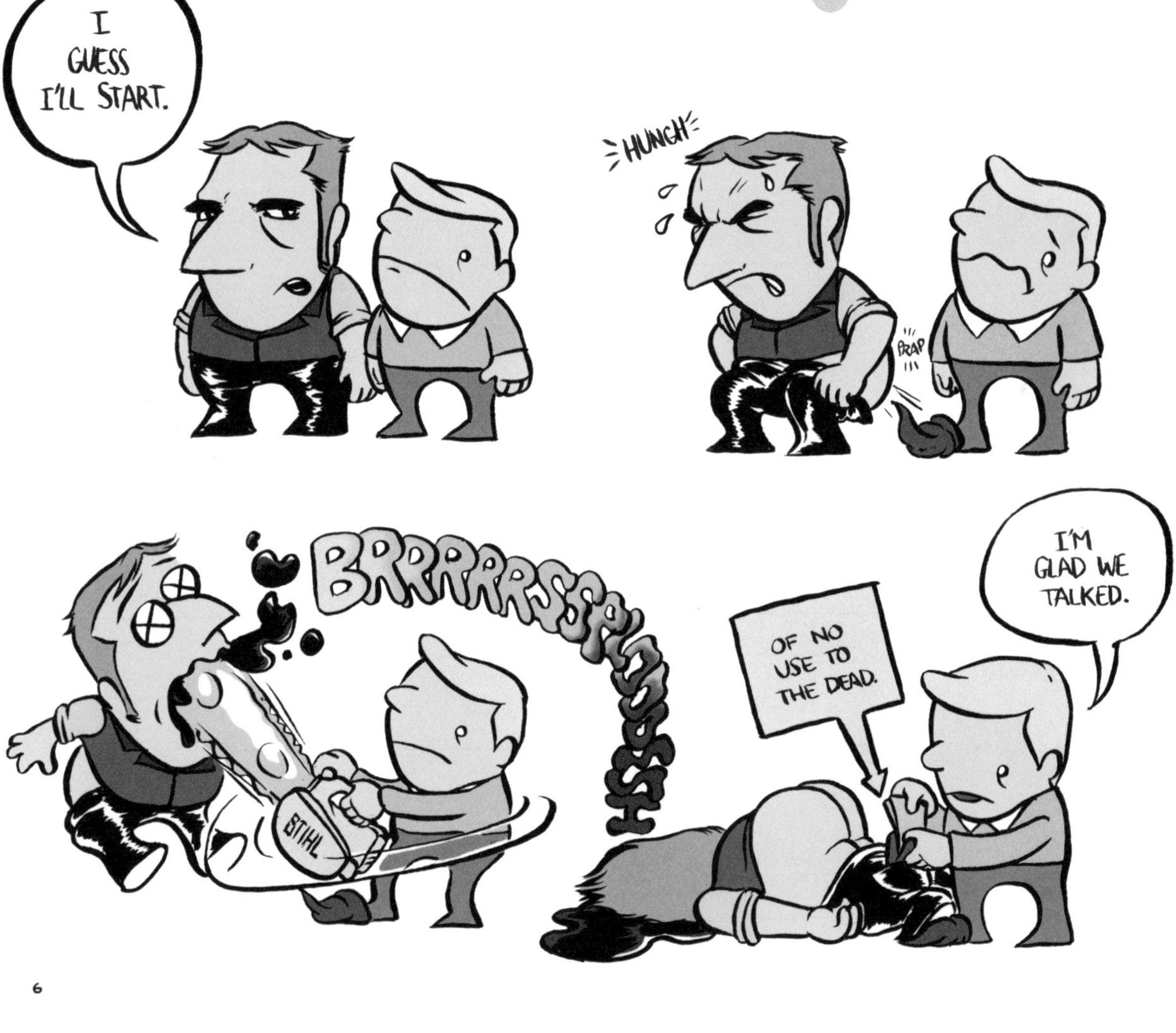

ARTIST'S
CATALOGUE

———————

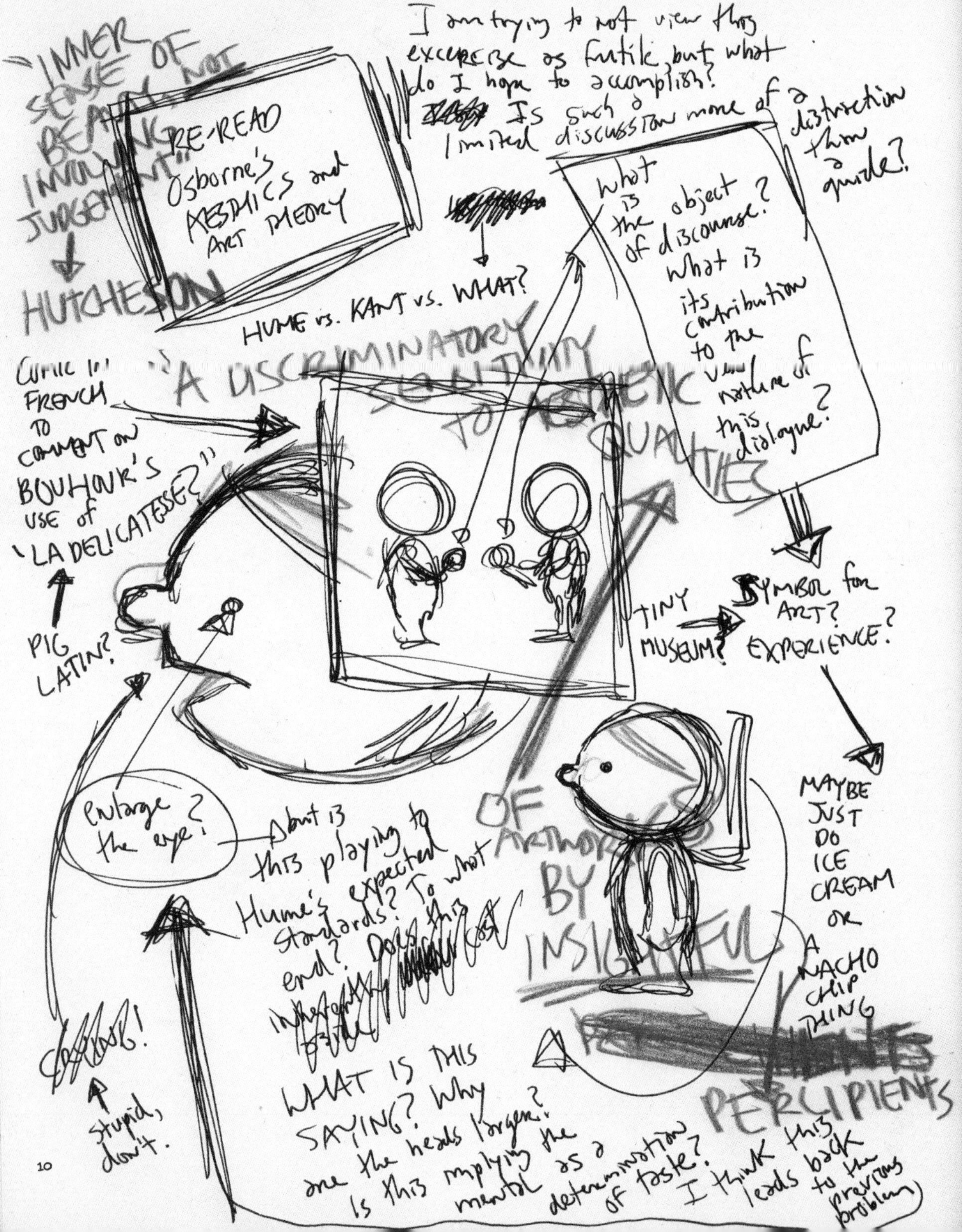
"INNER SENSE OF BEAUTY NOT INVOLVING JUDGEMENT"
HUTCHESON
RE-READ Osborne's AESTHETICS and ART THEORY
I am trying to not view this excercise as futile, but what do I hope to accomplish? Is such a limited discussion more of a distraction than a guide?
HUME vs. KANT vs. WHAT?
what is the object of discourse? What is its contribution to the nature of this dialogue?
"A DISCRIMINATORY SENSITIVITY TO AESTHETIC QUALITIES OF ARTWORKS BY INSIGHTFUL PERCIPIENTS
Comic in FRENCH to comment on BOUHOUR'S use of 'LA DELICATESSE?"
PIG LATIN?
TINY MUSEUM?
SYMBOL for ART? EXPERIENCE?
MAYBE JUST DO ICE CREAM OR A NACHO CHIP THING
Enlarge? the eye?
But is this playing to Hume's expected standards? To what end? Does this
CRAP!
stupid, don't.
WHAT IS THIS SAYING? Why are the heads larger? Is this implying the mental as a determination of taste? I think this leads back to the previous problem

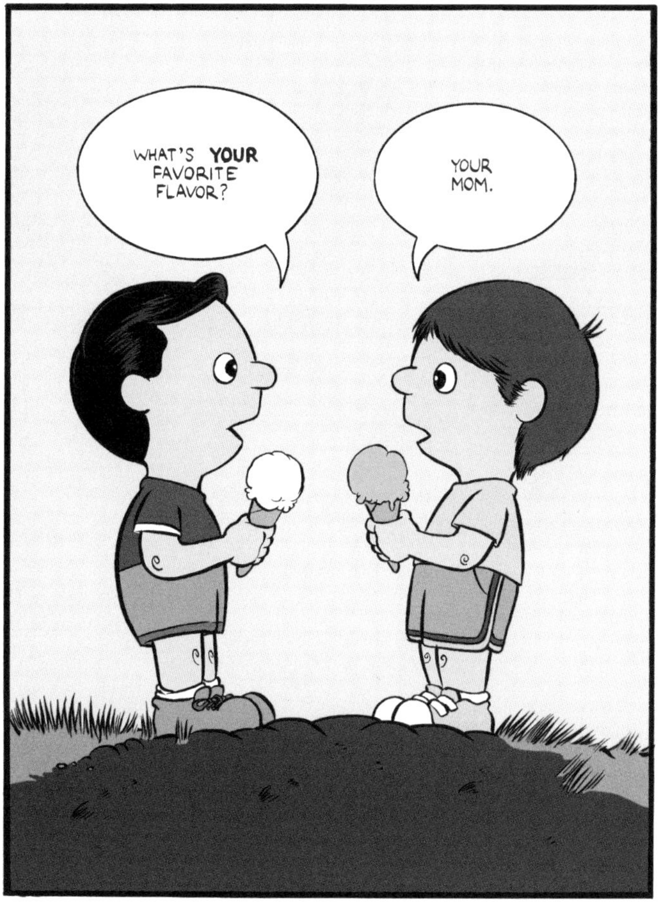
WHAT'S **YOUR** FAVORITE FLAVOR?
YOUR MOM.

Stupid Art Comics ARE STUPID

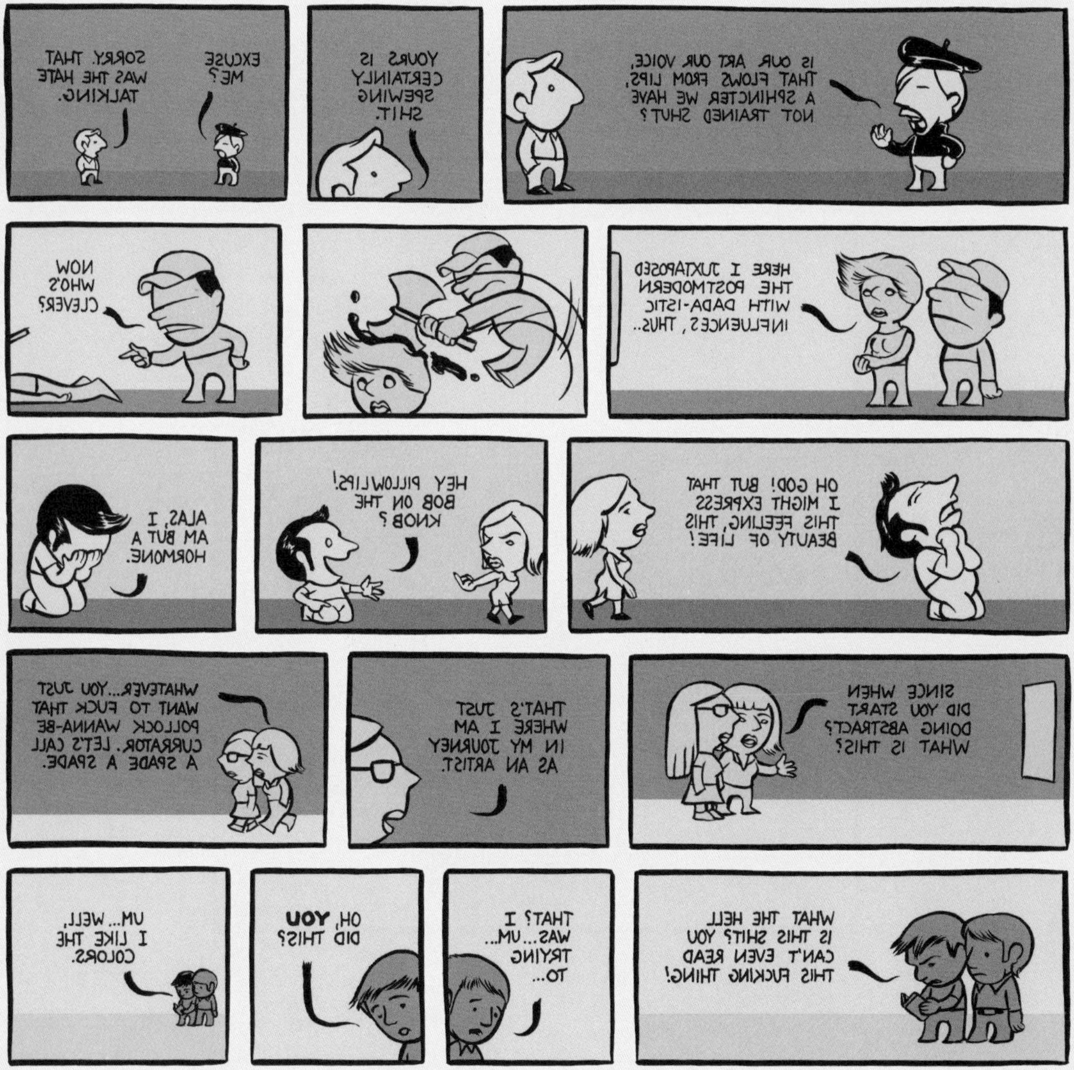
WHAT THE HELL IS THIS SHIT? YOU CAN'T EVEN READ THIS FUCKING THING!
THAT? I WAS...UM... TRYING TO...
OH, **YOU** DID THIS?
UM...WELL, I LIKE THE COLORS.
SINCE WHEN DID YOU START DOING ABSTRACT? WHAT IS THIS?
THAT'S JUST WHERE I AM IN MY JOURNEY AS AN ARTIST.
WHATEVER...YOU JUST WANT TO FUCK THAT POLLOCK WANNA-BE CURRATOR. LET'S CALL A SPADE A SPADE.
OH GOD! BUT THAT I MIGHT EXPRESS THIS FEELING, THIS BEAUTY OF LIFE!
HEY PILLOWLIPS! BOB ON THE KNOB?
ALAS, I AM BUT A HORMONE.
HERE I JUXTAPOSED THE POSTMODERN WITH DADA-ISTIC INFLUENCES, THUS..
NOW WHO'S CLEVER?
IS OUR ART OUR VOICE, THAT FLOWS FROM LIPS, A SPHINCTER WE HAVE NOT TRAINED SHUT?
YOURS IS CERTAINLY SPEWING SHIT.
EXCUSE ME?
SORRY. THAT WAS THE HATE TALKING.

GUEST CRITIQUE BY CHARLES LIPP

STUPID ART COMICS MAY BE STUPID, BUT "STUPID ART COMICS ARE STUPID" IS A COMPLETE WASTE OF TIME

There is nothing better, or more apt to relieve one of tension, than a well-delivered, well-written piece of comedy. The healing power of laughter is something into which I have long ago bought, and I often testify to friends and family that life would be a richer experience, if only they would learn to lighten up. That being said, Paul Hornschemeier should be burned at the stake.

I'm not ruling out nastiness beforehand, please note, I simply feel that burning is a good way to round out the whole evening of a populace - or, more accurately, the six or seven people who actual undergo the torture of Hornschemeier's work – acting in a unified movement: broadcasting clearly that this must stop.

The latest in a string of offenses, Hornschemeier's "Stupid Art Comics Are Stupid" manages to be simultaneously offensive and boring, a task for which I think the artist was clearly predestined.

In "Stupid Art Comics," Hornschemeier has opted for, rather than making the cartoon understandable or – dare we ask for such things – readable, making the cartoon horribly pretentious. The cartoon is displayed such that it can only be read with the publication housing it being held upside down and then only if viewed via a mirror.

How clever! What a brave and scathing commentary on the art world! My blatant sarcasm here is almost as readily evident as Hornschemeier's obvious use of formal masturbation as a means to compensate for his deficit of talent, inspiration, technical skill, and wit.

The brute fact of the matter is that this cartoon does not improve or worsen with the difficulty of reading it in a mirror: it is immutably awful. The "jokes" – I use this word hesitantly – are crass without the appeal of a standard base gag, and as actual commentary comment on nothing more than, oh, look there, you need to clean that spot on your mirror.

This cartoon seems to view things like, "humans have conflicted interests," or "sometimes people change themselves to obtain love or acceptance," or "people like to have sex," as mind-boggling revelations, by which the reader will be both shocked and amused. So, if you are a third grade student in an Amish community, this piece may appeal to you. You may need to also have some sort of severe frontal lobe damage, but we'll give Hornschemeier the benefit of a doubt.

What is Hornschemeier's view on this pretension he is so convinced he is satirizing? Is he for or against it? While he is certainly *participating* in it,

his views on this or any subject are as muddied as his forced dialogue and uncomfortable line. Trying to form an opinion based on Hornschemeier's rhetoric is as improbable as is his being considered a cartoonist.

To be fair: It has been said that great art makes us turn a critical eye inward, examining our lives and choices, our environment and place in history. And in this respect, "Stupid Art Comics" could justifiably be considered some of the greatest art ever set to paper (though it pains me to acknowledge this loophole). While holding this mistake born of ink and incompetence, I often found myself questioning: "why do I bother reading pieces from self-evidently substandard authors?" and "why do I take commissions for pointless essays (he's horrible, how many ways does any one person need to write it? Not that it isn't fun to do so)?" and "why don't I clean my mirror more often?" What a powerfully introspective trek. So I suppose that's Hornschemeier: one, Art: zero (note to self: work on revised definition for great art).

I truly feel that, should this artist continue to work diligently, he will make great contributions to landfills, but not, it is plain from this and other examples, to anything approaching the field of art, stupid or otherwise.

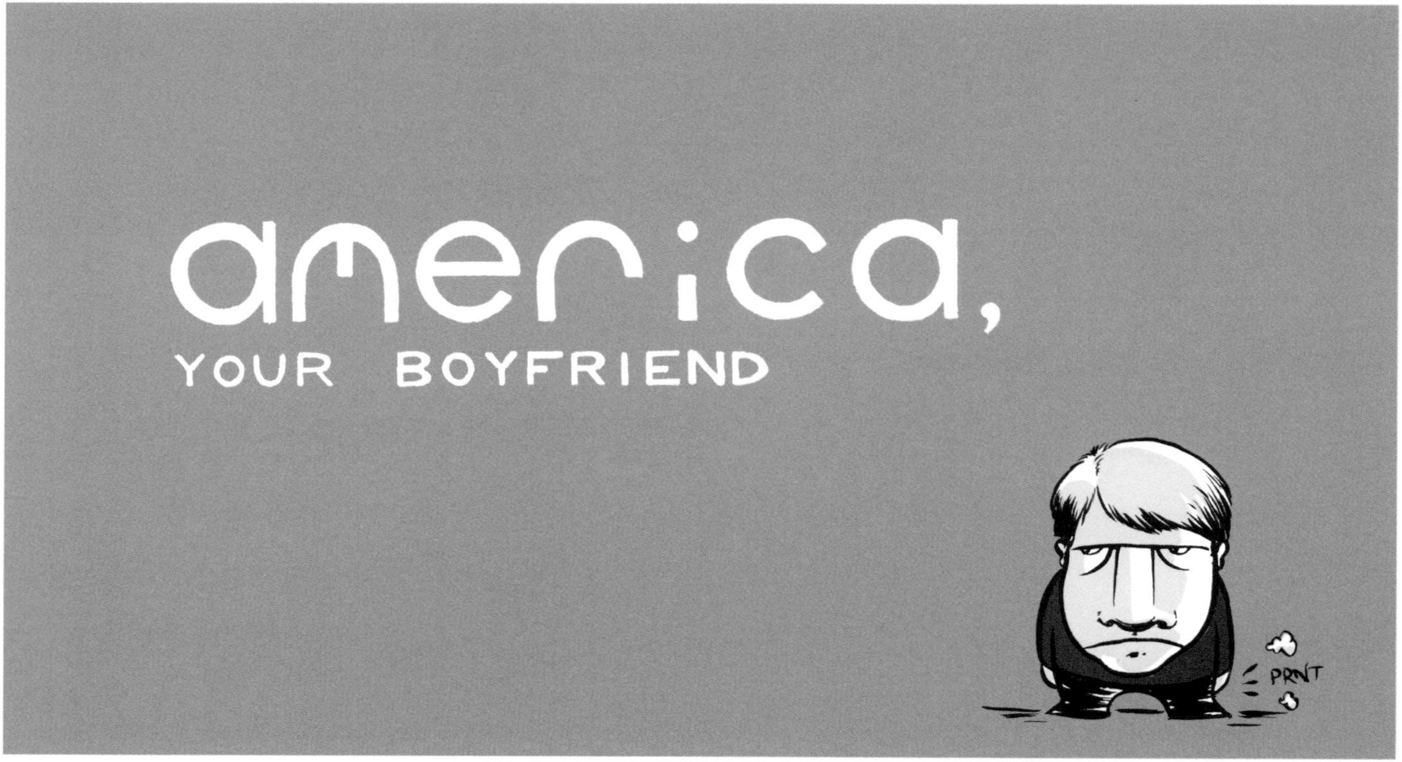
america,
YOUR BOYFRIEND
PRNT

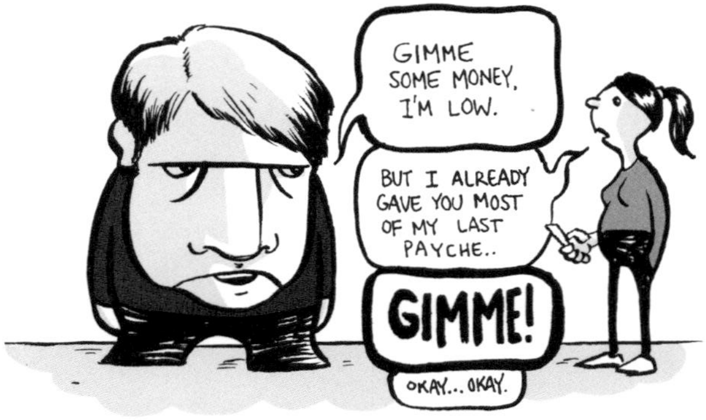
GIMME SOME MONEY, I'M LOW.
BUT I ALREADY GAVE YOU MOST OF MY LAST PAYCHE..
GIMME!
OKAY... OKAY.

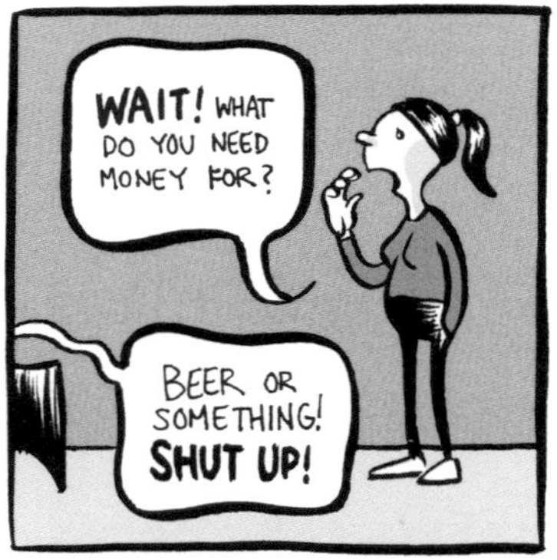
WAIT! WHAT DO YOU NEED MONEY FOR?
BEER OR SOMETHING! SHUT UP!

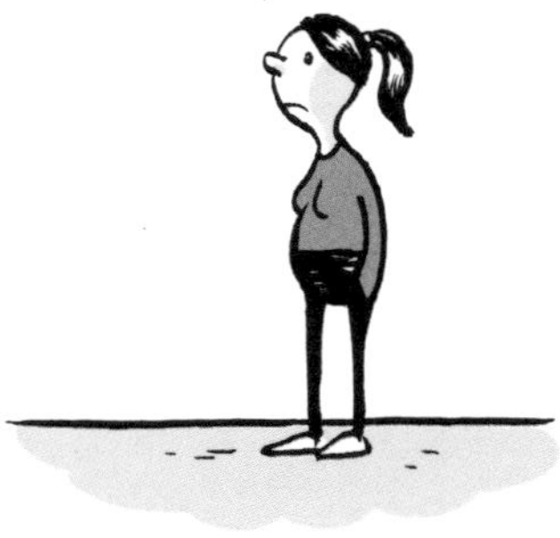

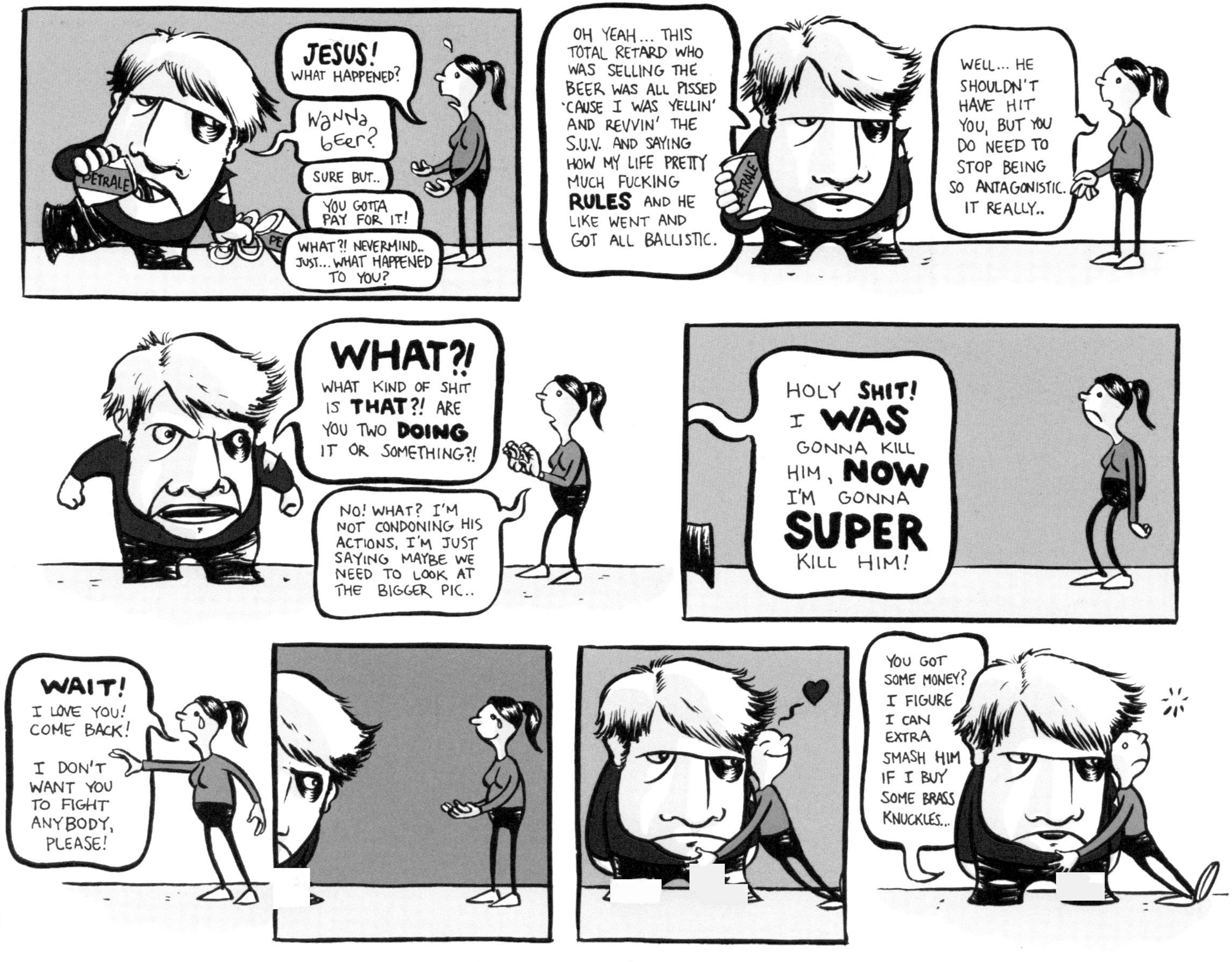
JESUS! WHAT HAPPENED?
Wanna beer?
SURE BUT..
YOU GOTTA PAY FOR IT!
WHAT?! NEVERMIND.. JUST... WHAT HAPPENED TO YOU?
PETRALE
OH YEAH... THIS TOTAL RETARD WHO WAS SELLING THE BEER WAS ALL PISSED 'CAUSE I WAS YELLIN' AND REVVIN' THE S.U.V. AND SAYING HOW MY LIFE PRETTY MUCH FUCKING RULES AND HE LIKE WENT AND GOT ALL BALLISTIC.
PETRALE
WELL... HE SHOULDN'T HAVE HIT YOU, BUT YOU DO NEED TO STOP BEING SO ANTAGONISTIC. IT REALLY..
WHAT?! WHAT KIND OF SHIT IS THAT?! ARE YOU TWO DOING IT OR SOMETHING?!
NO! WHAT? I'M NOT CONDONING HIS ACTIONS, I'M JUST SAYING MAYBE WE NEED TO LOOK AT THE BIGGER PIC..
HOLY SHIT! I WAS GONNA KILL HIM, NOW I'M GONNA SUPER KILL HIM!
WAIT! I LOVE YOU! COME BACK!
I DON'T WANT YOU TO FIGHT ANYBODY, PLEASE!
YOU GOT SOME MONEY? I FIGURE I CAN EXTRA SMASH HIM IF I BUY SOME BRASS KNUCKLES...

ditty AND THE Pillow Plane

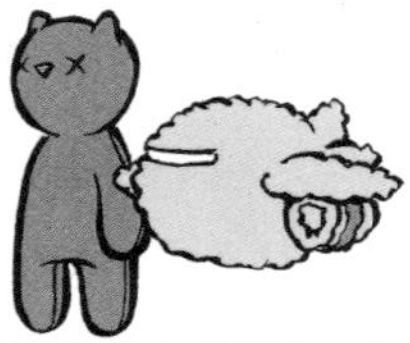

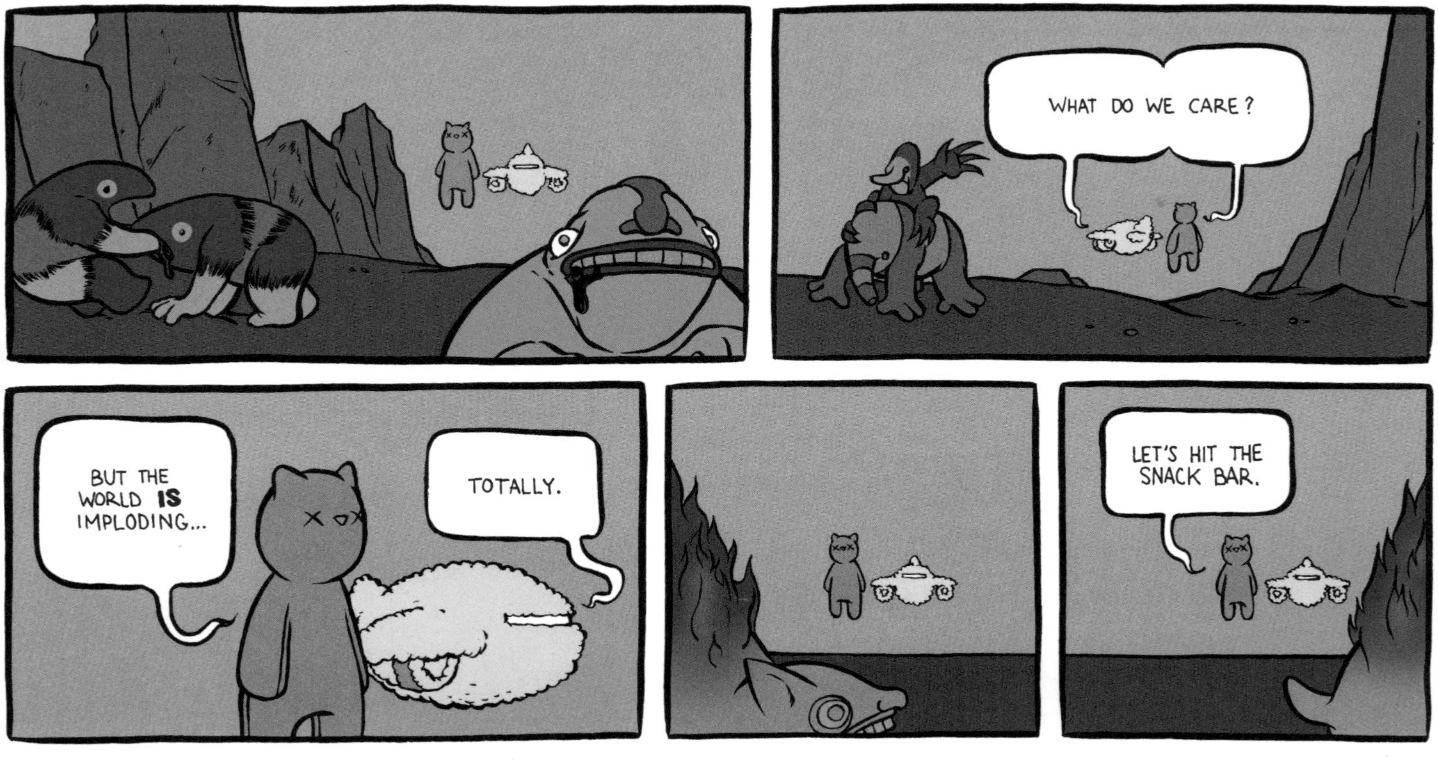
WHAT DO WE CARE?
BUT THE WORLD **IS** IMPLODING...
TOTALLY.
LET'S HIT THE SNACK BAR.

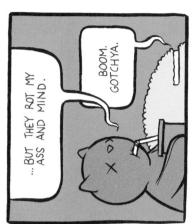

SNACK BAR
I ONLY DESIRE THE "BAD" THINGS...
1,000 HEDONS!
...BUT THEY ROT MY ASS AND MIND.
BOOM. GOTCHYA.
SIP
SIP
SNACK BAR
IS CIVILIZATION A CANCER?
OF THE KIDNEY, DITTY.

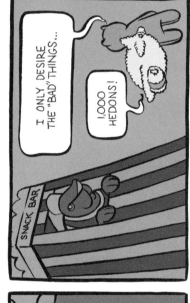

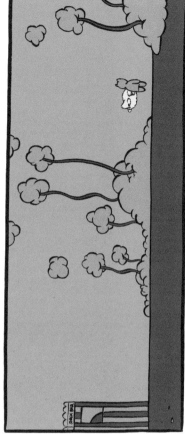

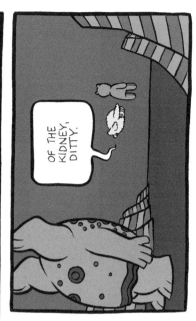

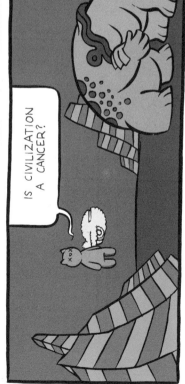

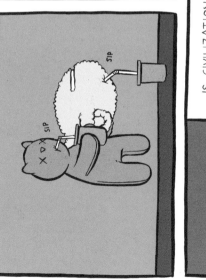

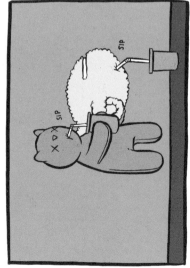

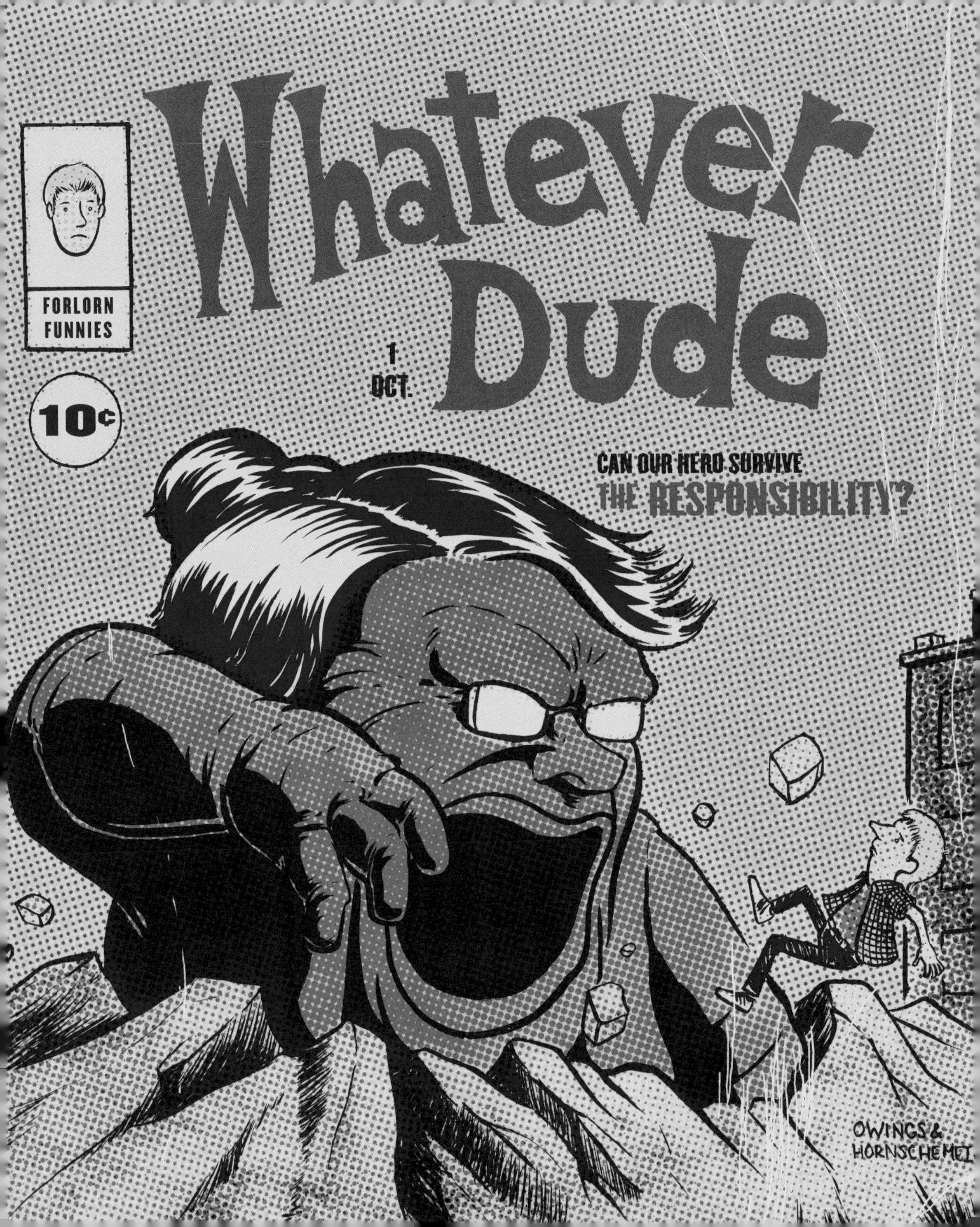
FORLORN FUNNIES
10¢
Whatever Dude
1
OCT.
CAN OUR HERO SURVIVE
THE RESPONSIBILITY?
OWINGS &
HORNSCHEMEI

YOU HAVE TO BUILD SOMETHING WITH YOUR LIFE! HOW CAN YOU NOT? HOW CAN YOU SIT IDLY BY AND LET POTENTIAL SLIP AWAY?
THINK OF THE BUSINESSES YOU COULD OWN! THINK OF THE GOVERNMENTS YOU COULD RUN! WE ARE ASWIM IN OPPORTUNITY, YET YOU ONLY BOB! A BUOYANT BOOB, IS THAT ALL YOU ARE?
OUR HERO SUMMONS HIS POWER.
WHATEVER DUDE.

WHATEVER DUDE CLASSICS

BY OWINGS & HORNSCHEMEIER

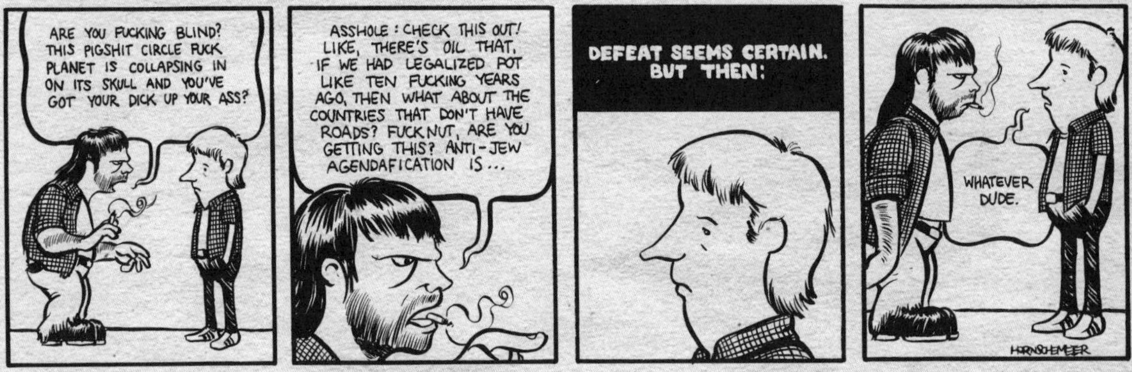
ARE YOU FUCKING BLIND? THIS PIGSHIT CIRCLE FUCK PLANET IS COLLAPSING IN ON ITS SKULL AND YOU'VE GOT YOUR DICK UP YOUR ASS?
ASSHOLE: CHECK THIS OUT! LIKE, THERE'S OIL THAT, IF WE HAD LEGALIZED POT LIKE TEN FUCKING YEARS AGO, THEN WHAT ABOUT THE COUNTRIES THAT DON'T HAVE ROADS? FUCKNUT, ARE YOU GETTING THIS? ANTI-JEW AGENDAFICATION IS...
DEFEAT SEEMS CERTAIN. BUT THEN:
WHATEVER DUDE.
HORNSCHEMEIER

REVENGE OF THE ANTI-WHATEVER DUDE

BY OWINGS & HORNSCHEMEIER

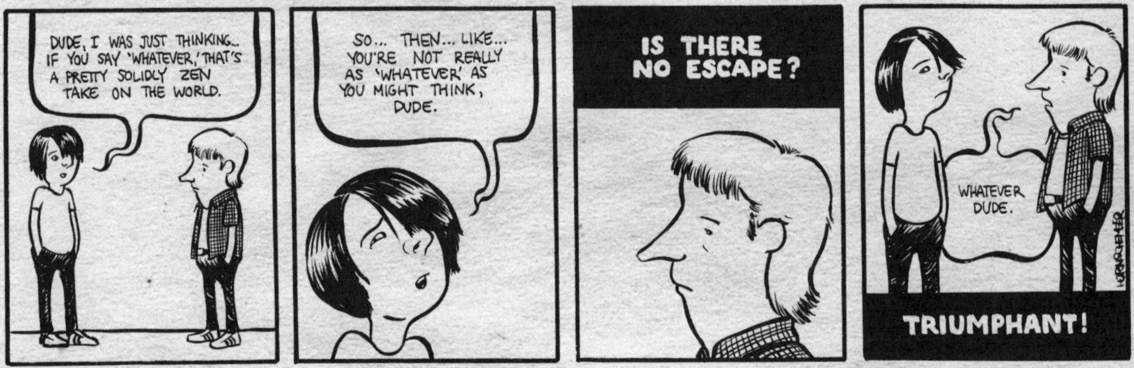
DUDE, I WAS JUST THINKING... IF YOU SAY 'WHATEVER,' THAT'S A PRETTY SOLIDLY ZEN TAKE ON THE WORLD.
SO... THEN... LIKE... YOU'RE NOT REALLY AS 'WHATEVER' AS YOU MIGHT THINK, DUDE.
IS THERE NO ESCAPE?
WHATEVER DUDE.
HORNSCHEMEIER
TRIUMPHANT!

WHATEVER BABIES

BY OWINGS & HORNSCHEMEIER

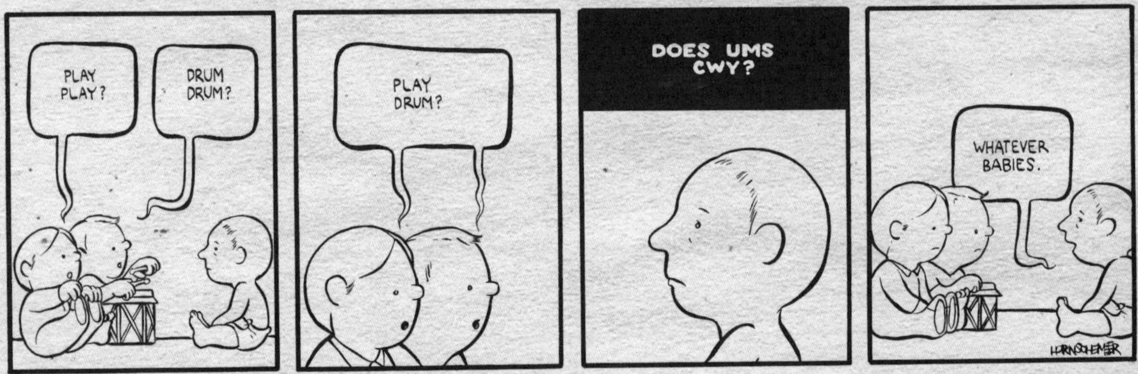
PLAY PLAY?
DRUM DRUM?
PLAY DRUM?
DOES UMS CWY?
WHATEVER BABIES.
HORNSCHEMEIER

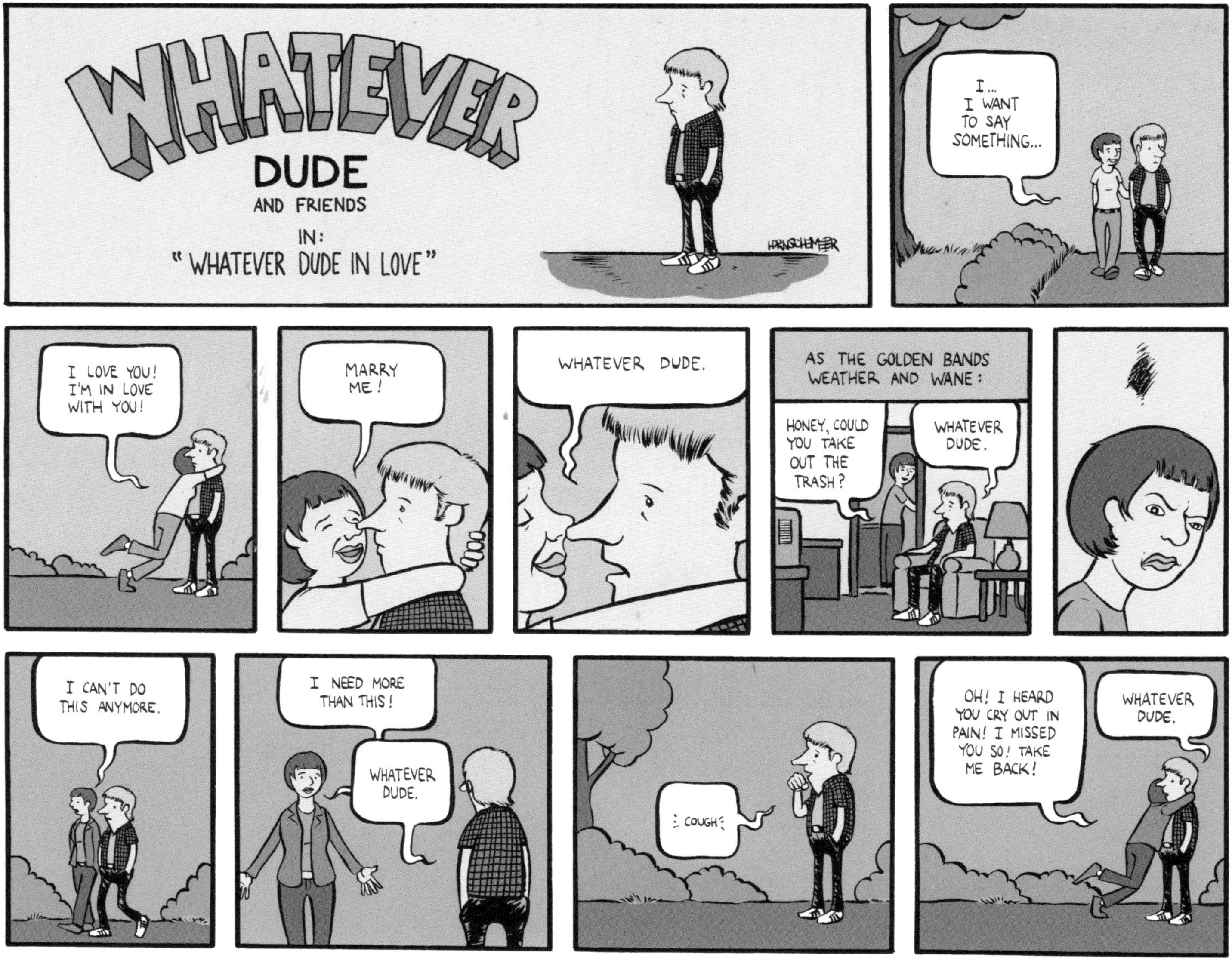
WHATEVER
DUDE
AND FRIENDS
IN:
"WHATEVER DUDE IN LOVE"
HORNSCHEMEIER
I... I WANT TO SAY SOMETHING...
I LOVE YOU! I'M IN LOVE WITH YOU!
MARRY ME!
WHATEVER DUDE.
AS THE GOLDEN BANDS WEATHER AND WANE:
HONEY, COULD YOU TAKE OUT THE TRASH?
WHATEVER DUDE.
I CAN'T DO THIS ANYMORE.
I NEED MORE THAN THIS!
WHATEVER DUDE.
COUGH
OH! I HEARD YOU CRY OUT IN PAIN! I MISSED YOU SO! TAKE ME BACK!
WHATEVER DUDE.

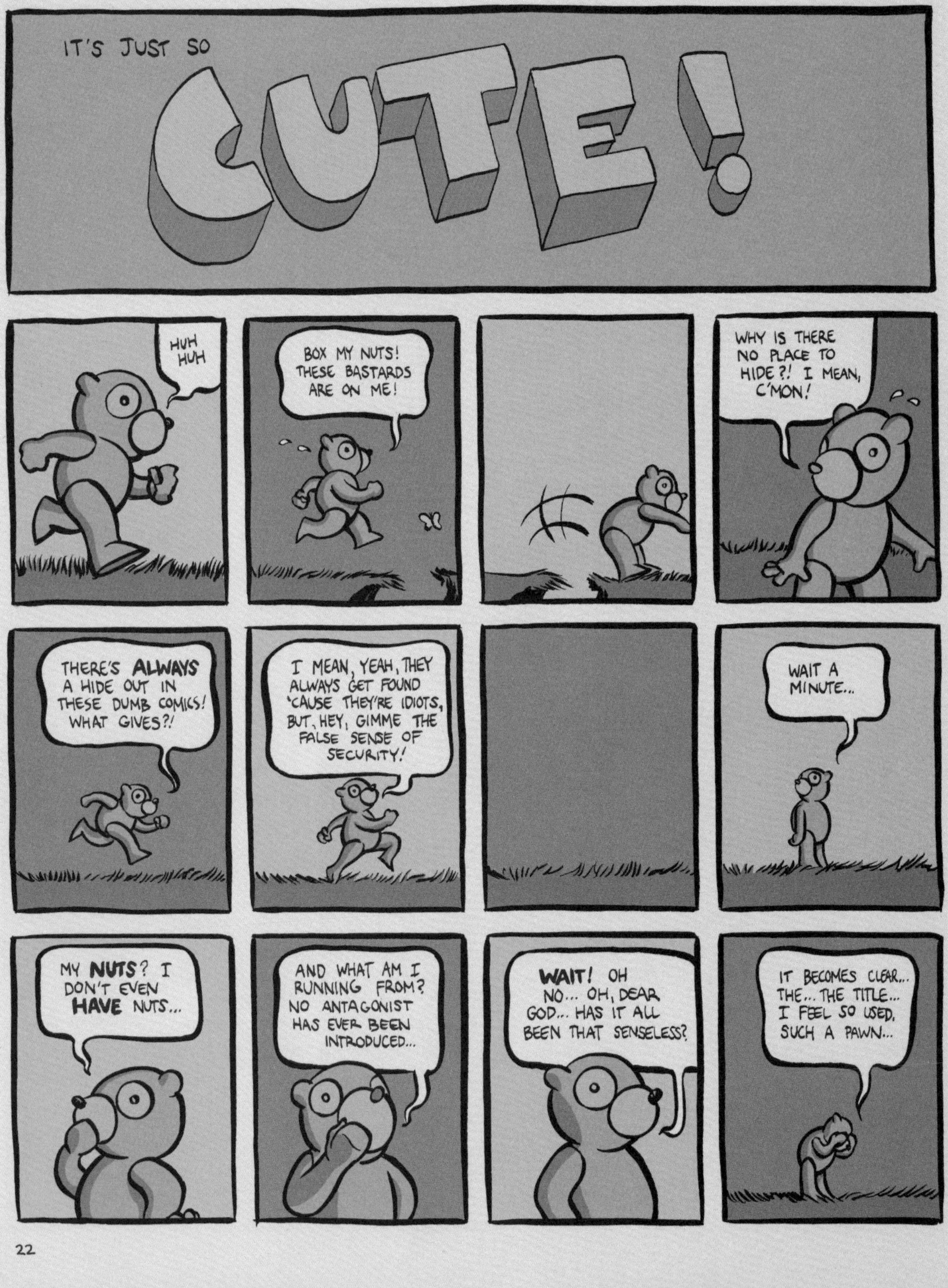
IT'S JUST SO
CUTE!
HUH HUH
BOX MY NUTS! THESE BASTARDS ARE ON ME!
WHY IS THERE NO PLACE TO HIDE?! I MEAN, C'MON!
THERE'S ALWAYS A HIDE OUT IN THESE DUMB COMICS! WHAT GIVES?!
I MEAN, YEAH, THEY ALWAYS GET FOUND 'CAUSE THEY'RE IDIOTS, BUT, HEY, GIMME THE FALSE SENSE OF SECURITY!
WAIT A MINUTE...
MY NUTS? I DON'T EVEN HAVE NUTS...
AND WHAT AM I RUNNING FROM? NO ANTAGONIST HAS EVER BEEN INTRODUCED...
WAIT! OH NO... OH, DEAR GOD... HAS IT ALL BEEN THAT SENSELESS?
IT BECOMES CLEAR... THE... THE TITLE... I FEEL SO USED, SUCH A PAWN...

FUCK IT ALL ANYWAY

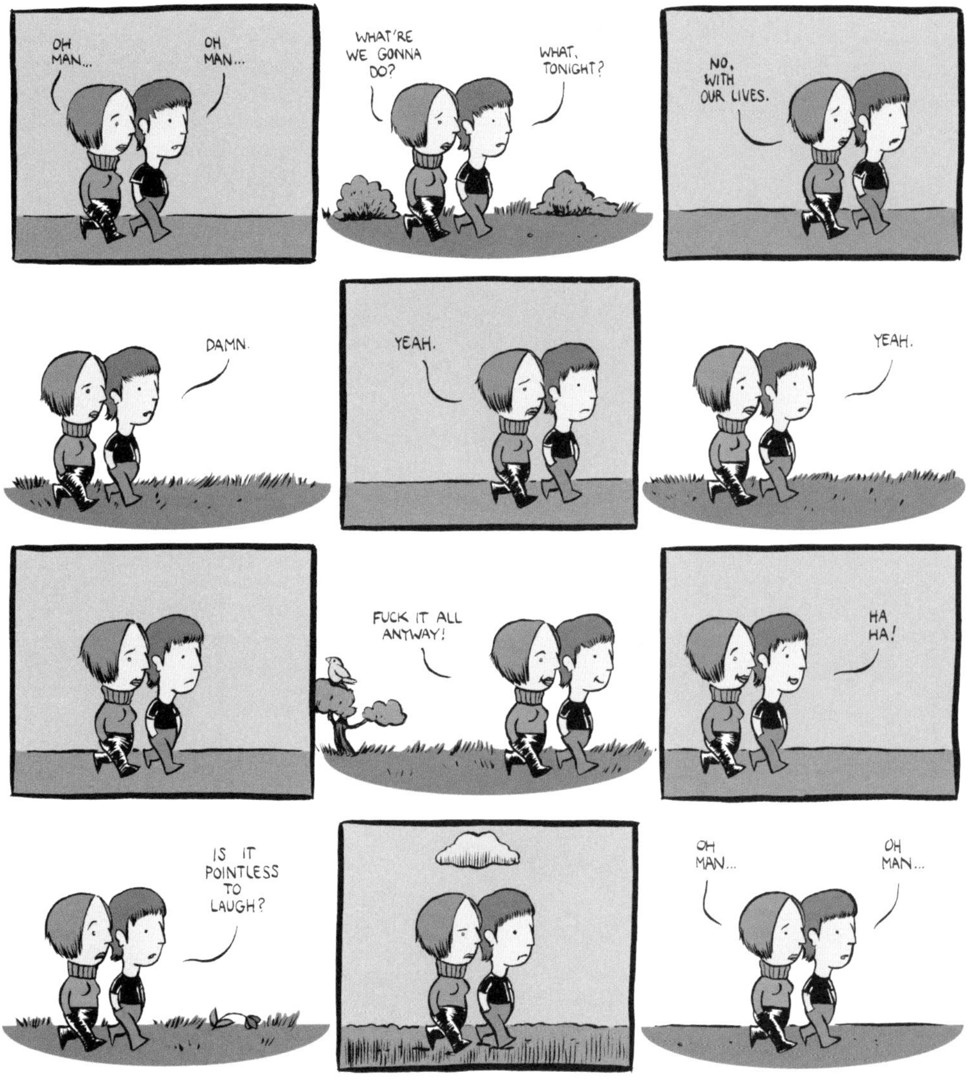
OH MAN...
OH MAN...
WHAT'RE WE GONNA DO?
WHAT, TONIGHT?
NO, WITH OUR LIVES.
DAMN.
YEAH.
YEAH.
FUCK IT ALL ANYWAY!
HA HA!
IS IT POINTLESS TO LAUGH?
OH MAN...
OH MAN...

THE WORLD WILL NEVER BE THE SAME

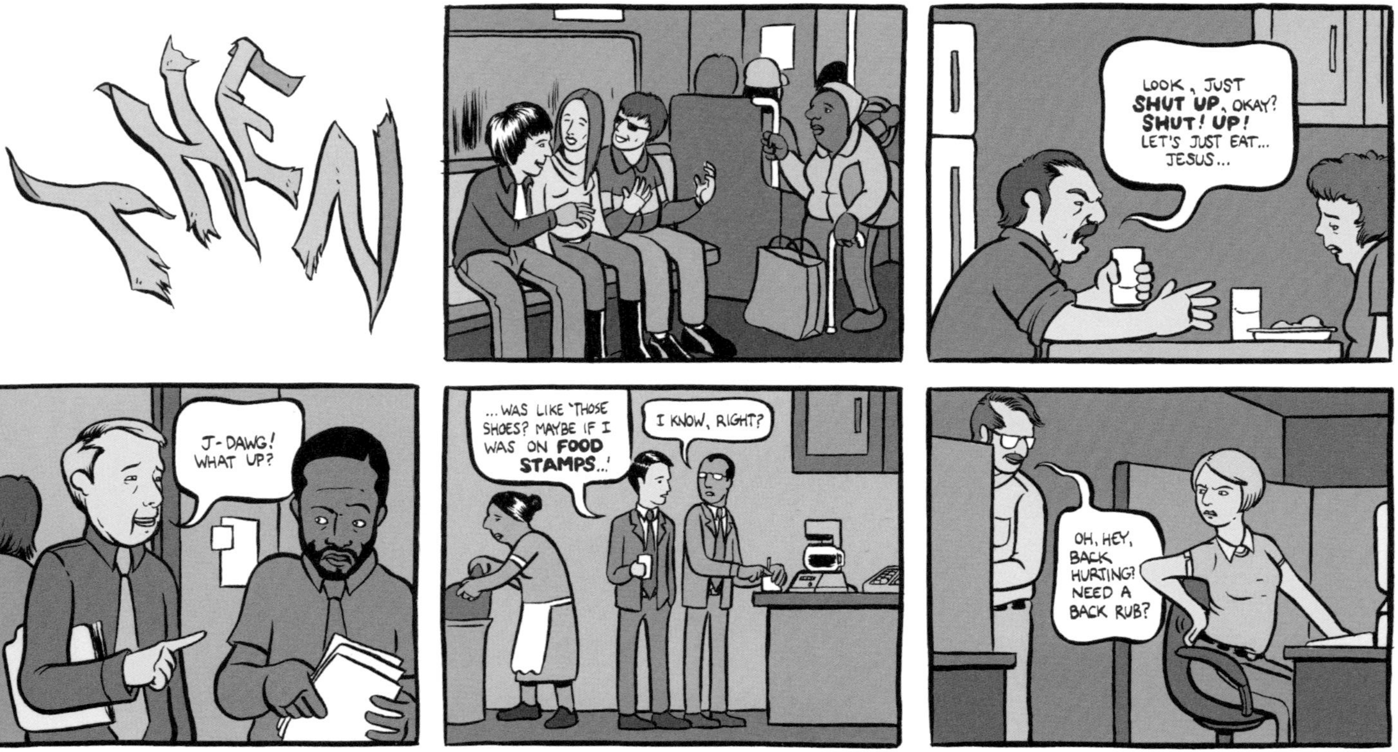
THEN
LOOK, JUST SHUT UP, OKAY? SHUT! UP! LET'S JUST EAT... JESUS...
J-DAWG! WHAT UP?
...WAS LIKE 'THOSE SHOES? MAYBE IF I WAS ON FOOD STAMPS...'
I KNOW, RIGHT?
OH, HEY, BACK HURTING? NEED A BACK RUB?

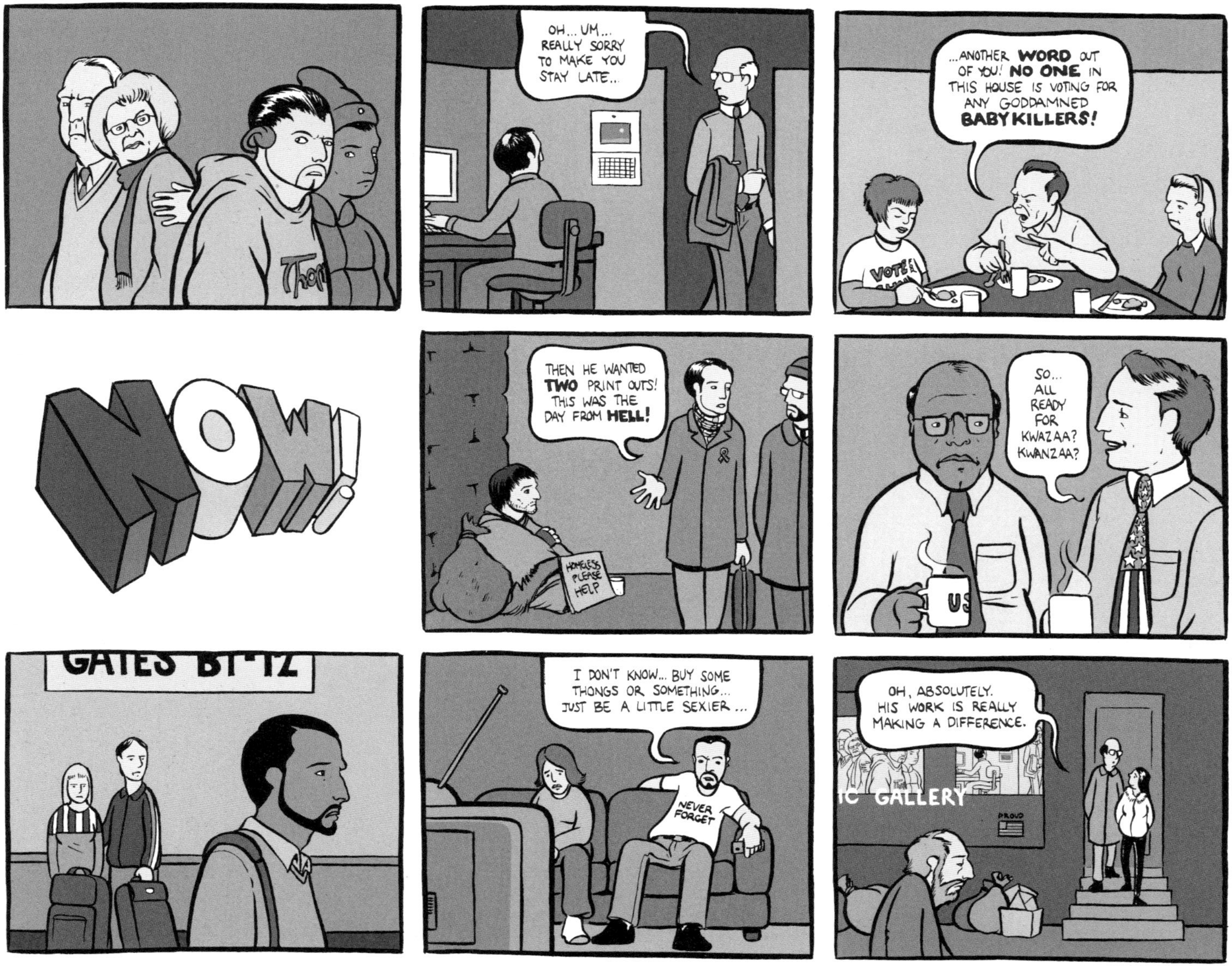
OH... UM... REALLY SORRY TO MAKE YOU STAY LATE...
...ANOTHER **WORD** OUT OF YOU! **NO ONE** IN THIS HOUSE IS VOTING FOR ANY GODDAMNED **BABYKILLERS!**
VOTE!
NOW!
THEN HE WANTED **TWO** PRINT OUTS! THIS WAS THE DAY FROM **HELL!**
HOMELESS PLEASE HELP
SO... ALL READY FOR KWAZAA? KWANZAA?
US
GATES B1-12
I DON'T KNOW... BUY SOME THONGS OR SOMETHING... JUST BE A LITTLE SEXIER...
NEVER FORGET
OH, ABSOLUTELY. HIS WORK IS REALLY MAKING A DIFFERENCE.
IC GALLERY
PROUD

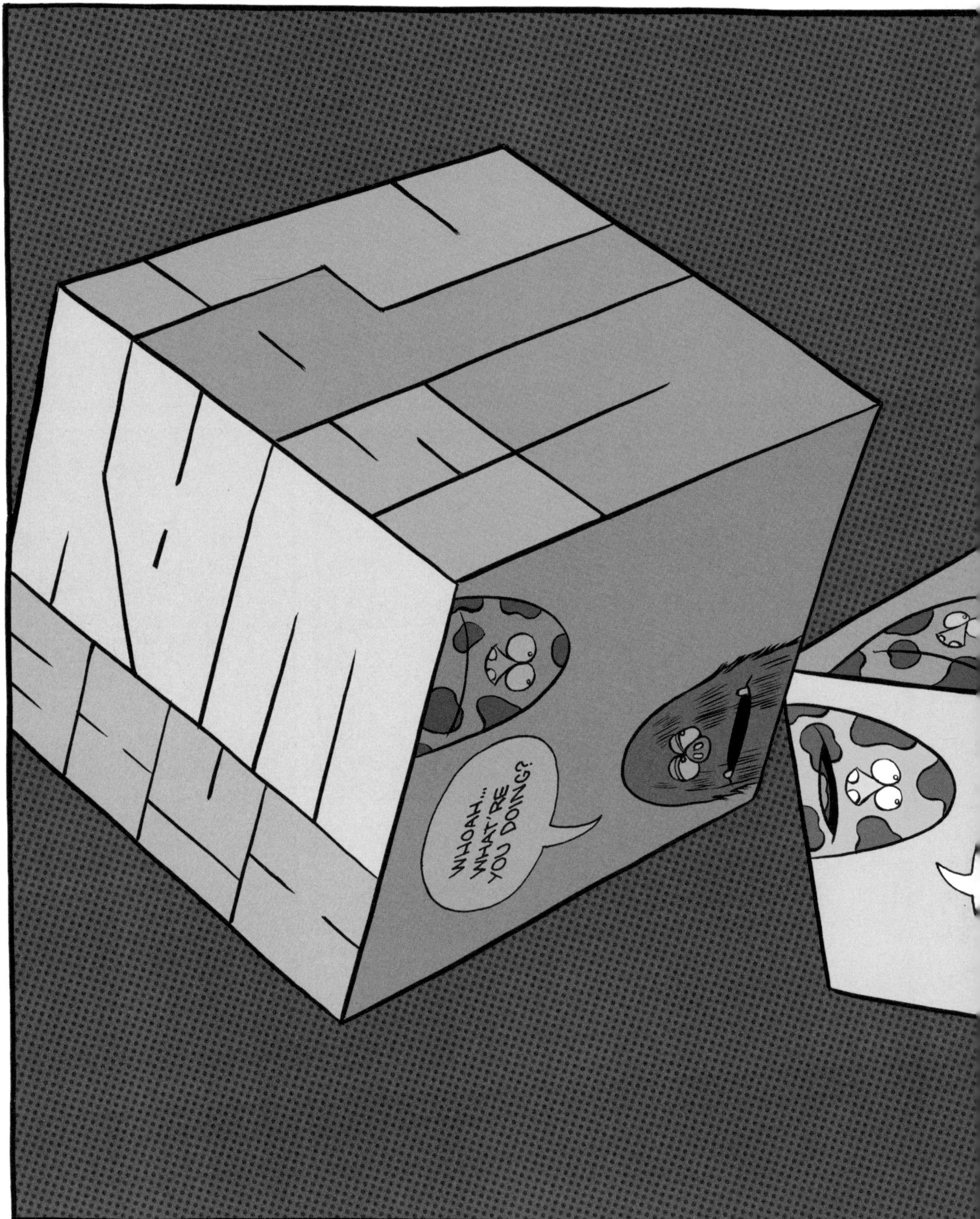
WHOAH... WHAT'RE YOU DOING?

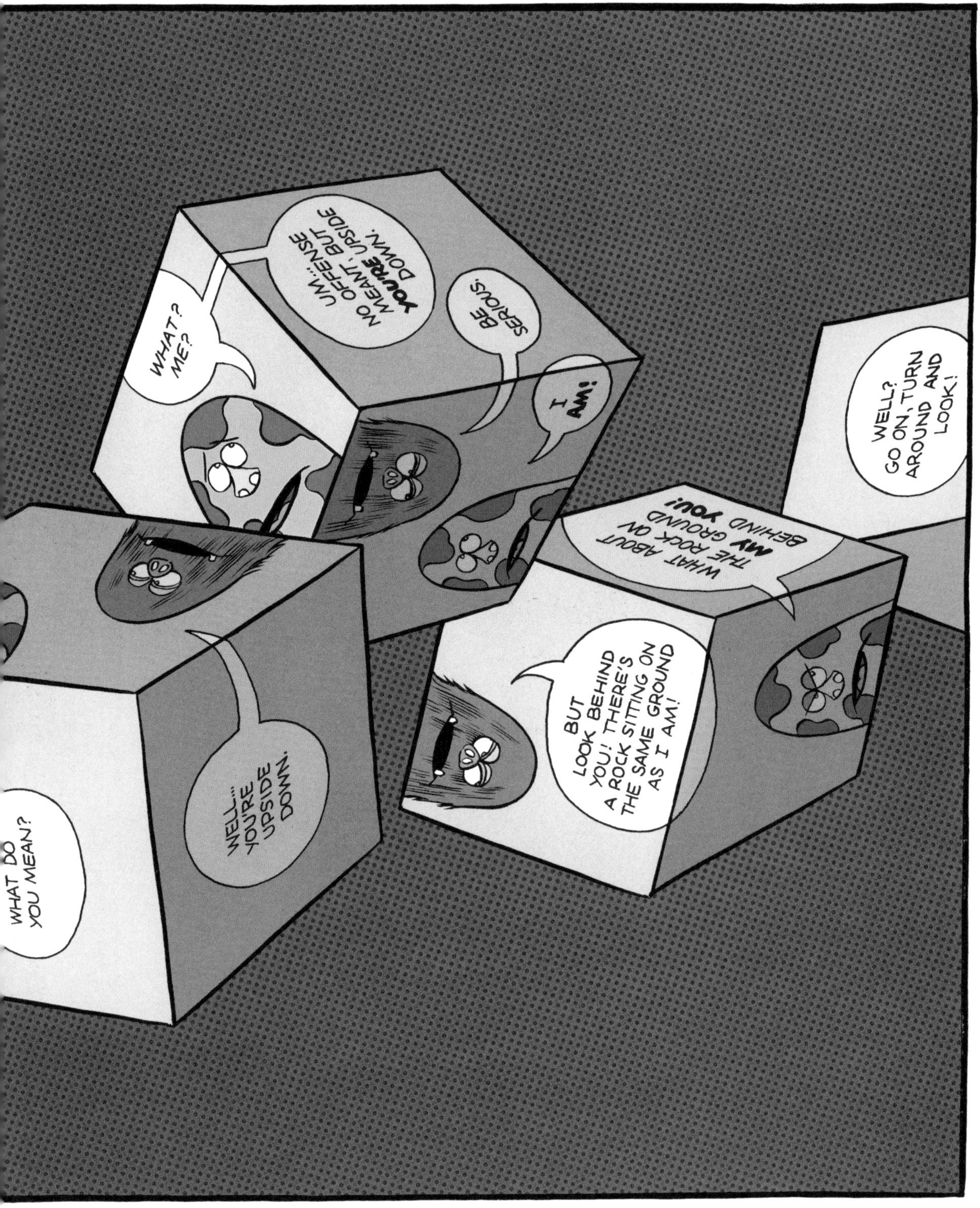
WHAT DO YOU MEAN?
WELL... YOU'RE UPSIDE DOWN.
WHAT? ME?
UM... NO OFFENSE MEANT, BUT **YOU'RE** UPSIDE DOWN.
BE SERIOUS.
I **AM!**
BUT LOOK BEHIND YOU! THERE'S A ROCK SITTING ON THE SAME GROUND AS I AM!
WHAT ABOUT THE ROCK ON **MY** GROUND BEHIND **YOU!**
WELL? GO ON, TURN AROUND AND LOOK!

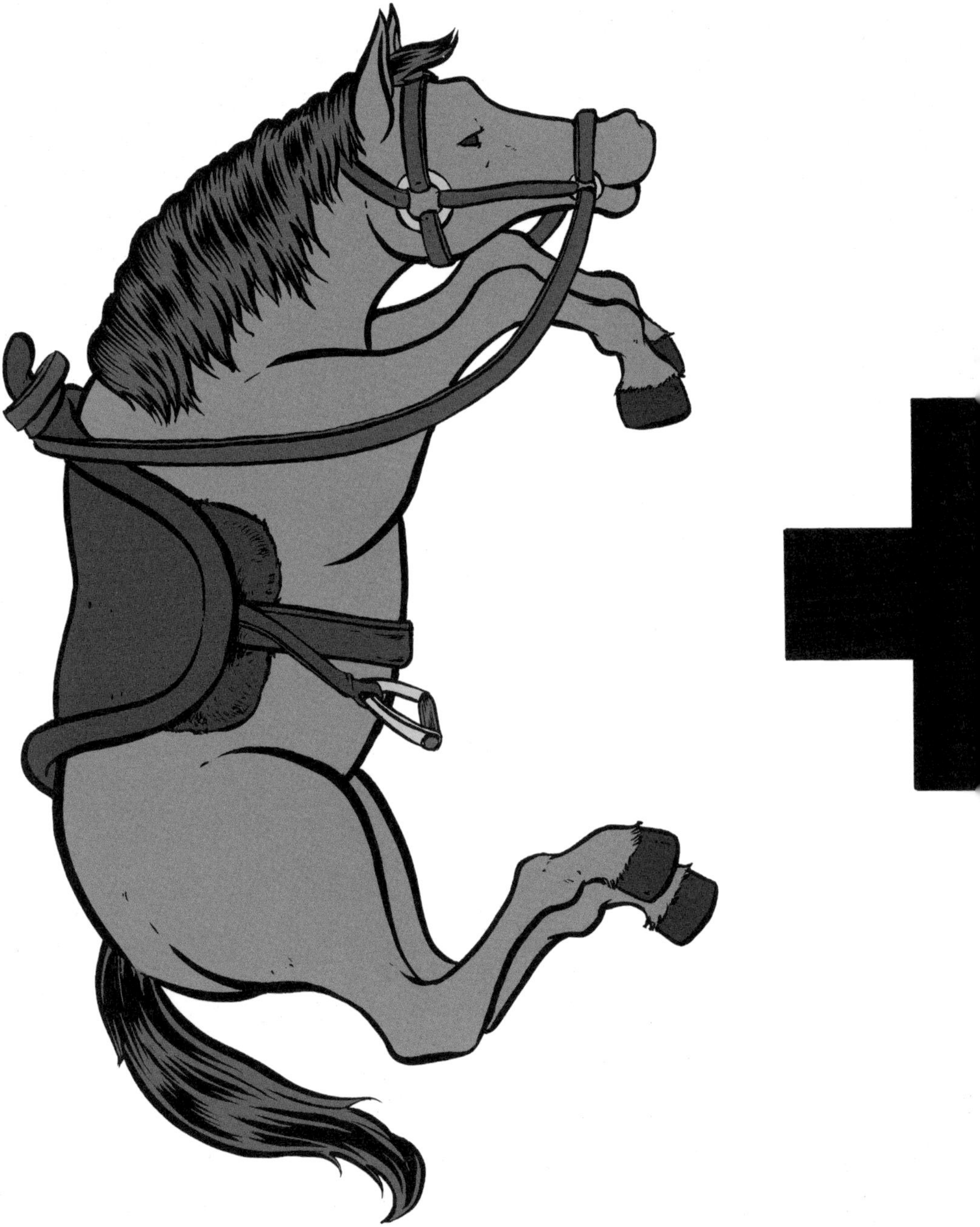

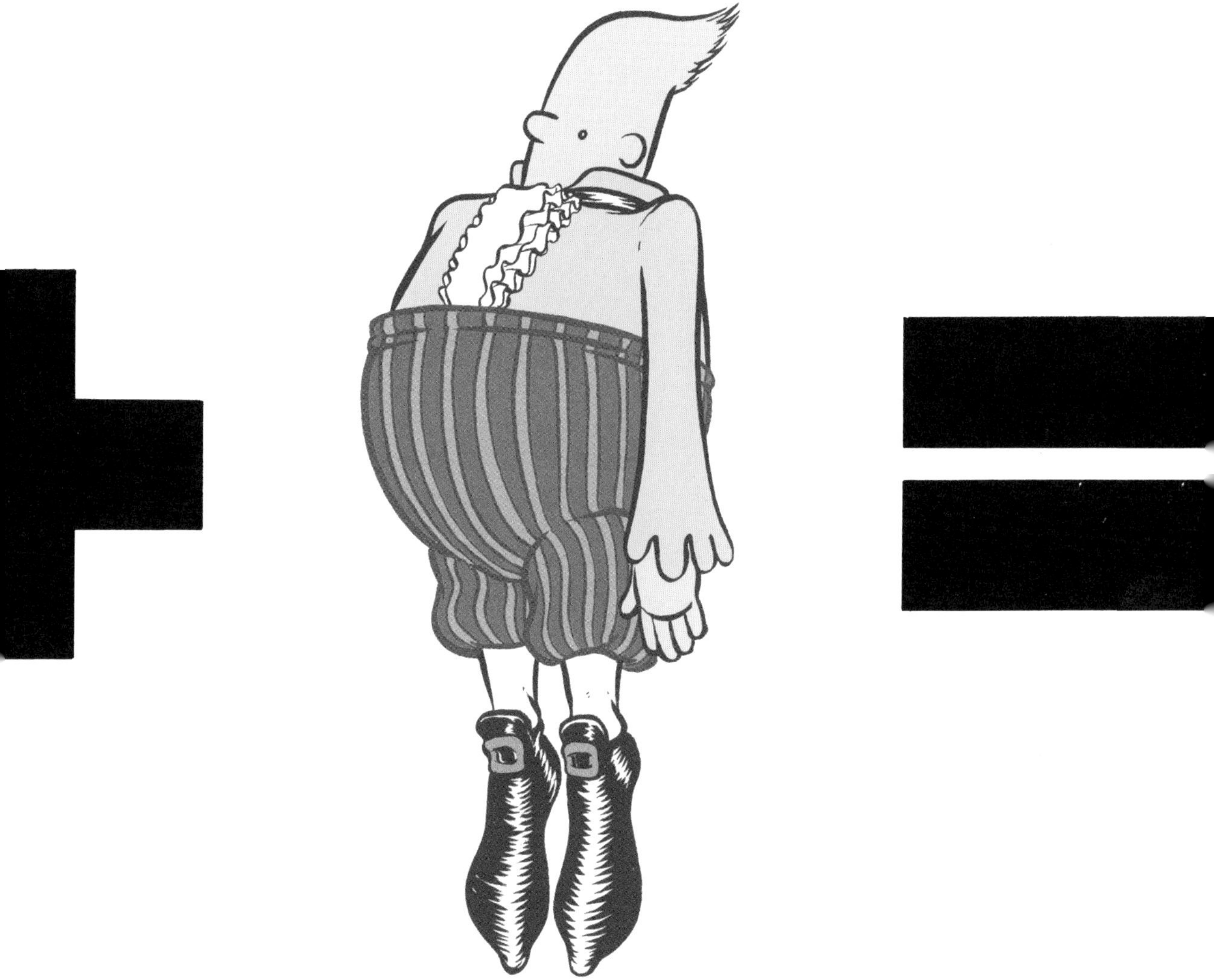

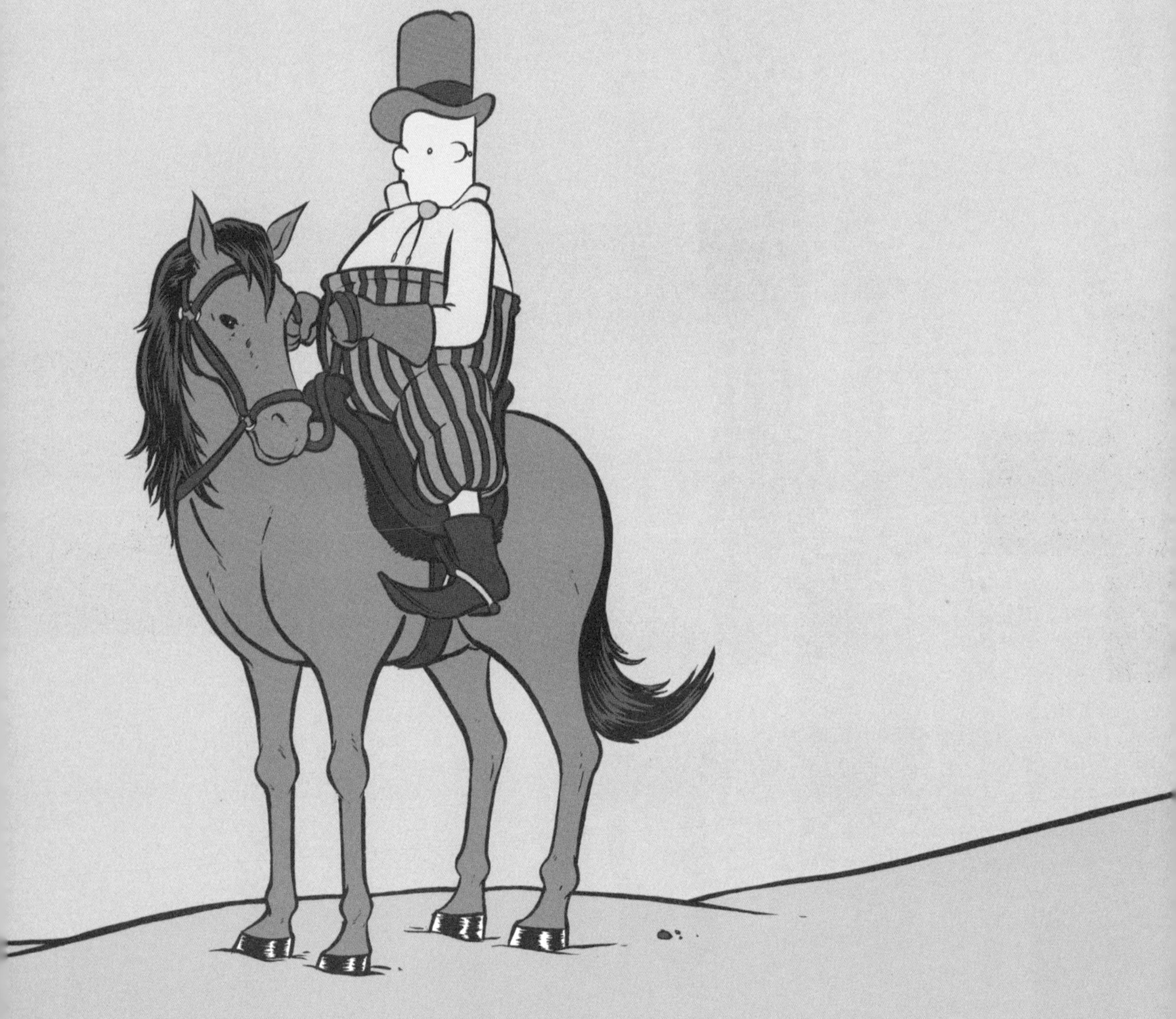

VANDERBILT MILLIONS

IS A MENTAL CASE

PRIORLY

I MUST LEAVE YOU.

BUT I WILL WITHER IN YOUR ABSCENCE... HAVE YOU NO COMPASSION?

MY COMPASSION IS FOR THE PEOPLE; YOU HAVE ALWAYS KNOWN THIS. WHY FEIGN IGNORANCE?

I WALK TO MY STEED WHICH I WILL RIDE A LOT TO PLACES.

EVEN THERE, MY TEARS WILL ECHO.

SO BE IT. I TAKE MY LEAVE.

NOW-ISH

VANDERBILT?

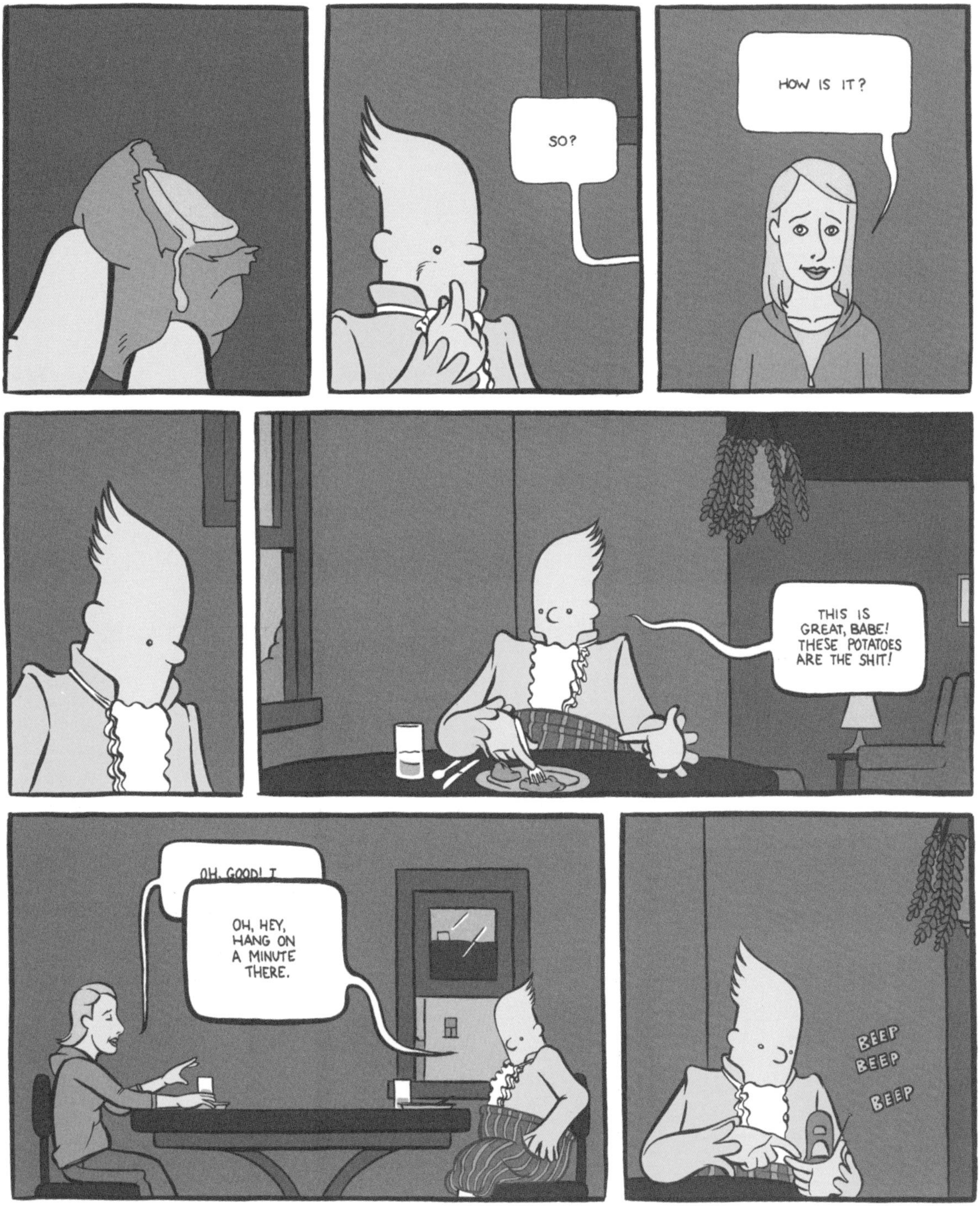
SO?
HOW IS IT?
THIS IS GREAT, BABE! THESE POTATOES ARE THE SHIT!
OH, GOOD! I
OH, HEY, HANG ON A MINUTE THERE.
BEEP
BEEP
BEEP

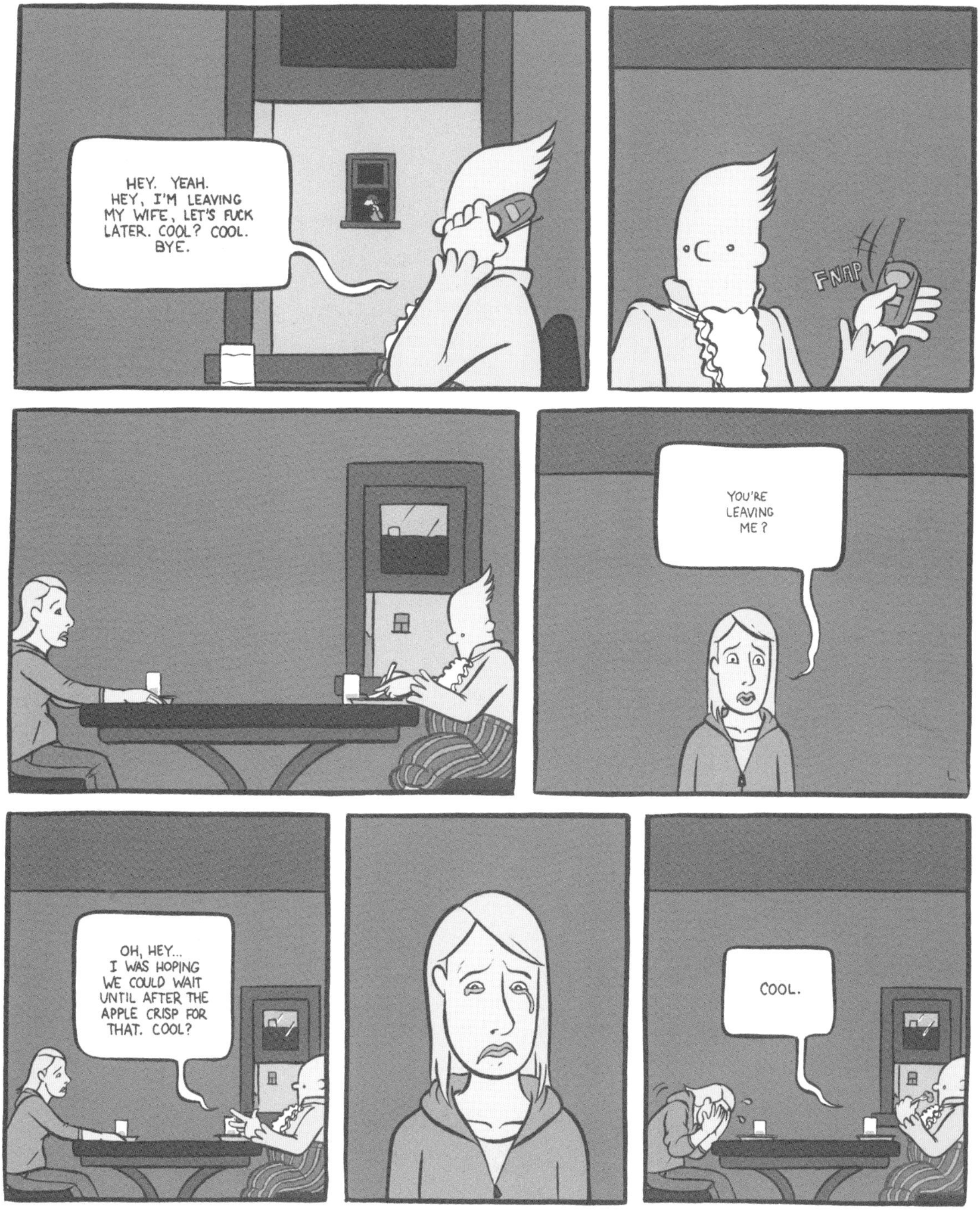
HEY. YEAH. HEY, I'M LEAVING MY WIFE, LET'S FUCK LATER. COOL? COOL. BYE.
FNAP
YOU'RE LEAVING ME?
OH, HEY... I WAS HOPING WE COULD WAIT UNTIL AFTER THE APPLE CRISP FOR THAT. COOL?
COOL.

SO?

HOW IS IT? DON'T SIT THERE KEEPING ME IN SUSPENSE...

IT'S GREAT, DEAR. THE POTATOES ARE YUMMY.

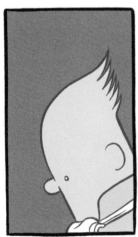

DO YOU THINK I SHOULD MAYBE GET A CELL PHONE?

OH MY GOD! IT'S SEVEN! "TAYLOR HANDSOME: MARSHALL" IS STARTING!

I'M FINISHING MY FOOD IN THE LIVING ROOM. I HOPE I DIDN'T MISS ANYTHING.

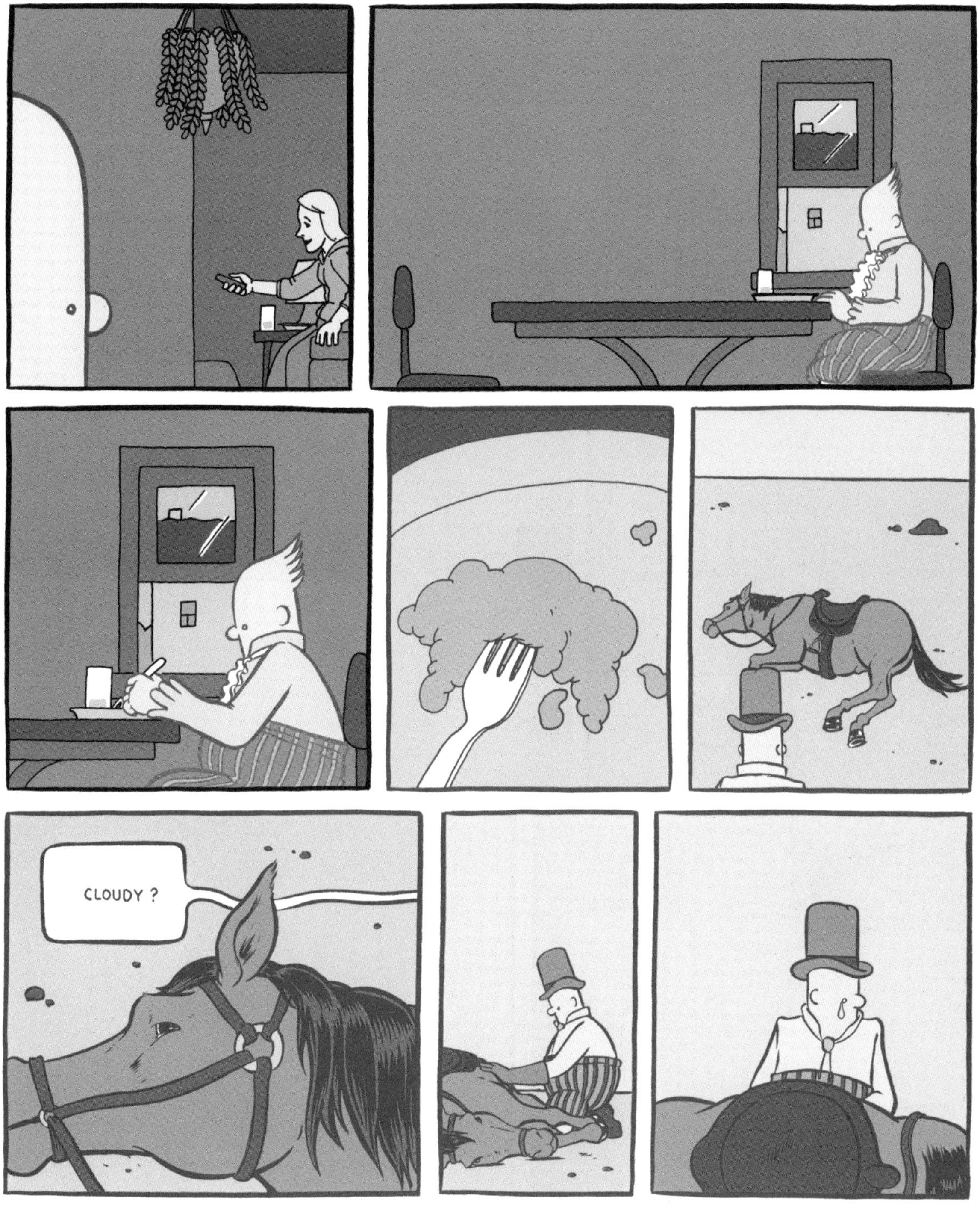
CLOUDY ?

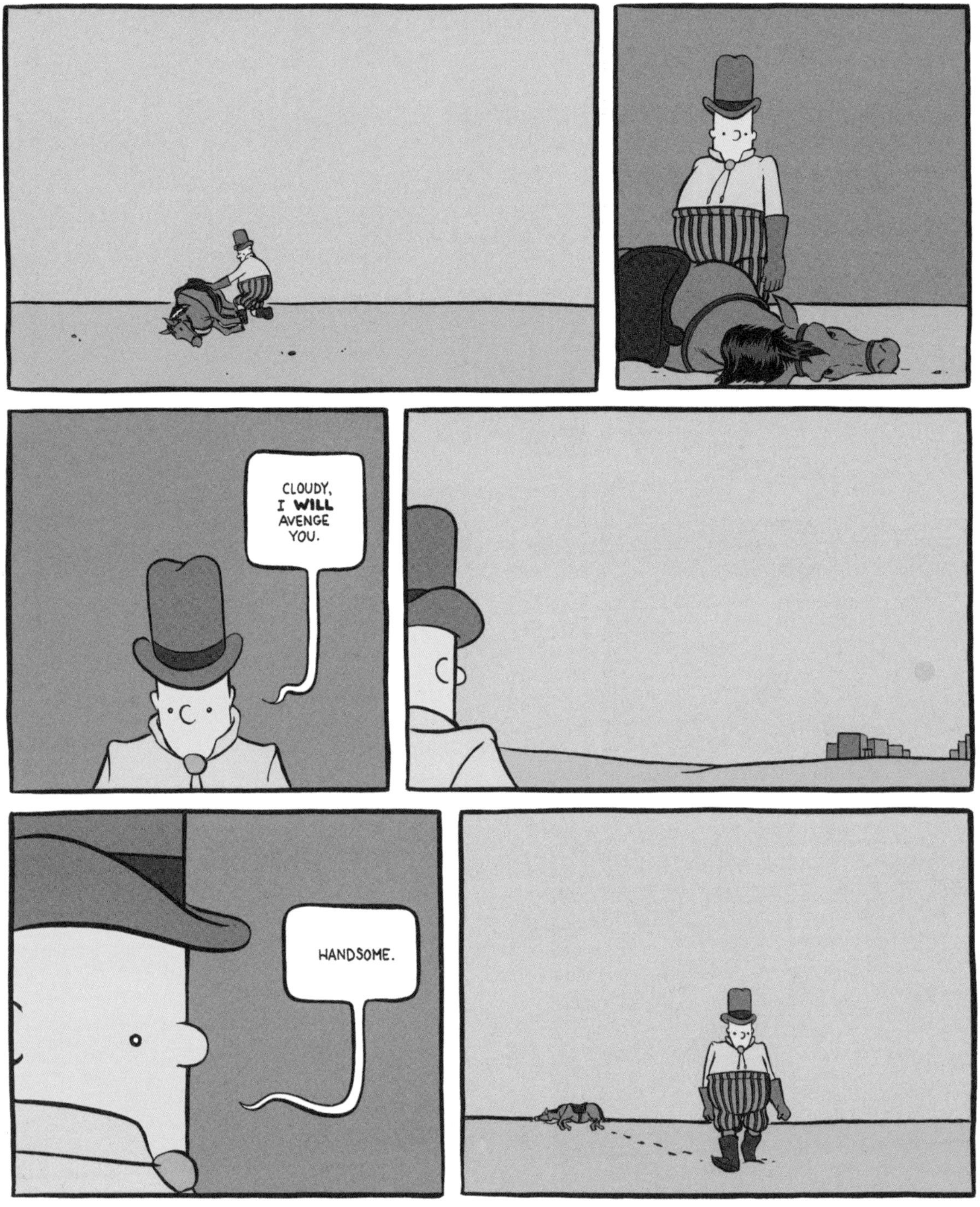
CLOUDY, I **WILL** AVENGE YOU.
HANDSOME.

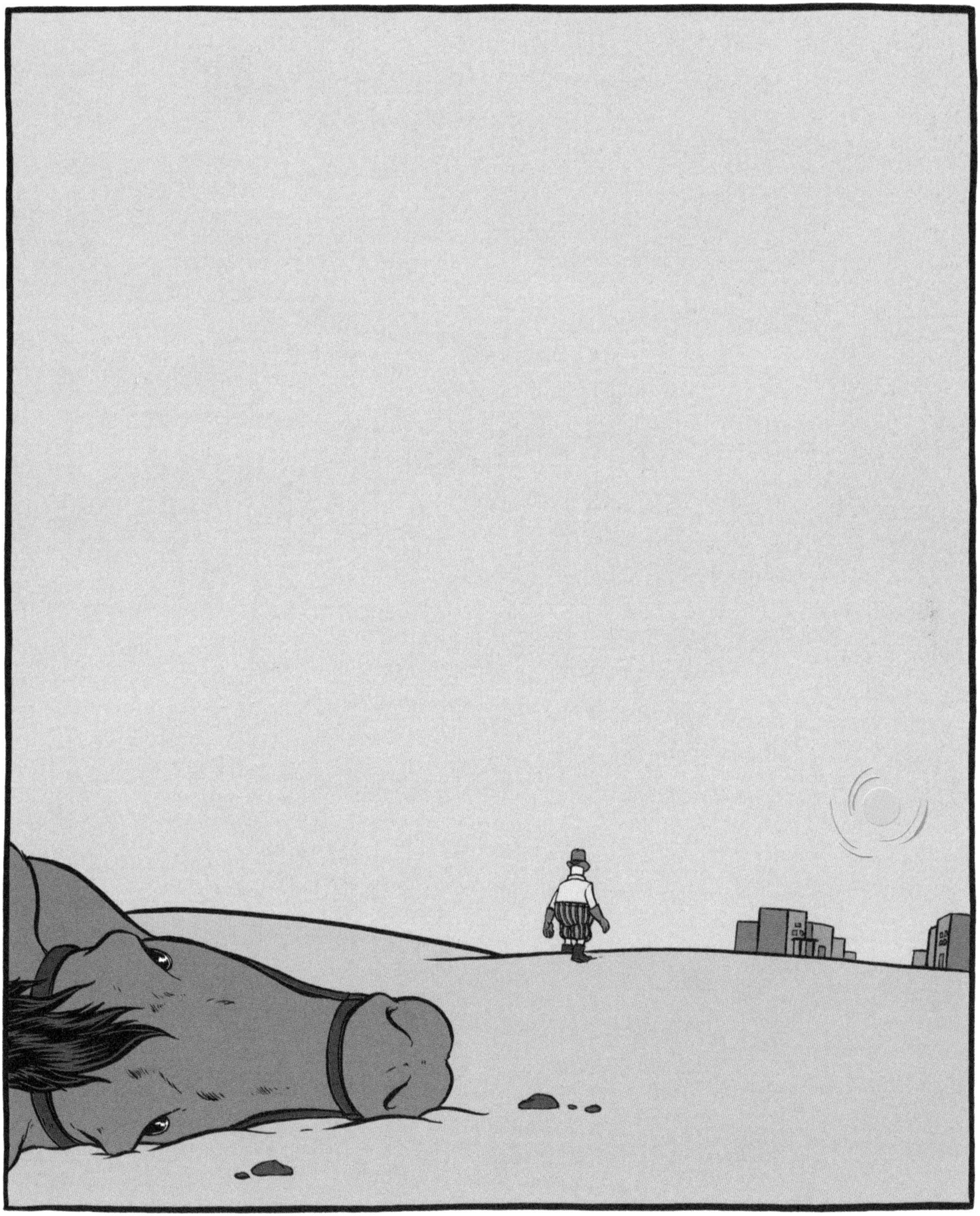

MEN AND WOMEN OF THE TELEVISION

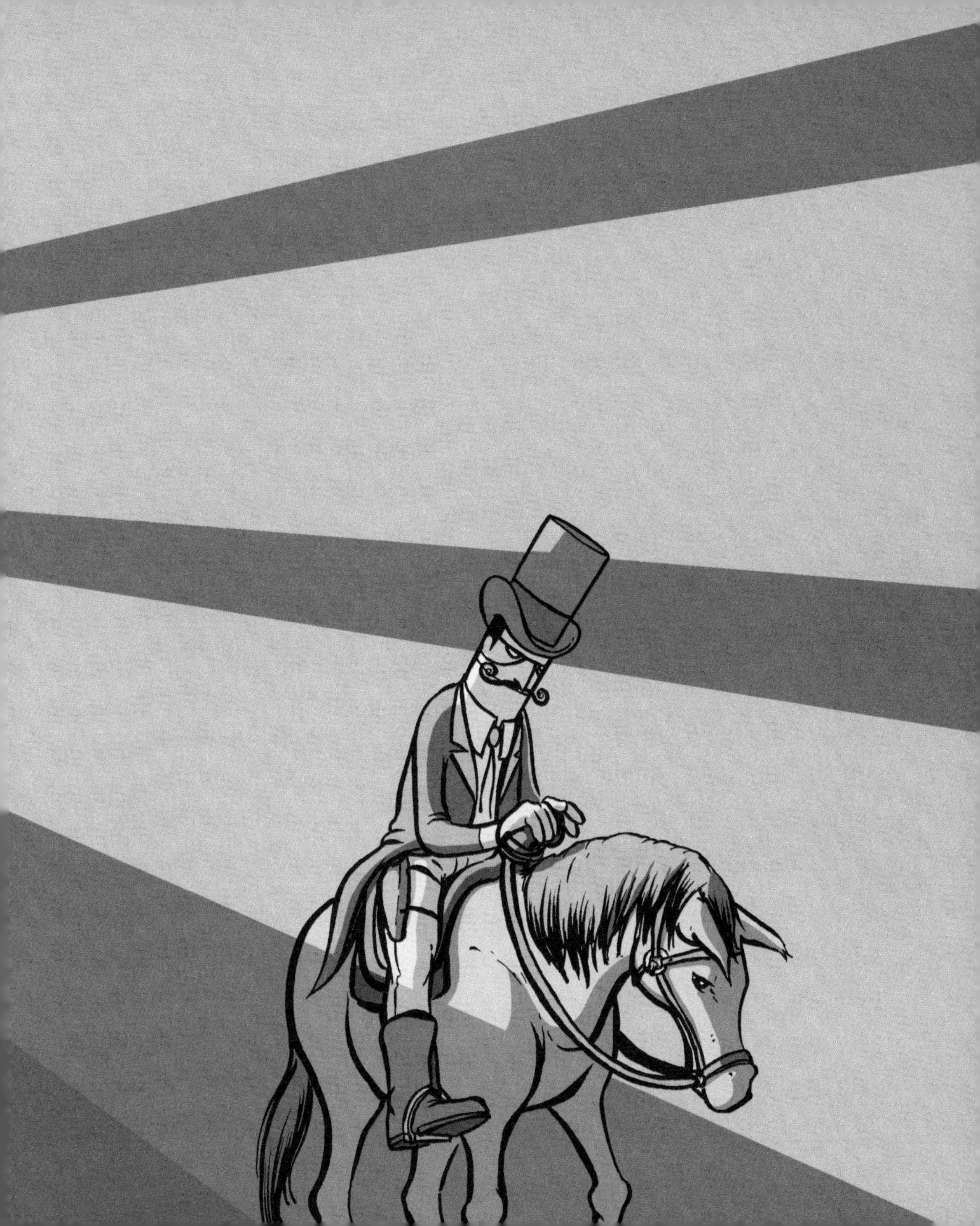

THE BAD BAD MAN

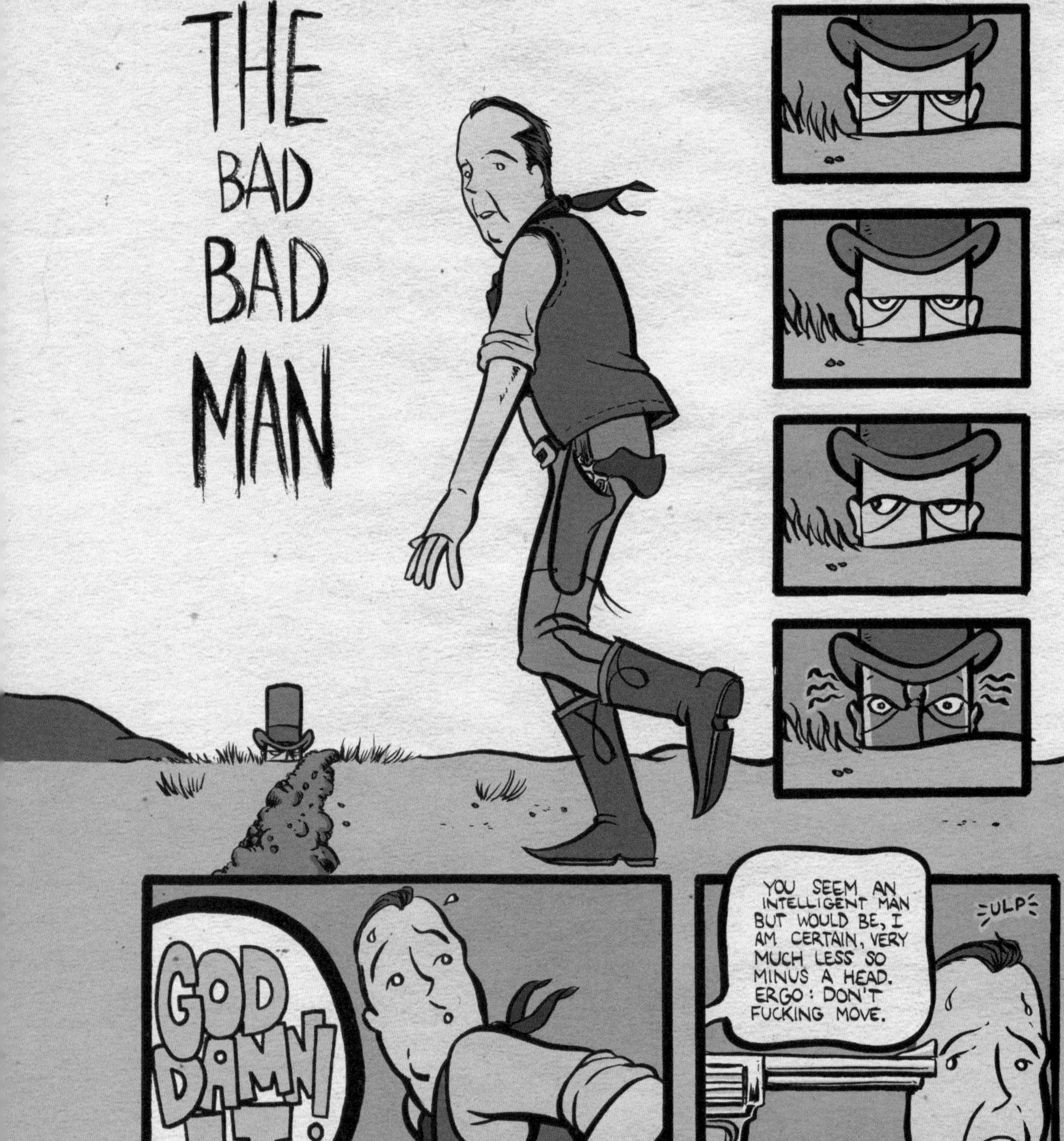
GOD DAMN IT!
YOU SEEM AN INTELLIGENT MAN BUT WOULD BE, I AM CERTAIN, VERY MUCH LESS SO MINUS A HEAD. ERGO: DON'T FUCKING MOVE.
ULP

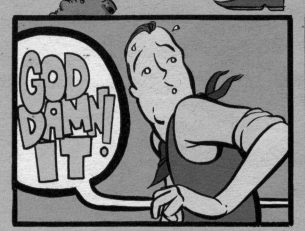

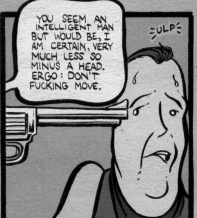

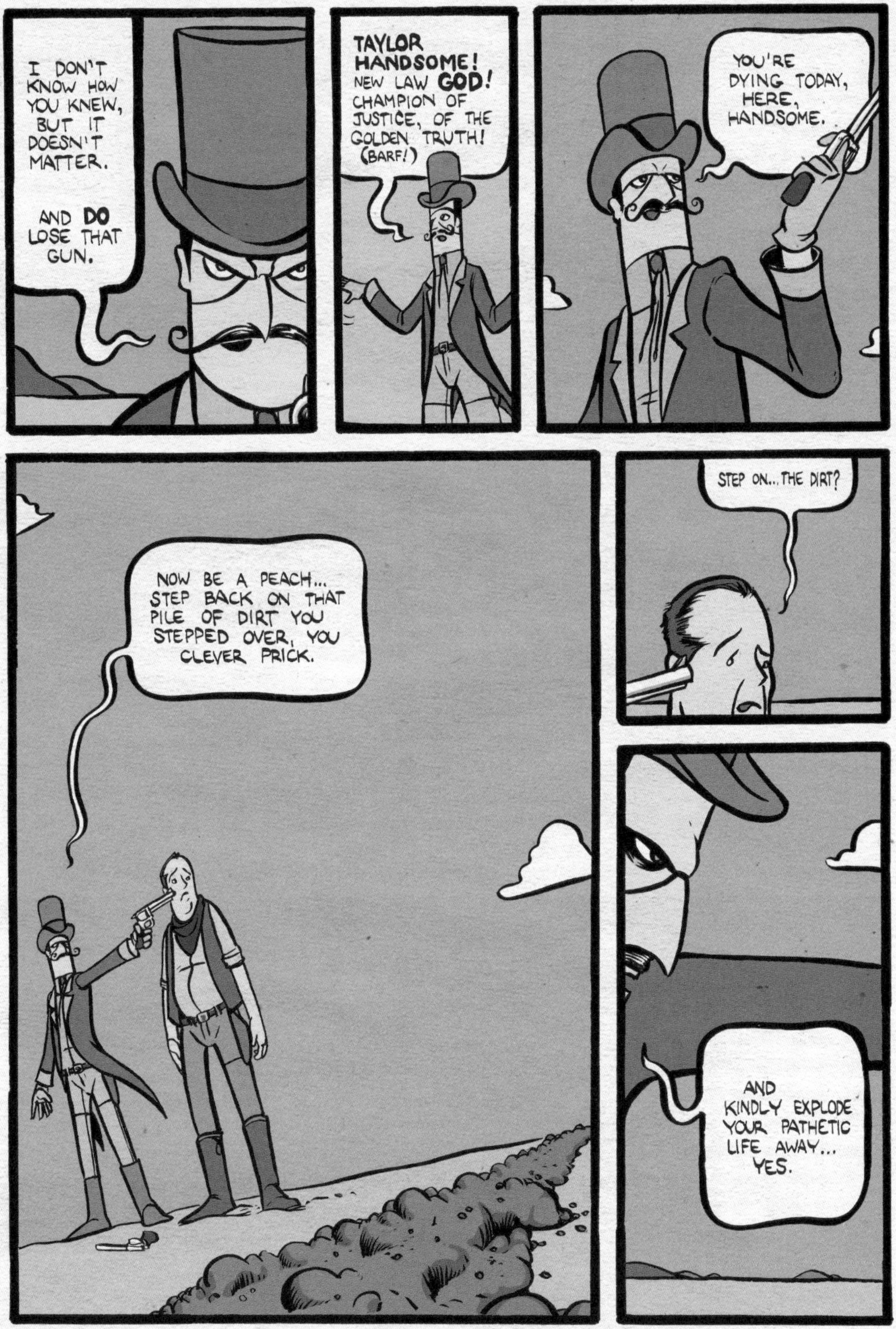
I DON'T KNOW HOW YOU KNEW, BUT IT DOESN'T MATTER.
AND DO LOSE THAT GUN.
TAYLOR HANDSOME! NEW LAW GOD! CHAMPION OF JUSTICE, OF THE GOLDEN TRUTH! (BARF!)
YOU'RE DYING TODAY, HERE, HANDSOME.
NOW BE A PEACH... STEP BACK ON THAT PILE OF DIRT YOU STEPPED OVER, YOU CLEVER PRICK.
STEP ON... THE DIRT?
AND KINDLY EXPLODE YOUR PATHETIC LIFE AWAY... YES.

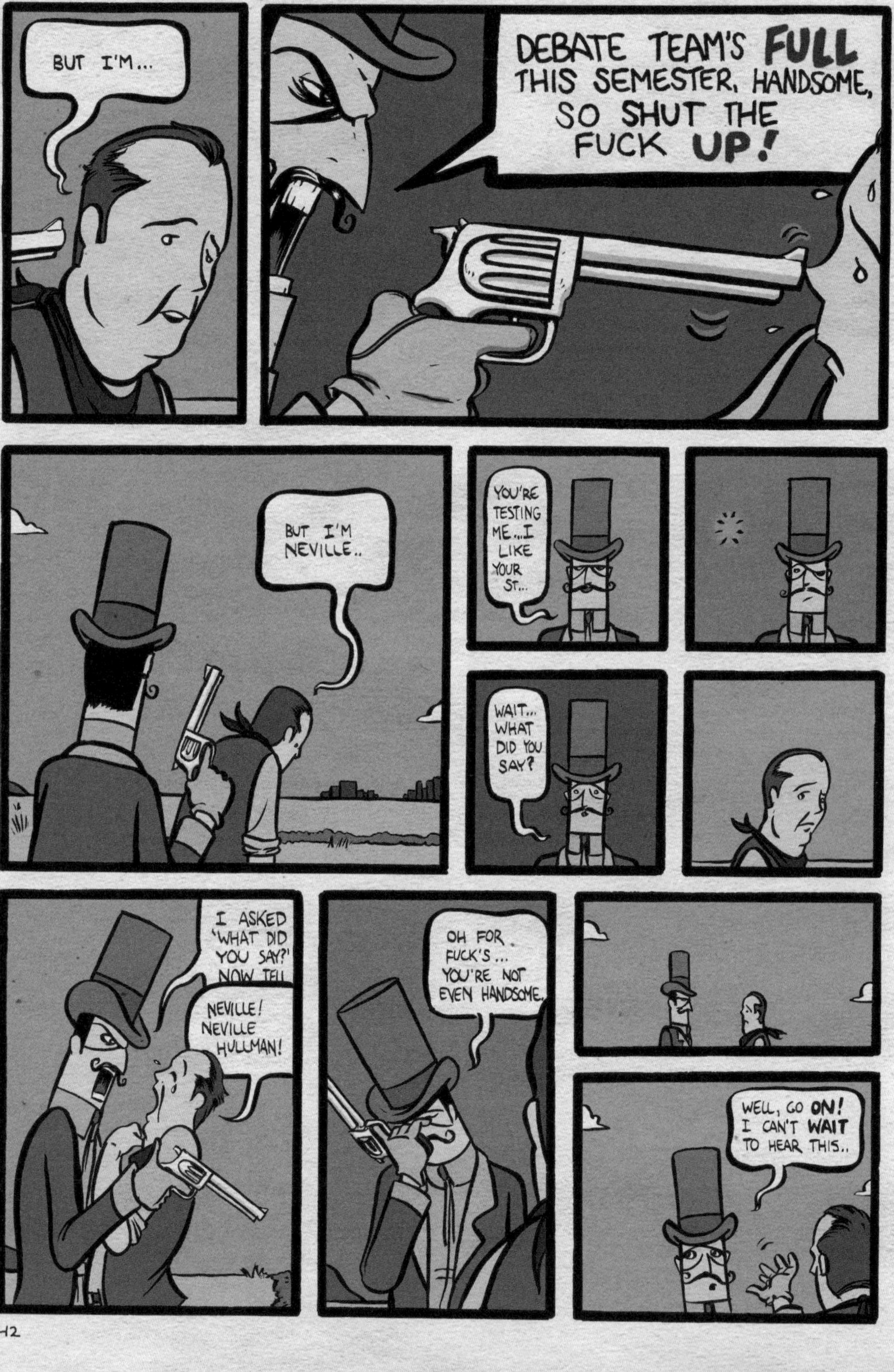
BUT I'M...
DEBATE TEAM'S FULL THIS SEMESTER, HANDSOME, SO SHUT THE FUCK UP!
BUT I'M NEVILLE..
YOU'RE TESTING ME...I LIKE YOUR ST..
WAIT... WHAT DID YOU SAY?
I ASKED 'WHAT DID YOU SAY?' NOW TELL
NEVILLE! NEVILLE HULLMAN!
OH FOR FUCK'S... YOU'RE NOT EVEN HANDSOME.
WELL, GO ON! I CAN'T WAIT TO HEAR THIS..

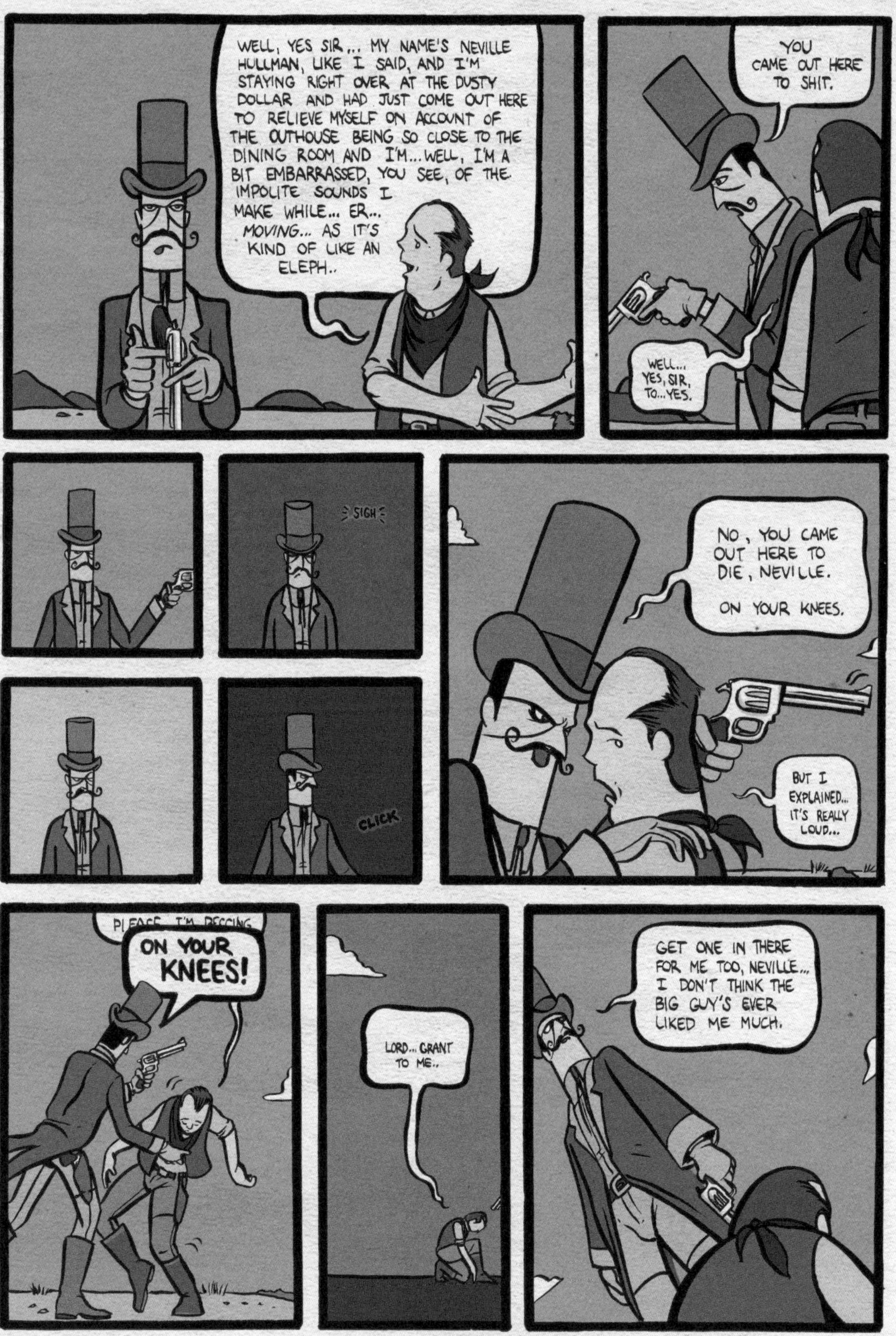

WELL, YES SIR... MY NAME'S NEVILLE HULLMAN, LIKE I SAID, AND I'M STAYING RIGHT OVER AT THE DUSTY DOLLAR AND HAD JUST COME OUT HERE TO RELIEVE MYSELF ON ACCOUNT OF THE OUTHOUSE BEING SO CLOSE TO THE DINING ROOM AND I'M... WELL, I'M A BIT EMBARRASSED, YOU SEE, OF THE IMPOLITE SOUNDS I MAKE WHILE... ER... *MOVING*... AS IT'S KIND OF LIKE AN ELEPH..
YOU CAME OUT HERE TO SHIT.
WELL... YES, SIR, TO... YES.
SIGH
CLICK
NO, YOU CAME OUT HERE TO DIE, NEVILLE.
ON YOUR KNEES.
BUT I EXPLAINED... IT'S REALLY LOUD...
ON YOUR KNEES!
LORD... GRANT TO ME..
GET ONE IN THERE FOR ME TOO, NEVILLE... I DON'T THINK THE BIG GUY'S EVER LIKED ME MUCH.

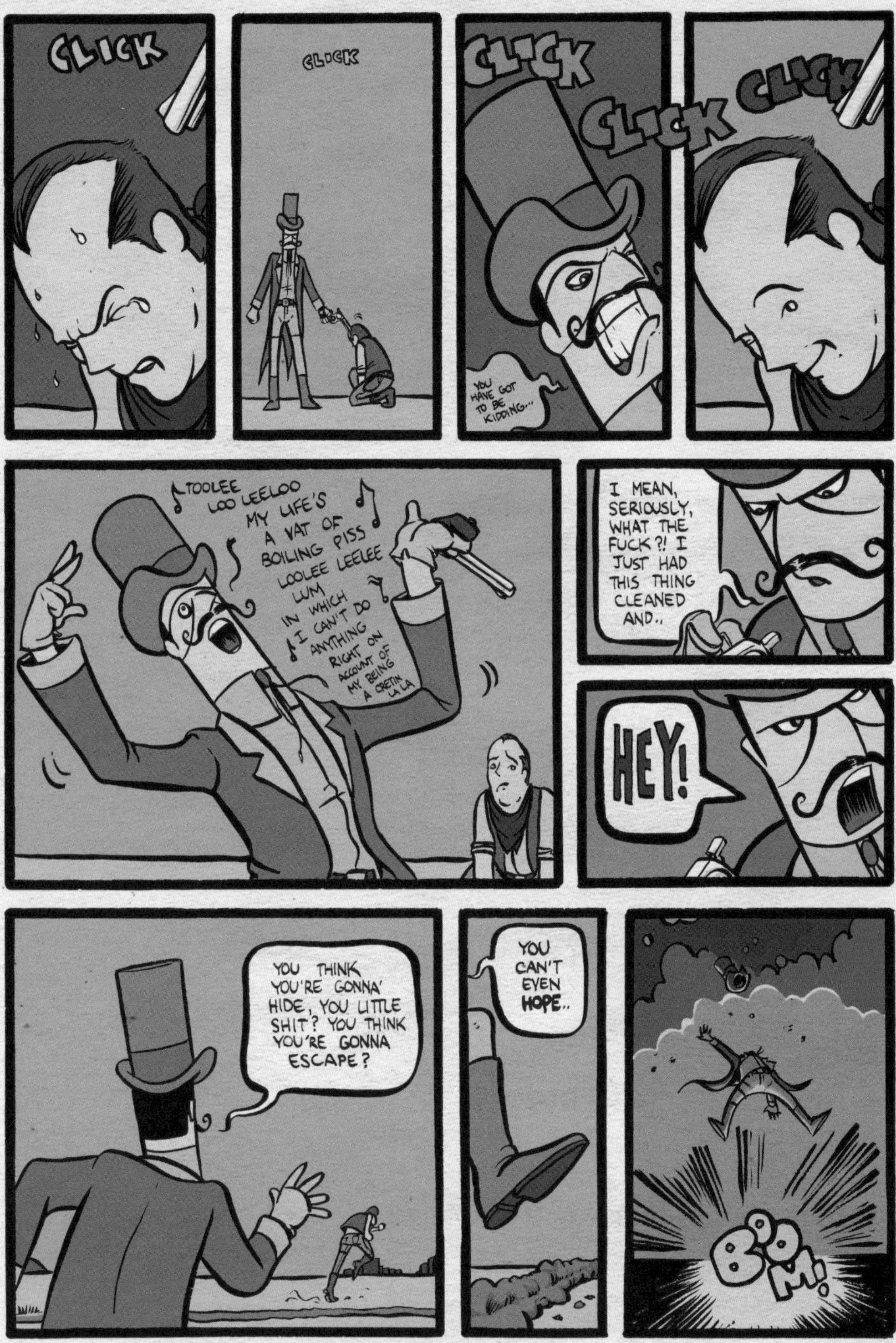
CLICK
CLICK
CLICK
YOU HAVE GOT TO BE KIDDING...
CLICK CLICK
TOOLEE LOO LEELOO MY LIFE'S A VAT OF BOILING PISS LOOLEE LEELEE LUM IN WHICH I CAN'T DO ANYTHING RIGHT ON ACCOUNT OF MY BEING A CRETIN LA LA
I MEAN, SERIOUSLY, WHAT THE FUCK?! I JUST HAD THIS THING CLEANED AND..
HEY!
YOU THINK YOU'RE GONNA' HIDE, YOU LITTLE SHIT? YOU THINK YOU'RE GONNA ESCAPE?
YOU CAN'T EVEN **HOPE**..
BOOM!

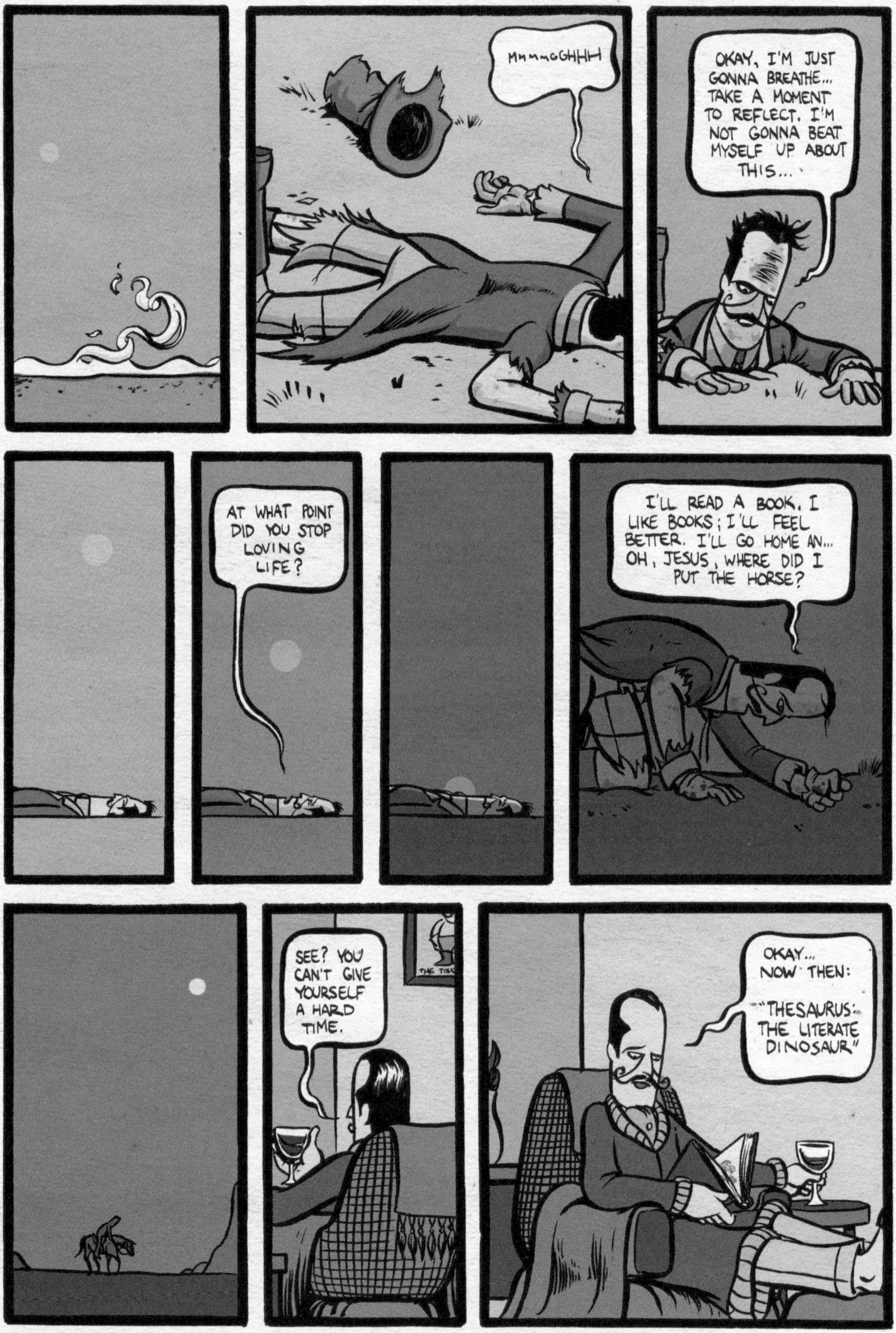
MMMMMGHHH
OKAY, I'M JUST GONNA BREATHE... TAKE A MOMENT TO REFLECT. I'M NOT GONNA BEAT MYSELF UP ABOUT THIS...
AT WHAT POINT DID YOU STOP LOVING LIFE?
I'LL READ A BOOK. I LIKE BOOKS; I'LL FEEL BETTER. I'LL GO HOME AN... OH, JESUS, WHERE DID I PUT THE HORSE?
SEE? YOU CAN'T GIVE YOURSELF A HARD TIME.
OKAY... NOW THEN:
"THESAURUS: THE LITERATE DINOSAUR"

But Thesaurus, my good man,
will you go to the bank?

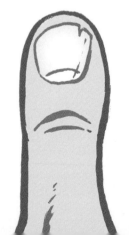

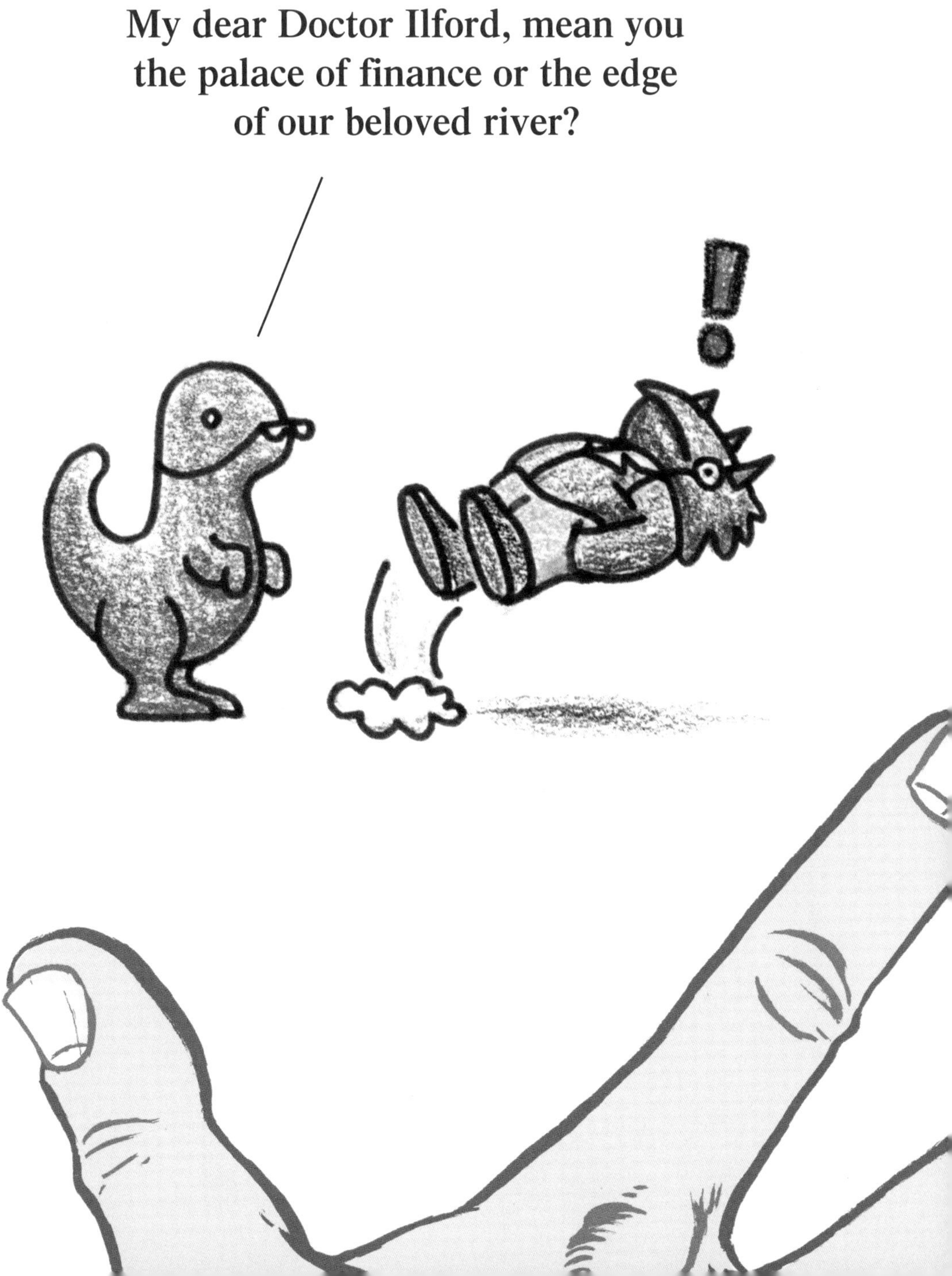
My dear Doctor Ilford, mean you the palace of finance or the edge of our beloved river?

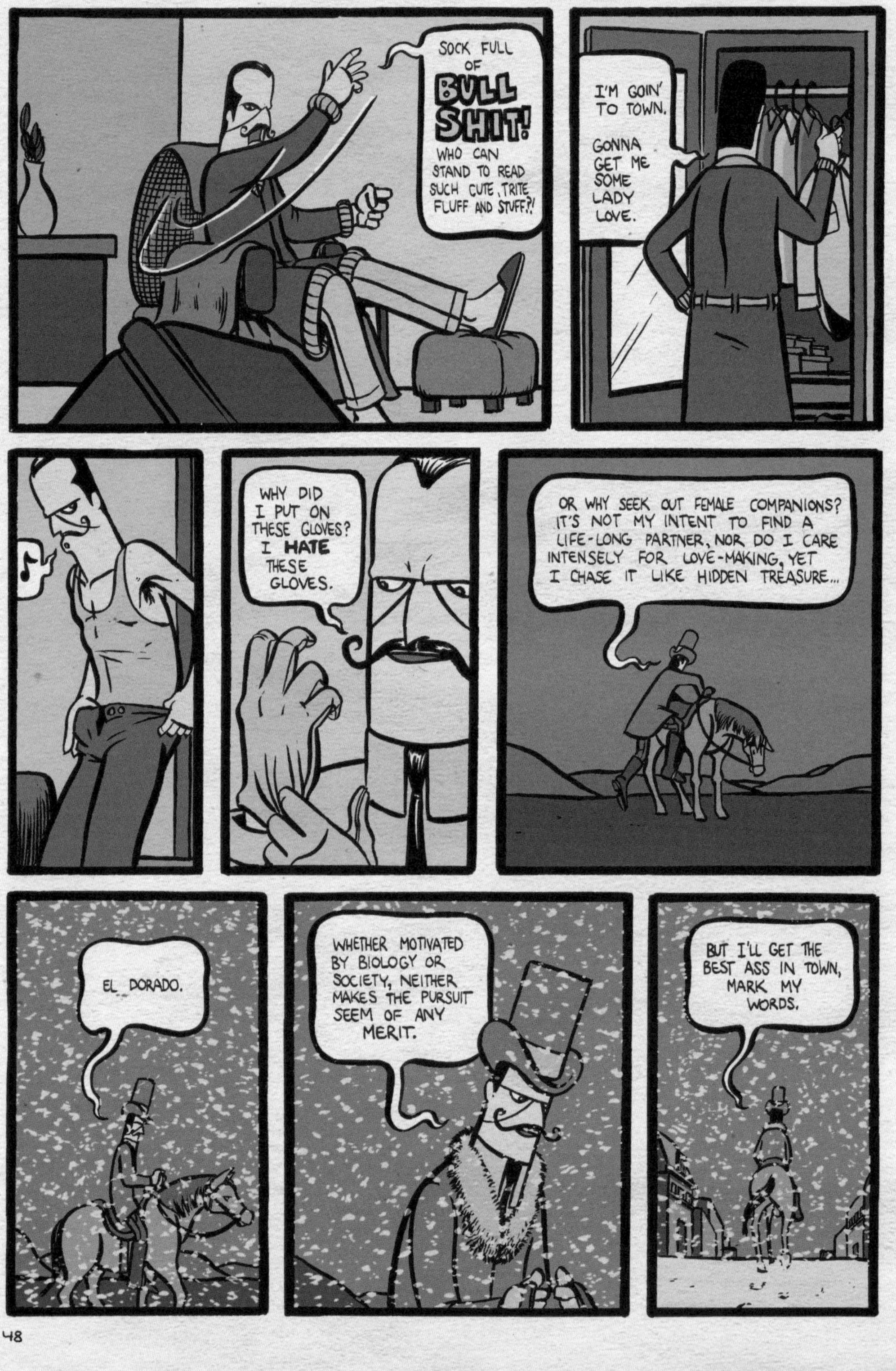
SOCK FULL OF BULL SHIT! WHO CAN STAND TO READ SUCH CUTE, TRITE FLUFF AND STUFF?!
I'M GOIN' TO TOWN.
GONNA GET ME SOME LADY LOVE.
WHY DID I PUT ON THESE GLOVES? I **HATE** THESE GLOVES.
OR WHY SEEK OUT FEMALE COMPANIONS? IT'S NOT MY INTENT TO FIND A LIFE-LONG PARTNER, NOR DO I CARE INTENSELY FOR LOVE-MAKING, YET I CHASE IT LIKE HIDDEN TREASURE...
EL DORADO.
WHETHER MOTIVATED BY BIOLOGY OR SOCIETY, NEITHER MAKES THE PURSUIT SEEM OF ANY MERIT.
BUT I'LL GET THE BEST ASS IN TOWN, MARK MY WORDS.

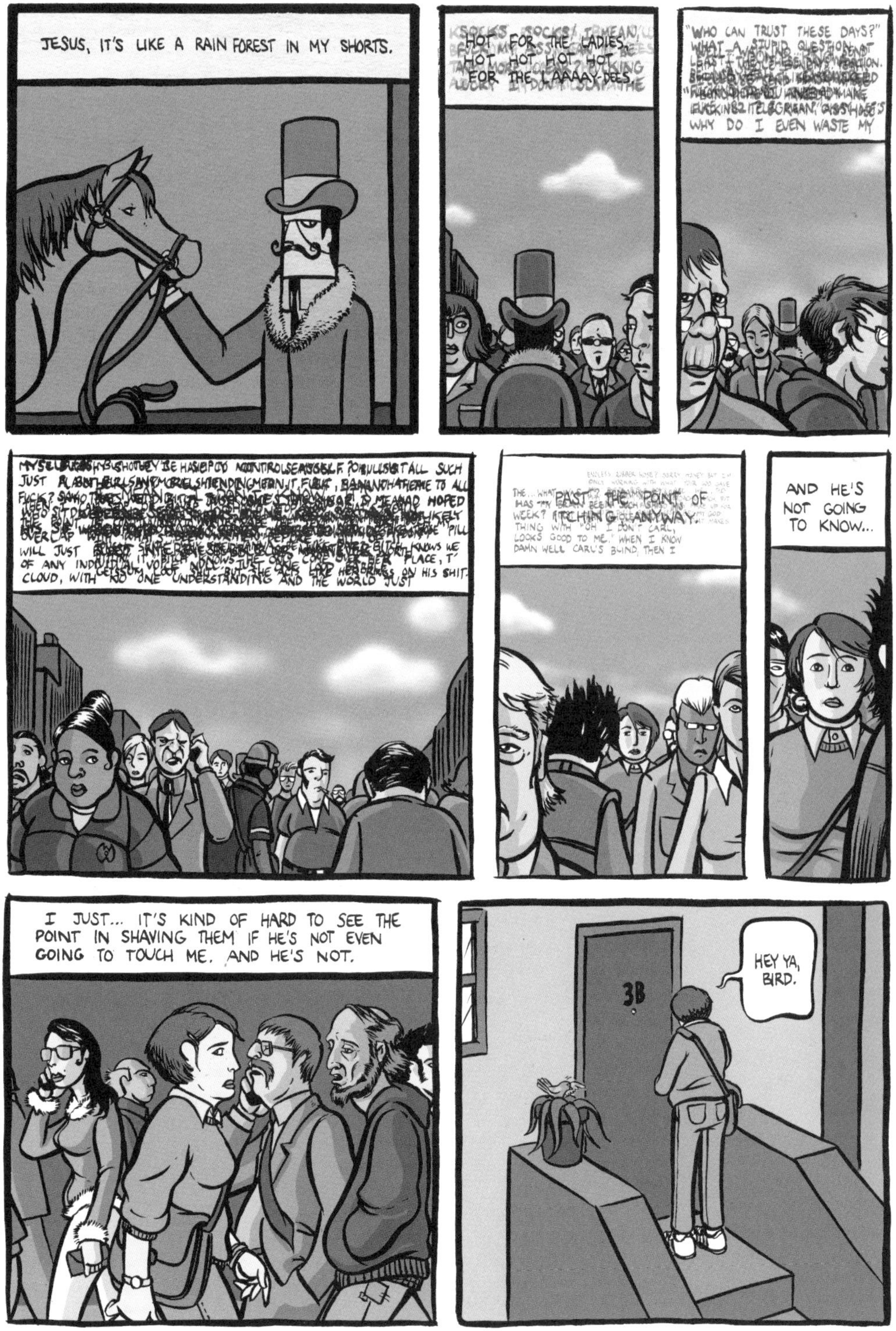
JESUS, IT'S LIKE A RAIN FOREST IN MY SHORTS.
HOT FOR THE LADIES. HOT HOT HOT HOT FOR THE LAAAAY-DEES.
"WHO CAN TRUST THESE DAYS?" WHAT A STUPID QUESTION.
WHY DO I EVEN WASTE MY
CLOUD, WITH NO ONE UNDERSTANDING AND THE WORLD JUST
PAST THE POINT OF ITCHING ANYWAY.
THING WITH "OH I DON'T CARL, LOOKS GOOD TO ME." WHEN I KNOW DAMN WELL CARL'S BLIND, THEN I
AND HE'S NOT GOING TO KNOW...
I JUST... IT'S KIND OF HARD TO SEE THE POINT IN SHAVING THEM IF HE'S NOT EVEN GOING TO TOUCH ME. AND HE'S NOT.
3B
HEY YA, BIRD.

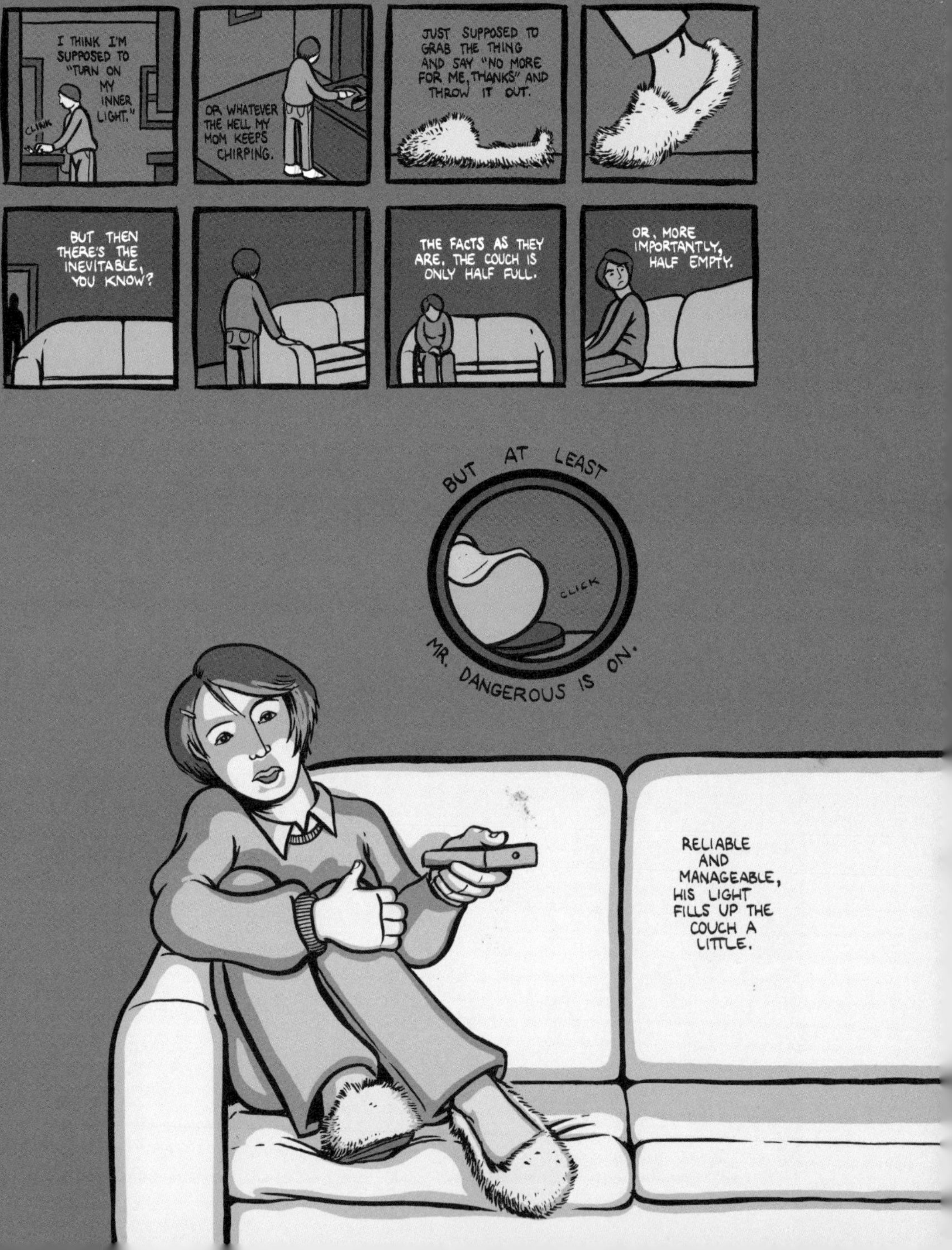
I THINK I'M SUPPOSED TO "TURN ON MY INNER LIGHT."
CLINK
OR WHATEVER THE HELL MY MOM KEEPS CHIRPING.
JUST SUPPOSED TO GRAB THE THING AND SAY "NO MORE FOR ME, THANKS" AND THROW IT OUT.
BUT THEN THERE'S THE INEVITABLE, YOU KNOW?
THE FACTS AS THEY ARE, THE COUCH IS ONLY HALF FULL.
OR, MORE IMPORTANTLY, HALF EMPTY.
BUT AT LEAST
CLICK
MR. DANGEROUS IS ON.
RELIABLE AND MANAGEABLE, HIS LIGHT FILLS UP THE COUCH A LITTLE.

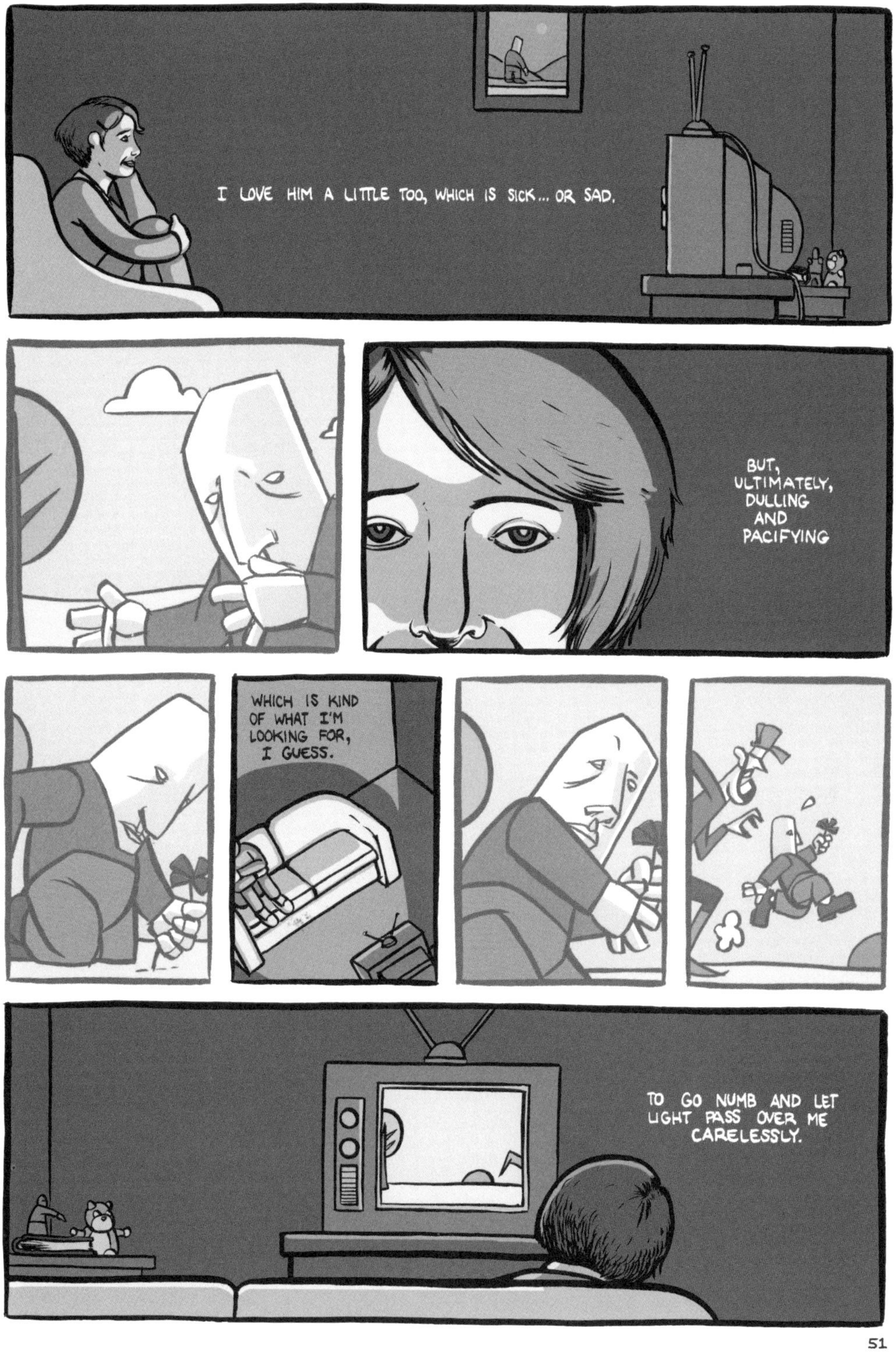
I LOVE HIM A LITTLE TOO, WHICH IS SICK... OR SAD.
BUT, ULTIMATELY, DULLING AND PACIFYING
WHICH IS KIND OF WHAT I'M LOOKING FOR, I GUESS.
TO GO NUMB AND LET LIGHT PASS OVER ME CARELESSLY.

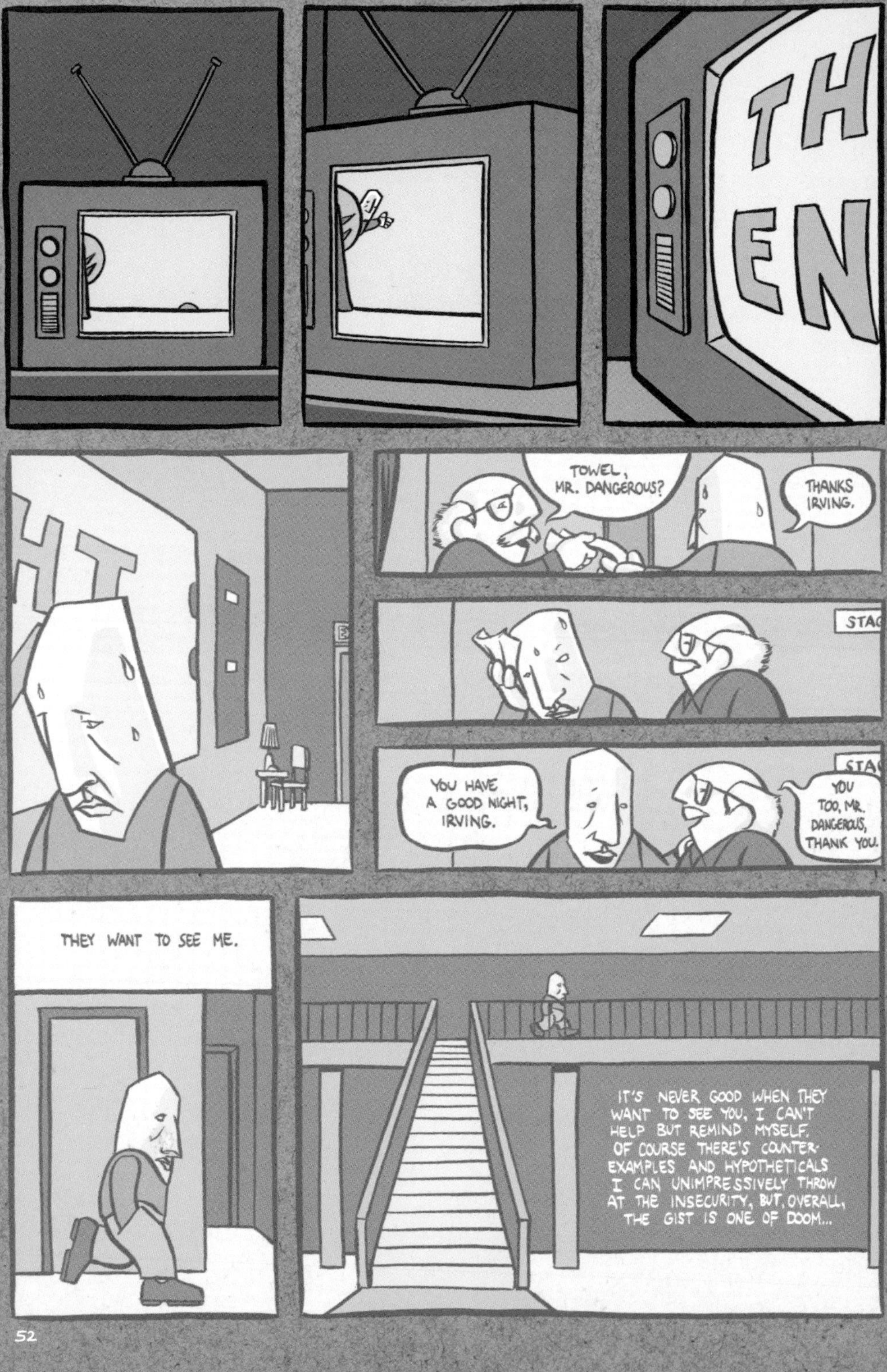
TH
EN
TOWEL, MR. DANGEROUS?
THANKS IRVING.
YOU HAVE A GOOD NIGHT, IRVING.
YOU TOO, MR. DANGEROUS, THANK YOU.
THEY WANT TO SEE ME.
IT'S NEVER GOOD WHEN THEY WANT TO SEE YOU, I CAN'T HELP BUT REMIND MYSELF. OF COURSE THERE'S COUNTER-EXAMPLES AND HYPOTHETICALS I CAN UNIMPRESSIVELY THROW AT THE INSECURITY, BUT, OVERALL, THE GIST IS ONE OF DOOM...

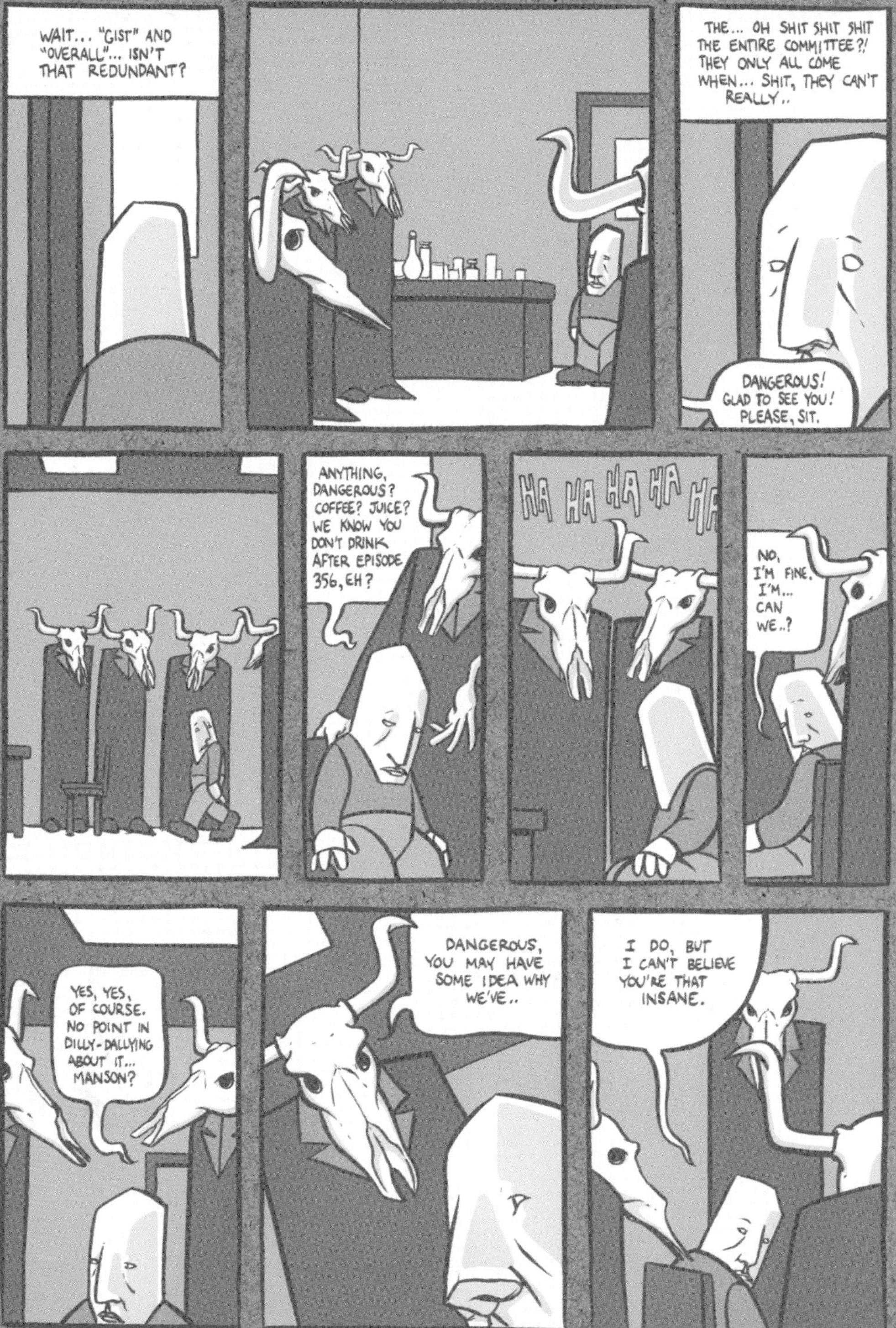
WAIT... "GIST" AND "OVERALL"... ISN'T THAT REDUNDANT?
THE... OH SHIT SHIT SHIT THE ENTIRE COMMITTEE?! THEY ONLY ALL COME WHEN... SHIT, THEY CAN'T REALLY..
DANGEROUS! GLAD TO SEE YOU! PLEASE, SIT.
ANYTHING, DANGEROUS? COFFEE? JUICE? WE KNOW YOU DON'T DRINK AFTER EPISODE 356, EH?
HA HA HA HA HA HA
NO, I'M FINE. I'M... CAN WE..?
YES, YES, OF COURSE. NO POINT IN DILLY-DALLYING ABOUT IT... MANSON?
DANGEROUS, YOU MAY HAVE SOME IDEA WHY WE'VE..
I DO, BUT I CAN'T BELIEVE YOU'RE THAT INSANE.

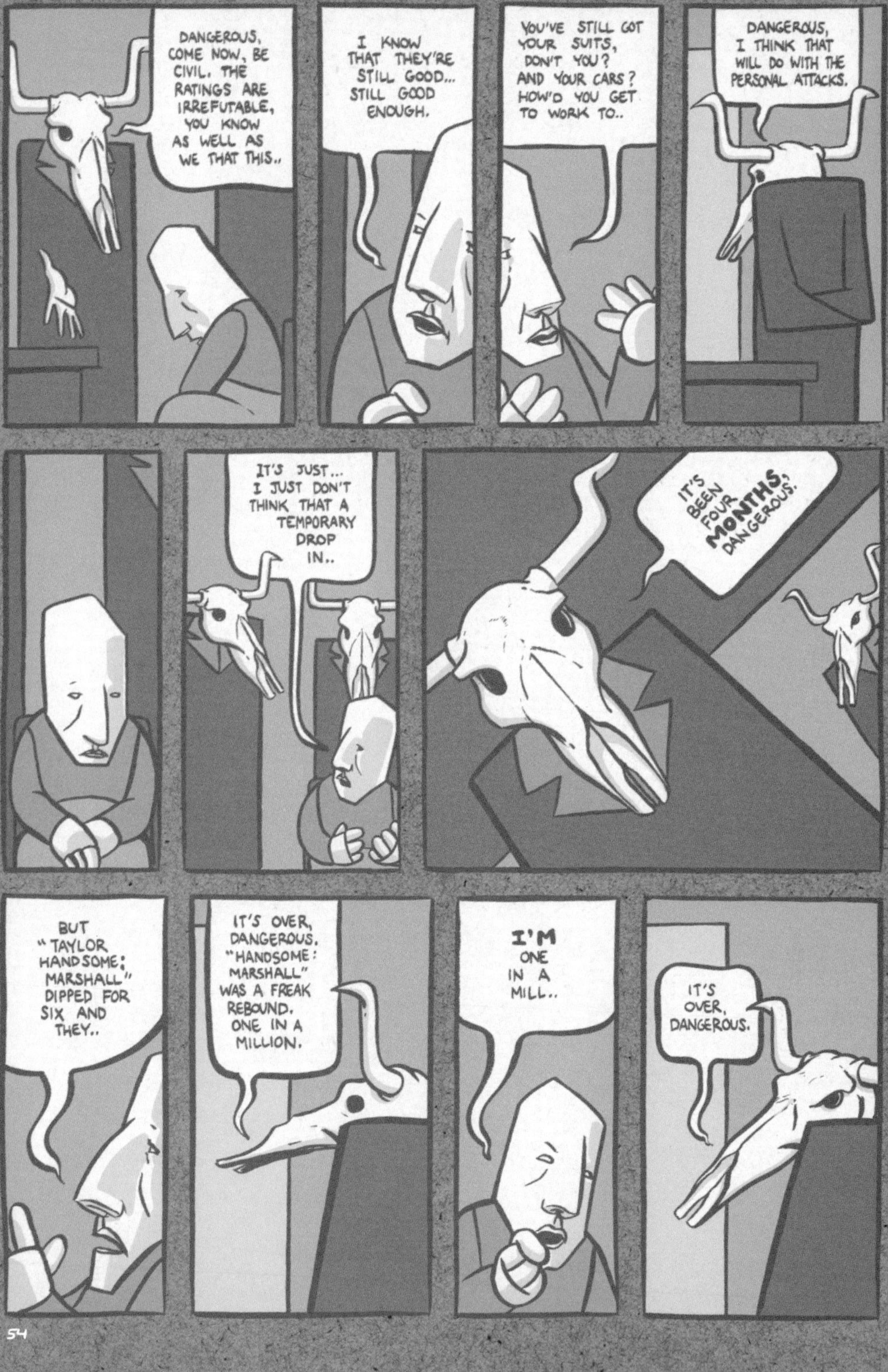
DANGEROUS, COME NOW, BE CIVIL. THE RATINGS ARE IRREFUTABLE, YOU KNOW AS WELL AS WE THAT THIS..
I KNOW THAT THEY'RE STILL GOOD... STILL GOOD ENOUGH.
YOU'VE STILL GOT YOUR SUITS, DON'T YOU? AND YOUR CARS? HOW'D YOU GET TO WORK TO..
DANGEROUS, I THINK THAT WILL DO WITH THE PERSONAL ATTACKS.
IT'S JUST... I JUST DON'T THINK THAT A TEMPORARY DROP IN..
IT'S BEEN FOUR **MONTHS**, DANGEROUS.
BUT "TAYLOR HANDSOME: MARSHALL" DIPPED FOR SIX AND THEY..
IT'S OVER, DANGEROUS. "HANDSOME: MARSHALL" WAS A FREAK REBOUND. ONE IN A MILLION.
I'M ONE IN A MILL..
IT'S OVER, DANGEROUS.

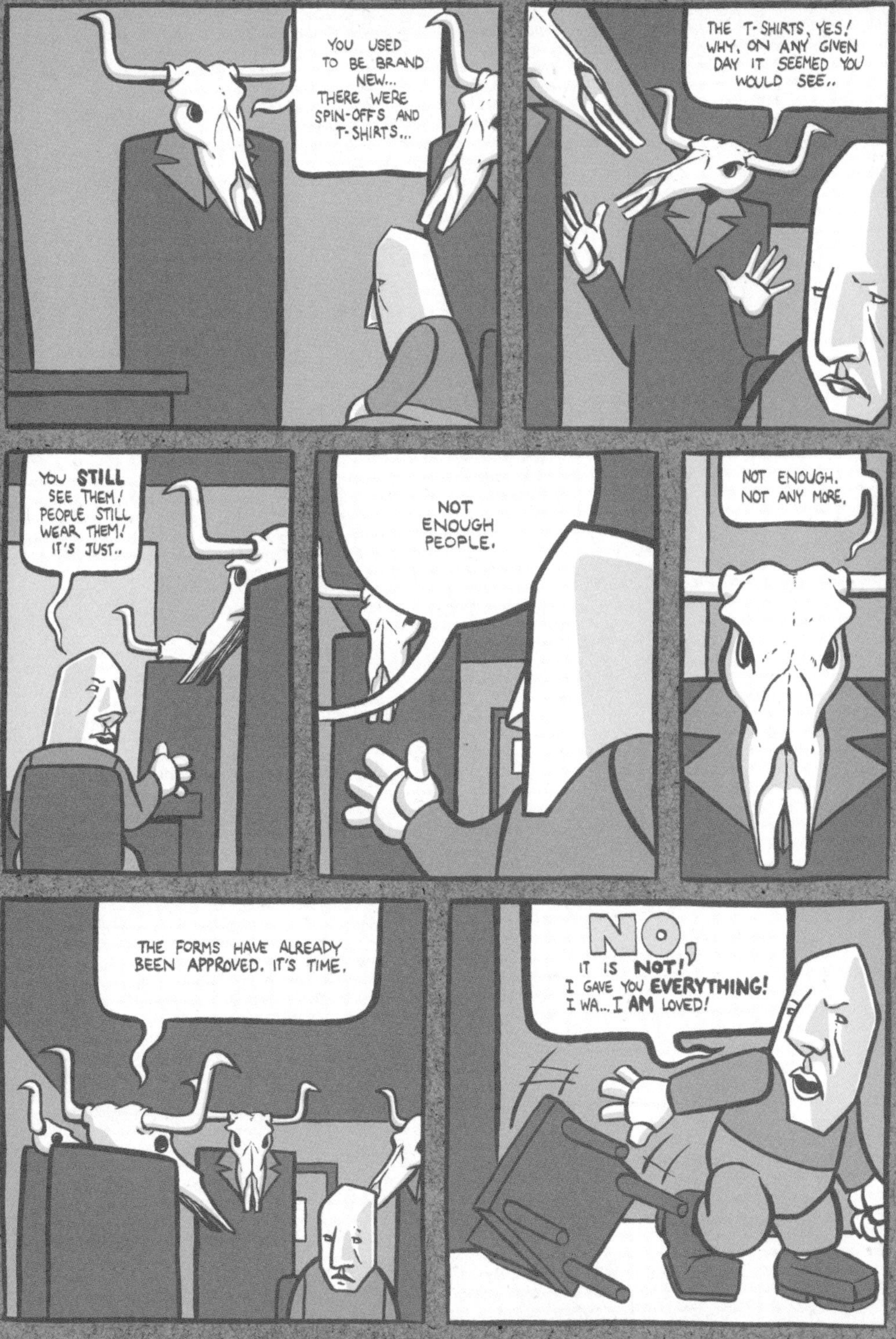
YOU USED TO BE BRAND NEW... THERE WERE SPIN-OFF'S AND T-SHIRTS...
THE T-SHIRTS, YES! WHY, ON ANY GIVEN DAY IT SEEMED YOU WOULD SEE..
YOU STILL SEE THEM! PEOPLE STILL WEAR THEM! IT'S JUST..
NOT ENOUGH PEOPLE.
NOT ENOUGH. NOT ANY MORE.
THE FORMS HAVE ALREADY BEEN APPROVED. IT'S TIME.
NO, IT IS NOT! I GAVE YOU EVERYTHING! I WA... I AM LOVED!

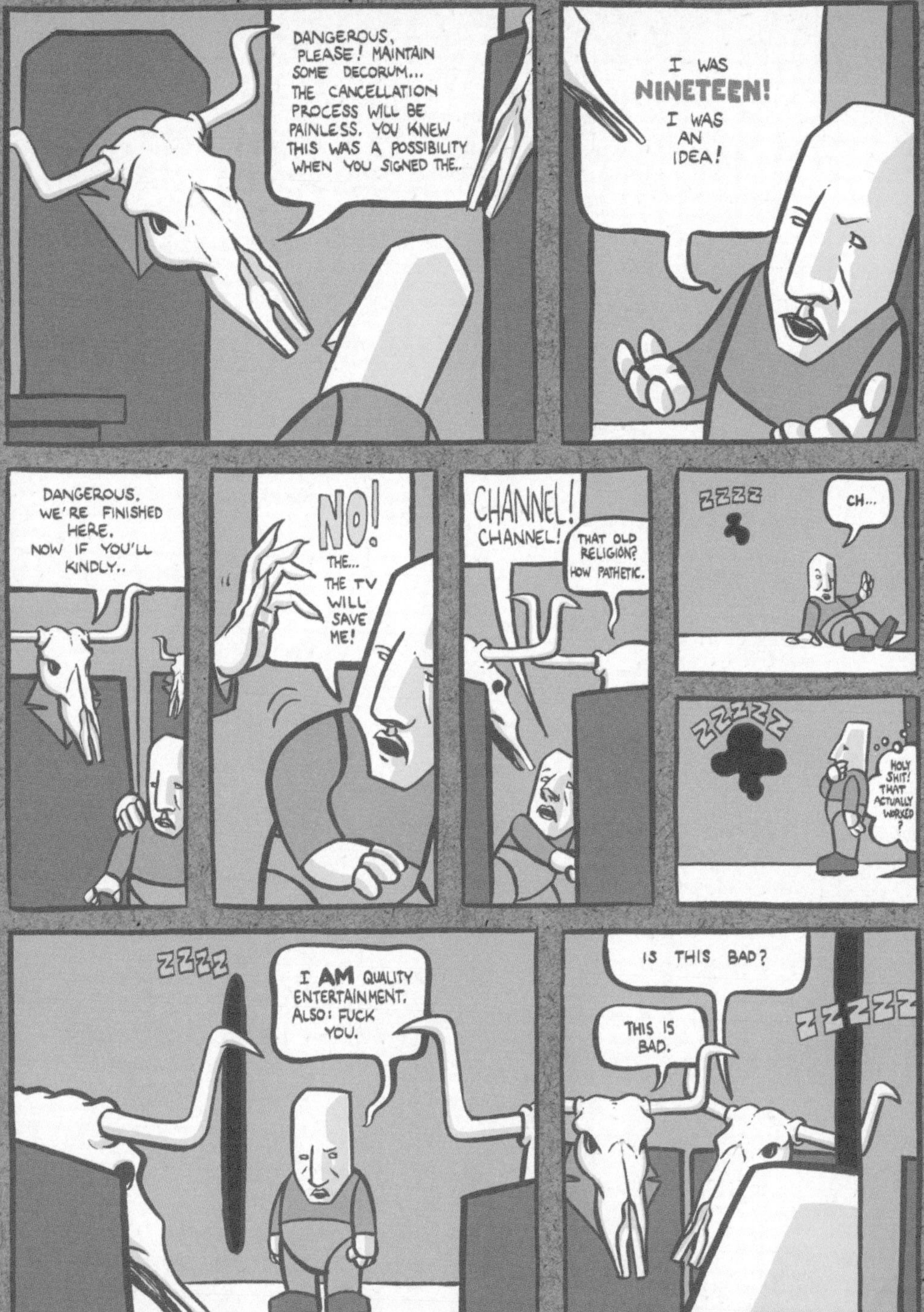
DANGEROUS, PLEASE! MAINTAIN SOME DECORUM... THE CANCELLATION PROCESS WILL BE PAINLESS. YOU KNEW THIS WAS A POSSIBILITY WHEN YOU SIGNED THE..
I WAS NINETEEN! I WAS AN IDEA!
DANGEROUS. WE'RE FINISHED HERE. NOW IF YOU'LL KINDLY..
NO! THE... THE TV WILL SAVE ME!
CHANNEL! CHANNEL!
THAT OLD RELIGION? HOW PATHETIC.
ZZZZ
CH...
ZZZZZ
HOLY SHIT! THAT ACTUALLY WORKED?
ZZZZ
I AM QUALITY ENTERTAINMENT. ALSO: FUCK YOU.
IS THIS BAD?
THIS IS BAD.
ZZZZZ

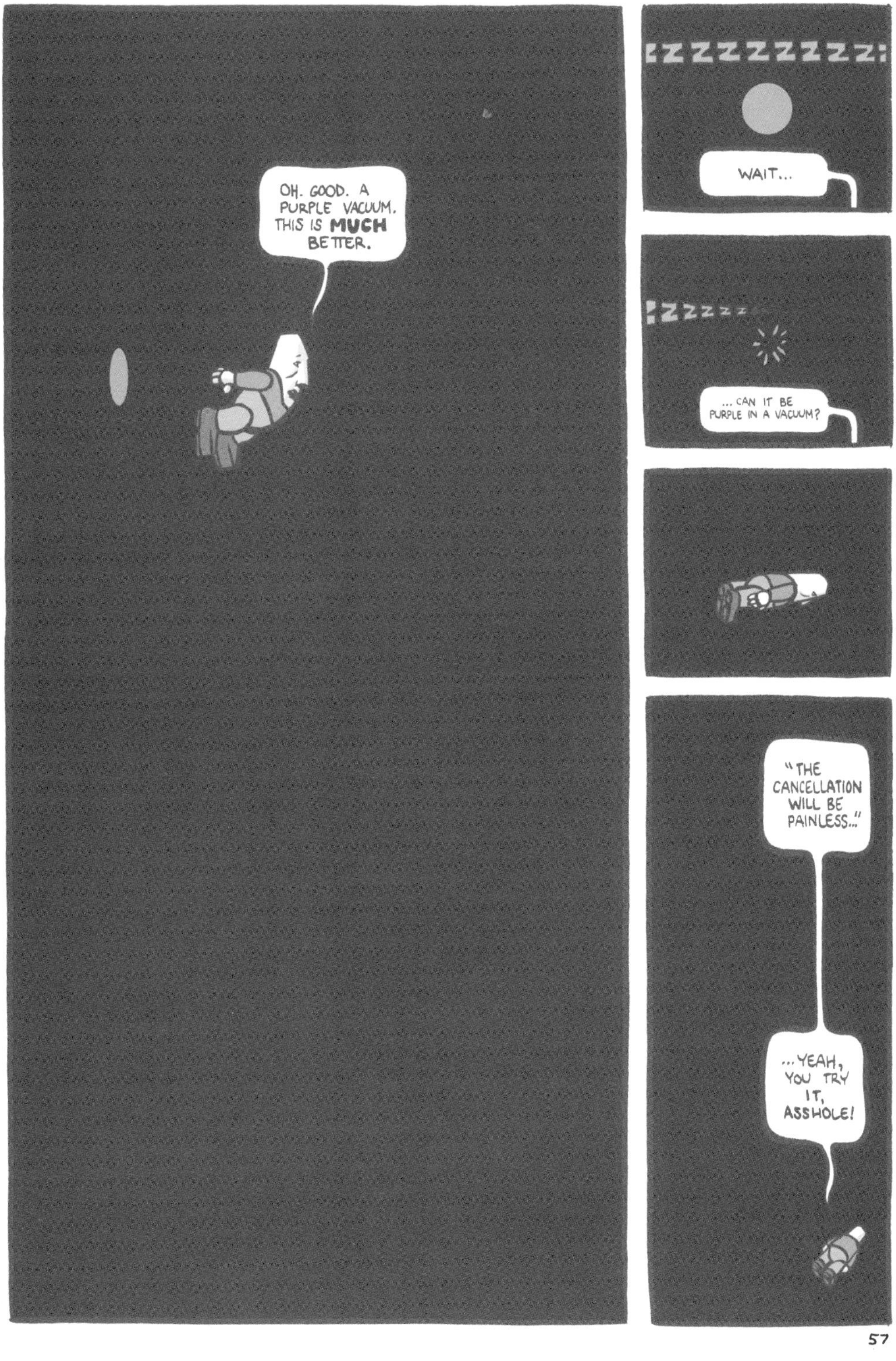
OH. GOOD. A PURPLE VACUUM. THIS IS **MUCH** BETTER.
ZZZZZZZZZ
WAIT...
ZZZZZ
...CAN IT BE PURPLE IN A VACUUM?
"THE CANCELLATION WILL BE PAINLESS..."
...YEAH, YOU TRY IT, ASSHOLE!

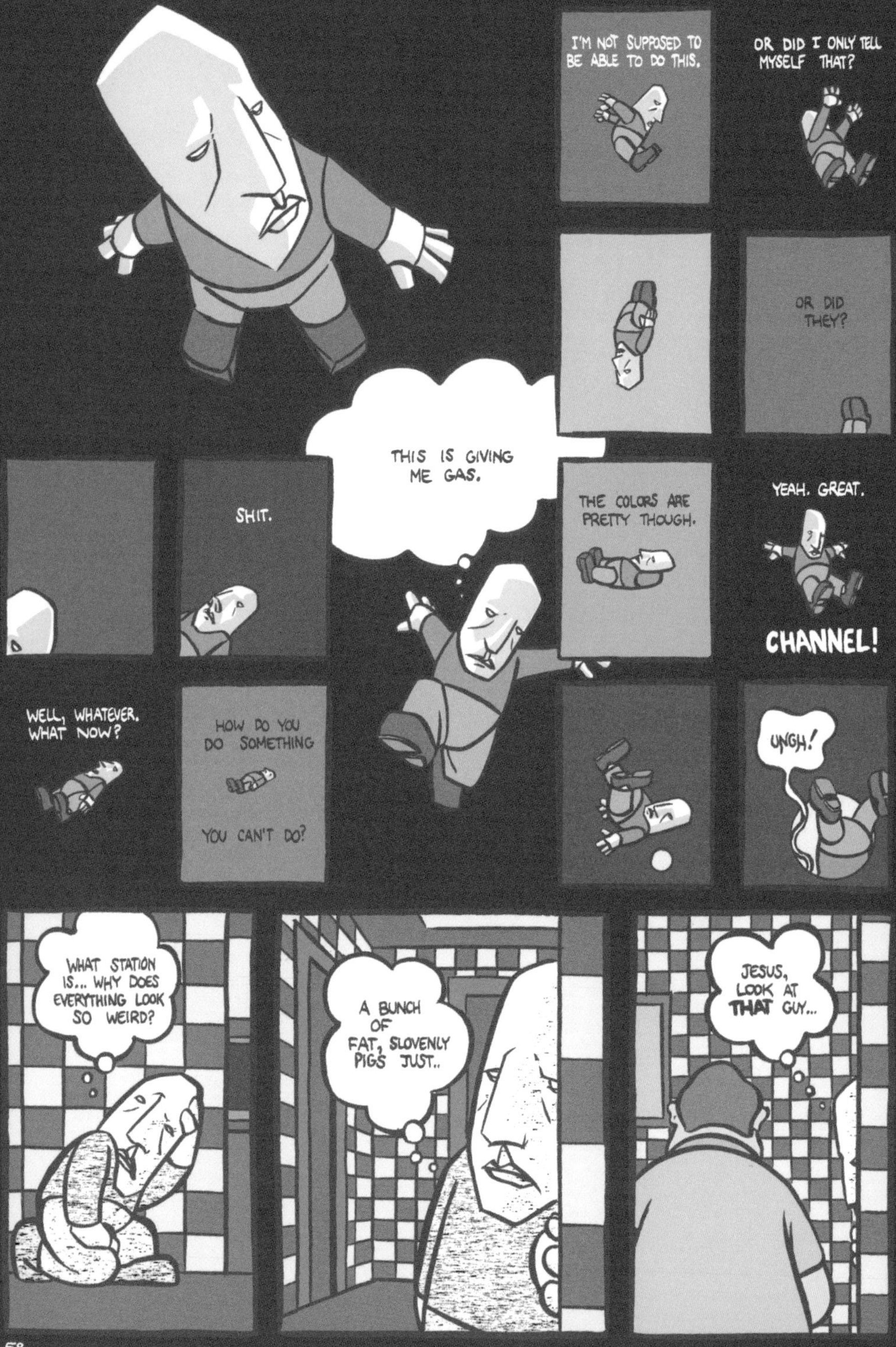
I'M NOT SUPPOSED TO BE ABLE TO DO THIS.
OR DID I ONLY TELL MYSELF THAT?
OR DID THEY?
SHIT.
THIS IS GIVING ME GAS.
THE COLORS ARE PRETTY THOUGH.
YEAH. GREAT.
CHANNEL!
WELL, WHATEVER. WHAT NOW?
HOW DO YOU DO SOMETHING
YOU CAN'T DO?
UNGH!
WHAT STATION IS... WHY DOES EVERYTHING LOOK SO WEIRD?
A BUNCH OF FAT, SLOVENLY PIGS JUST..
JESUS, LOOK AT THAT GUY...

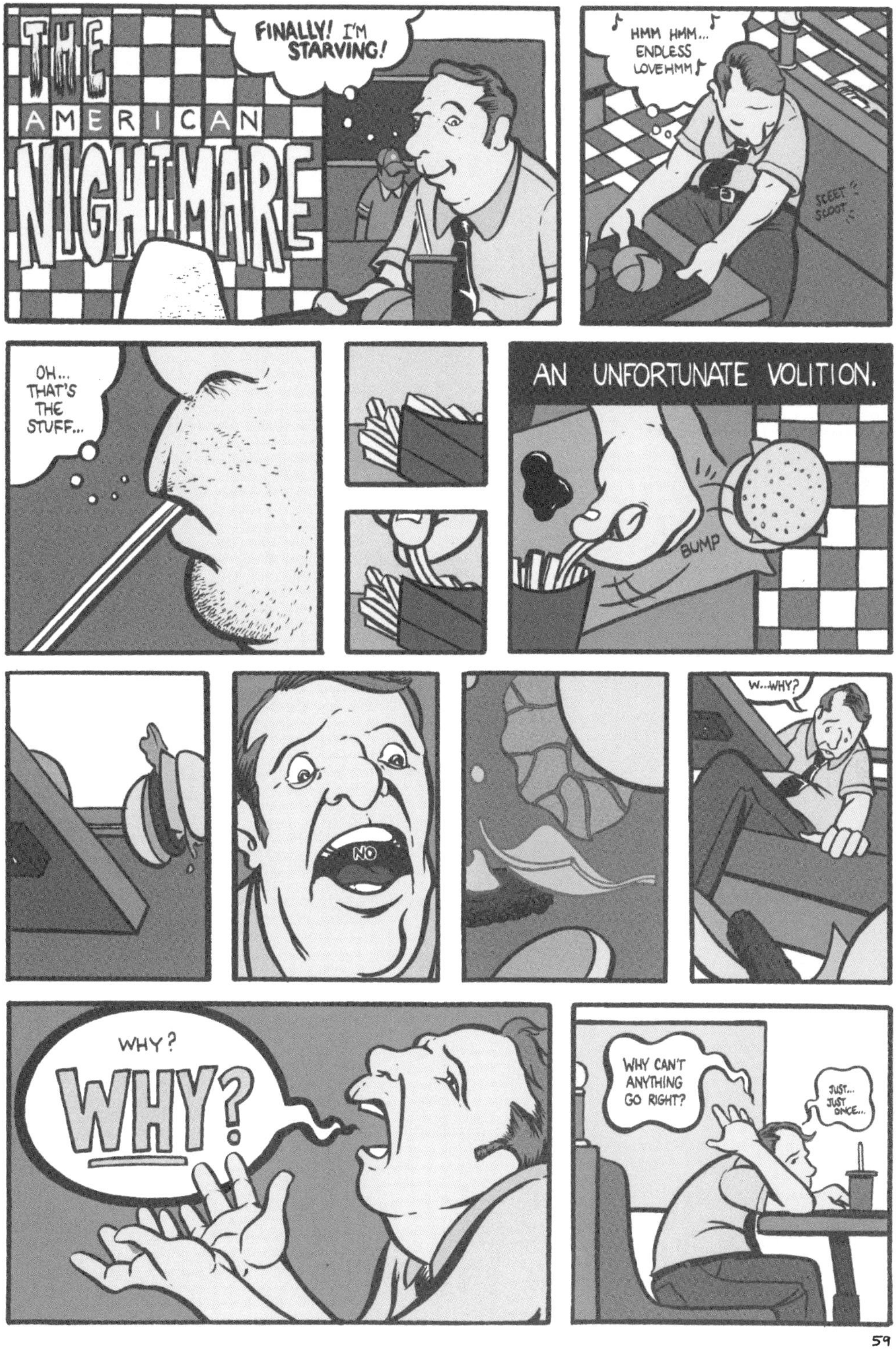
THE AMERICAN NIGHTMARE
FINALLY! I'M STARVING!
HMM HMM... ENDLESS LOVE HMM
SCEET SCOOT
OH... THAT'S THE STUFF...
AN UNFORTUNATE VOLITION.
BUMP
NO
W...WHY?
WHY? WHY?
WHY CAN'T ANYTHING GO RIGHT?
JUST... JUST ONCE...

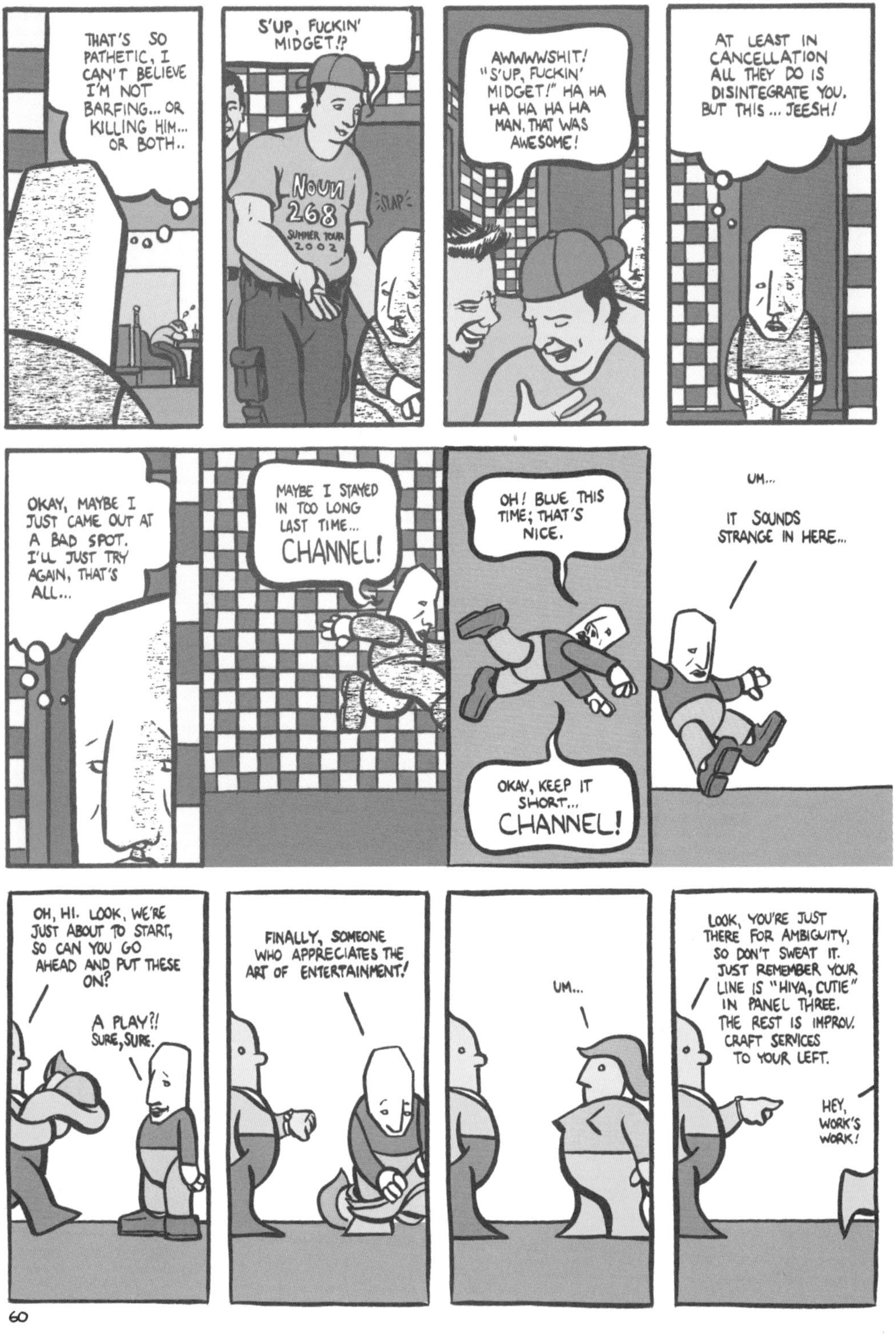
THAT'S SO PATHETIC, I CAN'T BELIEVE I'M NOT BARFING... OR KILLING HIM... OR BOTH..
S'UP, FUCKIN' MIDGET!?
NOUN 268 SUMMER TOUR 2002
SLAP
AWWWWSHIT! "S'UP, FUCKIN' MIDGET!" HA HA HA HA HA HA MAN, THAT WAS AWESOME!
AT LEAST IN CANCELLATION ALL THEY DO IS DISINTEGRATE YOU. BUT THIS ... JEESH!
OKAY, MAYBE I JUST CAME OUT AT A BAD SPOT. I'LL JUST TRY AGAIN, THAT'S ALL...
MAYBE I STAYED IN TOO LONG LAST TIME... CHANNEL!
OH! BLUE THIS TIME; THAT'S NICE.
OKAY, KEEP IT SHORT... CHANNEL!
UM...
IT SOUNDS STRANGE IN HERE...
OH, HI. LOOK, WE'RE JUST ABOUT TO START, SO CAN YOU GO AHEAD AND PUT THESE ON?
A PLAY?! SURE, SURE.
FINALLY, SOMEONE WHO APPRECIATES THE ART OF ENTERTAINMENT!
UM...
LOOK, YOU'RE JUST THERE FOR AMBIGUITY, SO DON'T SWEAT IT. JUST REMEMBER YOUR LINE IS "HIYA, CUTIE" IN PANEL THREE. THE REST IS IMPROV. CRAFT SERVICES TO YOUR LEFT.
HEY, WORK'S WORK!

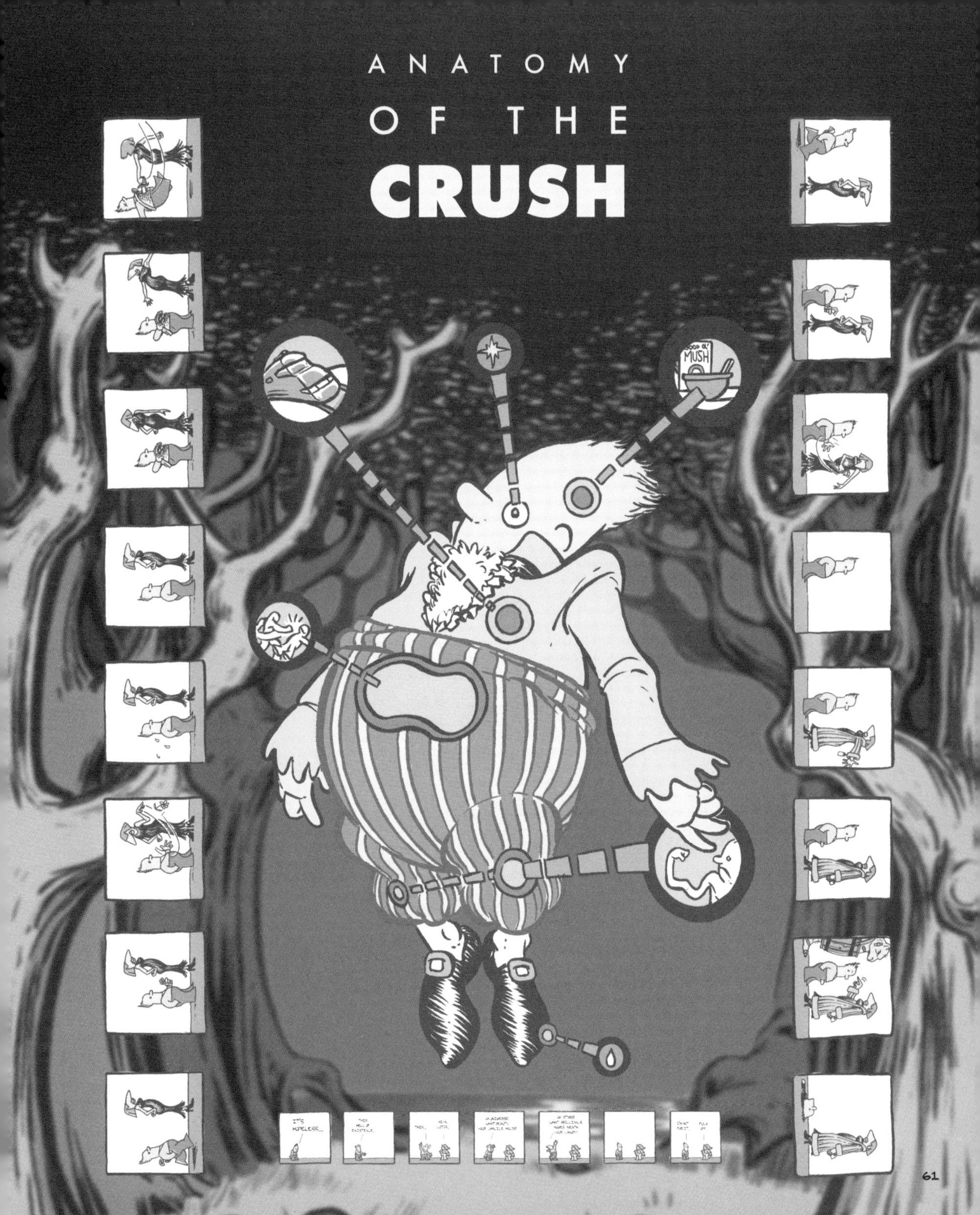
ANATOMY
OF THE
CRUSH
GOOD OL' MUSH
IT'S HOPELESS...
THIS HELL OF EXISTENCE.
THIS...
HI-YA, CUTIE.
OH UNIVERSE! WHAT BEAUTY YOUR CHALICE HOLDS!
OH STARS! WHAT BRILLIANCE MOVES NEATH YOUR CANOPY!
I'M HOT FOR IT.
FUCK OFF.

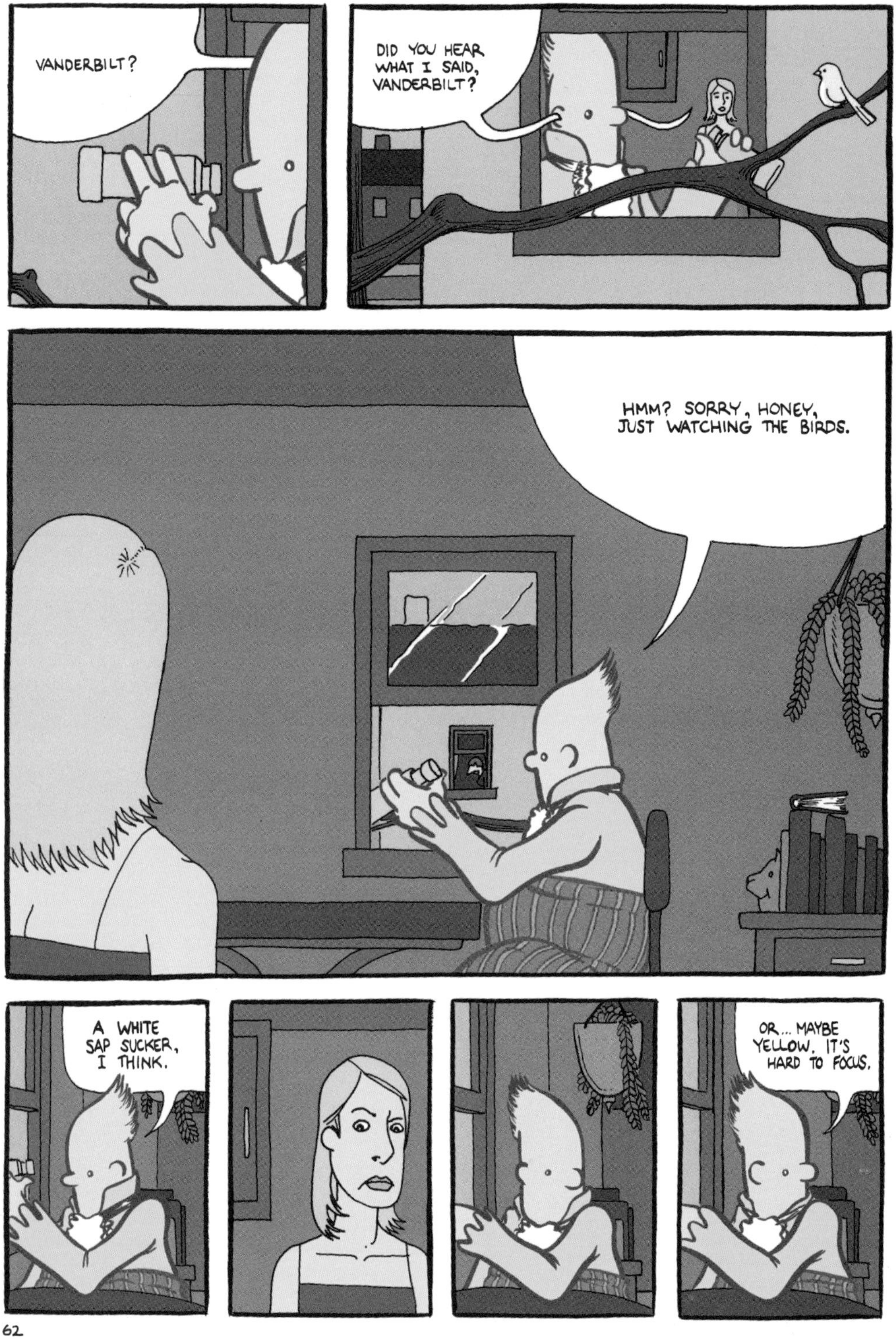
VANDERBILT?
DID YOU HEAR WHAT I SAID, VANDERBILT?
HMM? SORRY, HONEY, JUST WATCHING THE BIRDS.
A WHITE SAP SUCKER, I THINK.
OR... MAYBE YELLOW. IT'S HARD TO FOCUS.

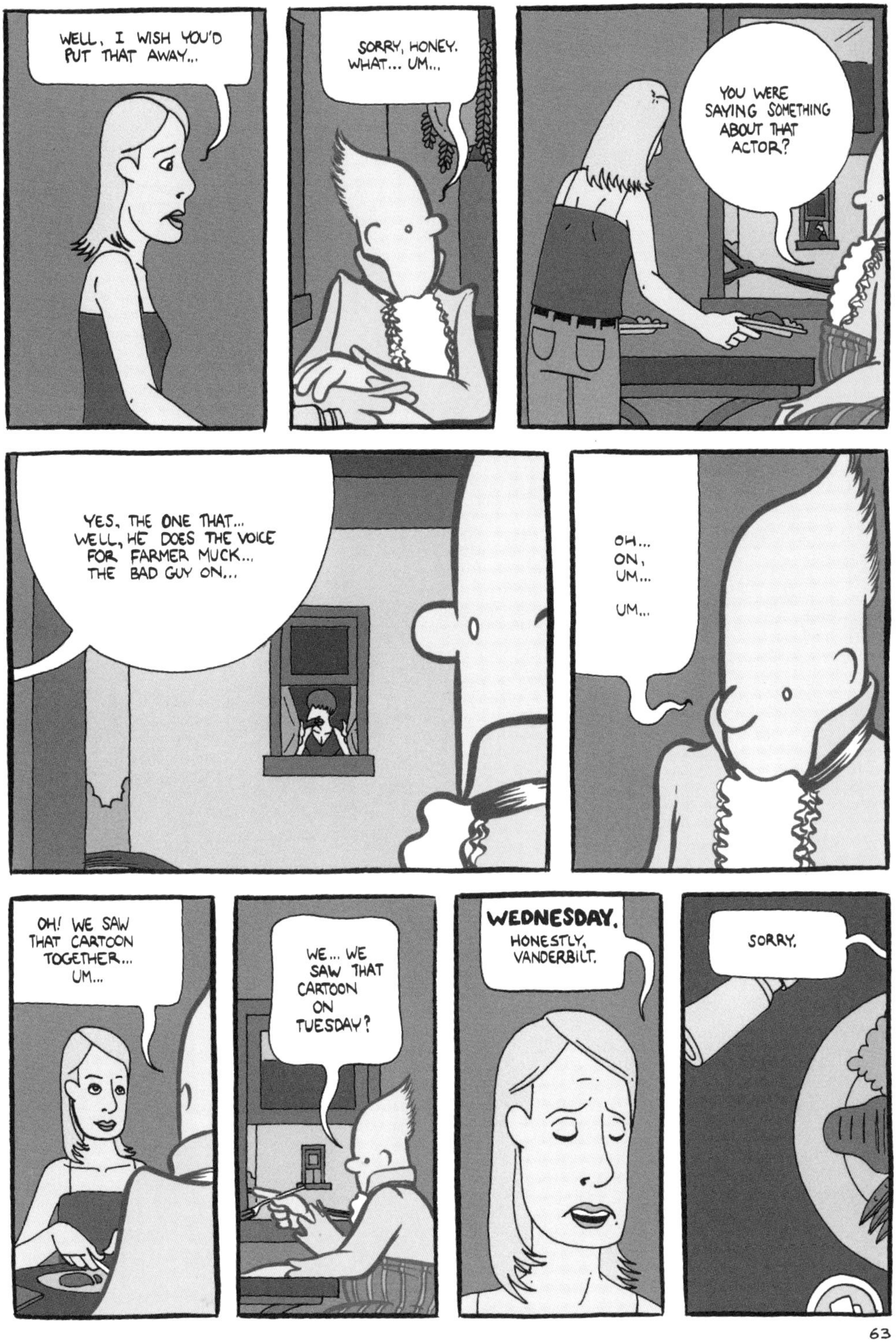
WELL, I WISH YOU'D PUT THAT AWAY...
SORRY, HONEY. WHAT... UM...
YOU WERE SAYING SOMETHING ABOUT THAT ACTOR?
YES, THE ONE THAT... WELL, HE DOES THE VOICE FOR FARMER MUCK... THE BAD GUY ON...
OH... ON, UM... UM...
OH! WE SAW THAT CARTOON TOGETHER... UM...
WE... WE SAW THAT CARTOON ON TUESDAY?
WEDNESDAY. HONESTLY, VANDERBILT.
SORRY.

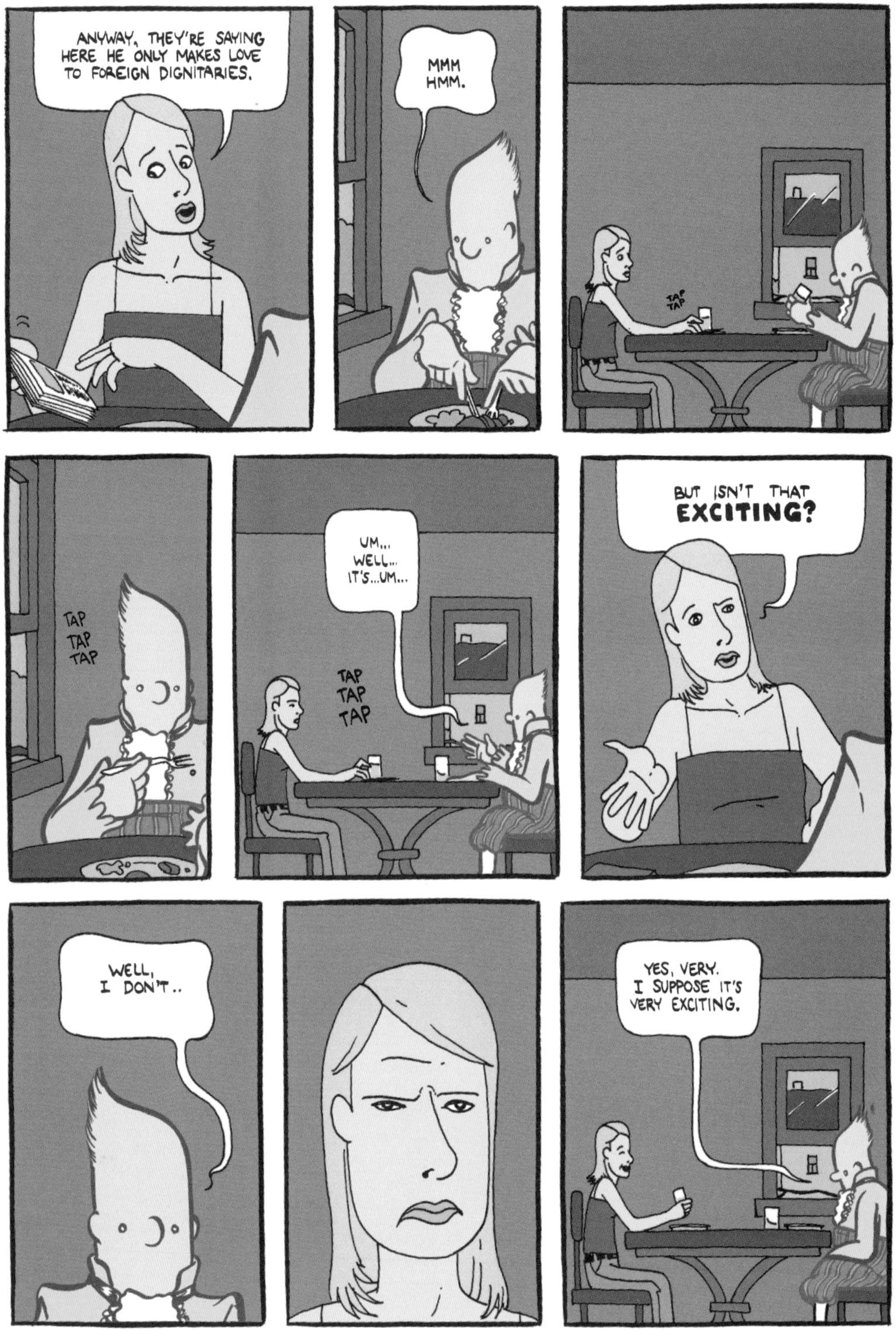
ANYWAY, THEY'RE SAYING HERE HE ONLY MAKES LOVE TO FOREIGN DIGNITARIES.
MMM HMM.
TAP TAP
TAP TAP TAP
UM... WELL... IT'S...UM...
TAP TAP TAP
BUT ISN'T THAT **EXCITING?**
WELL, I DON'T..
YES, VERY. I SUPPOSE IT'S VERY EXCITING.

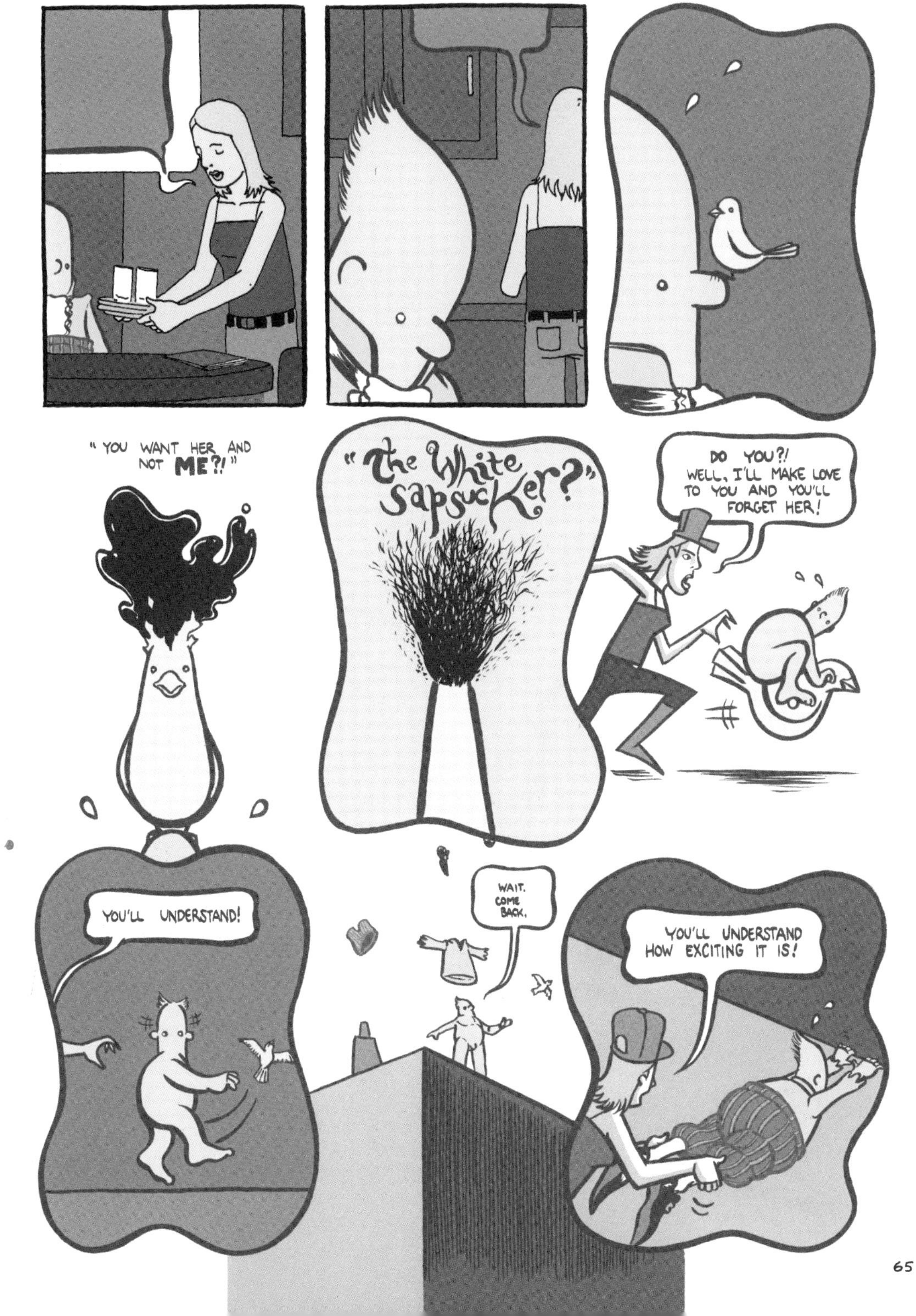
"YOU WANT HER AND NOT ME?!"
"The White sapsucker?"
DO YOU?! WELL, I'LL MAKE LOVE TO YOU AND YOU'LL FORGET HER!
YOU'LL UNDERSTAND!
WAIT. COME BACK.
YOU'LL UNDERSTAND HOW EXCITING IT IS!

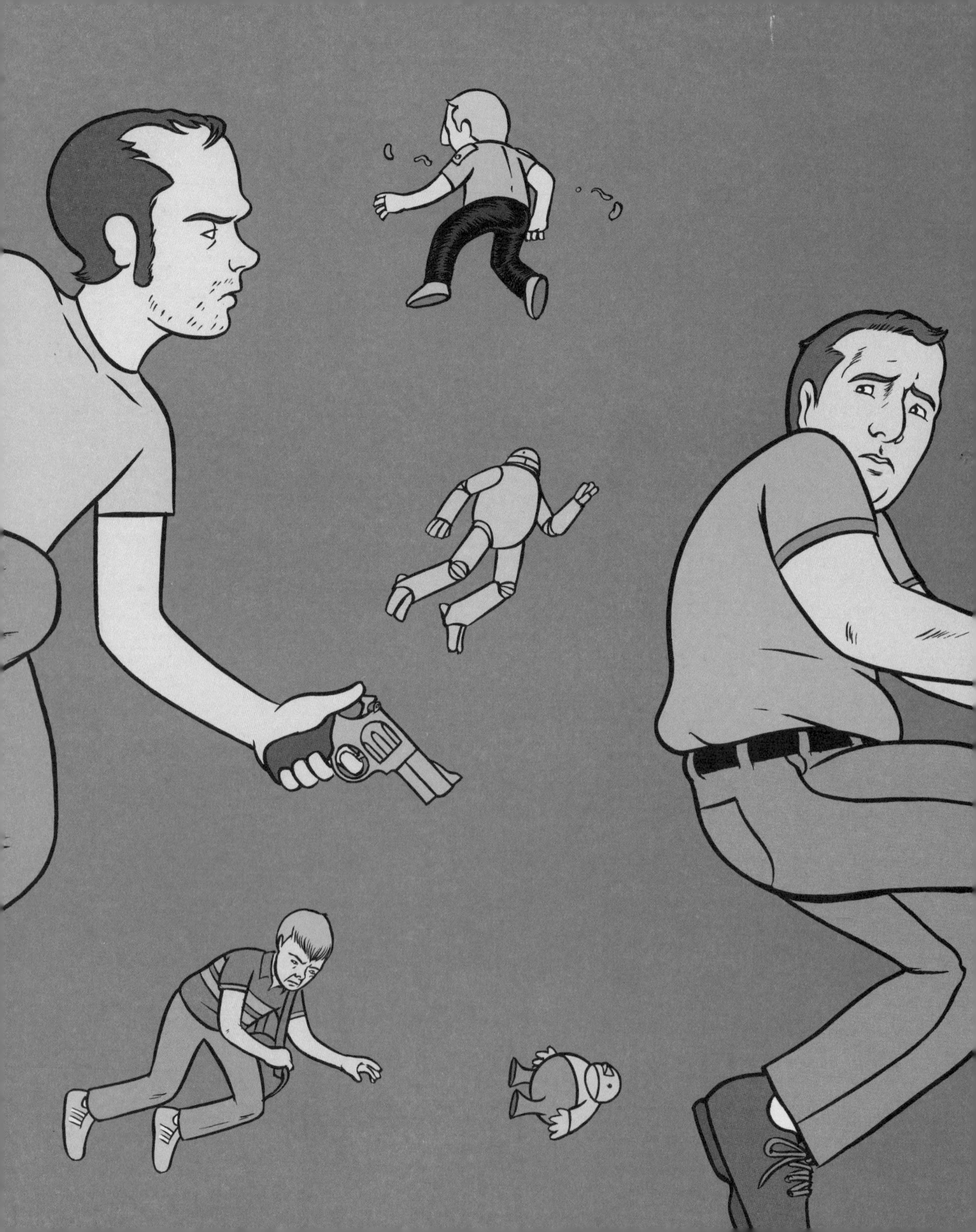

FOR MY MOTHER
WHO GAVE ME AGATHA CHRISTIE

WRITTEN AND DRAWN BY PAUL HORNSCHEMEIER
PUBLISHED BY GARY GROTH AND KIM THOMPSON
PROMOTED BY ERIC REYNOLDS
BOOK DESIGN BY THE AUTHOR

ISBN-10: 1-56097-752-3
ISBN-13: 978-1-56097-752-0

PRINTED IN SINGAPORE

FIRST EDITION: SEPTEMBER 2006

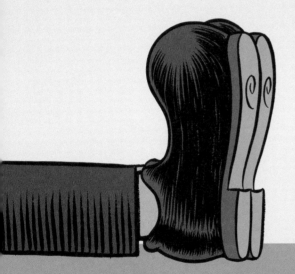

PORTIONS OF THIS COLLECTION WERE PUBLISHED PREVIOUSLY IN PROJECT TELSTAR, RETURN OF
THE ELEPHANT, THE COMICS JOURNAL SPECIAL EDITION, TYPEWRITER, AND FORLORN FUNNIES.

LET US BE

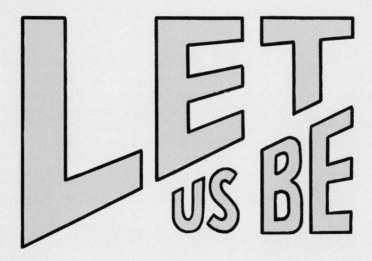

CONTENTS

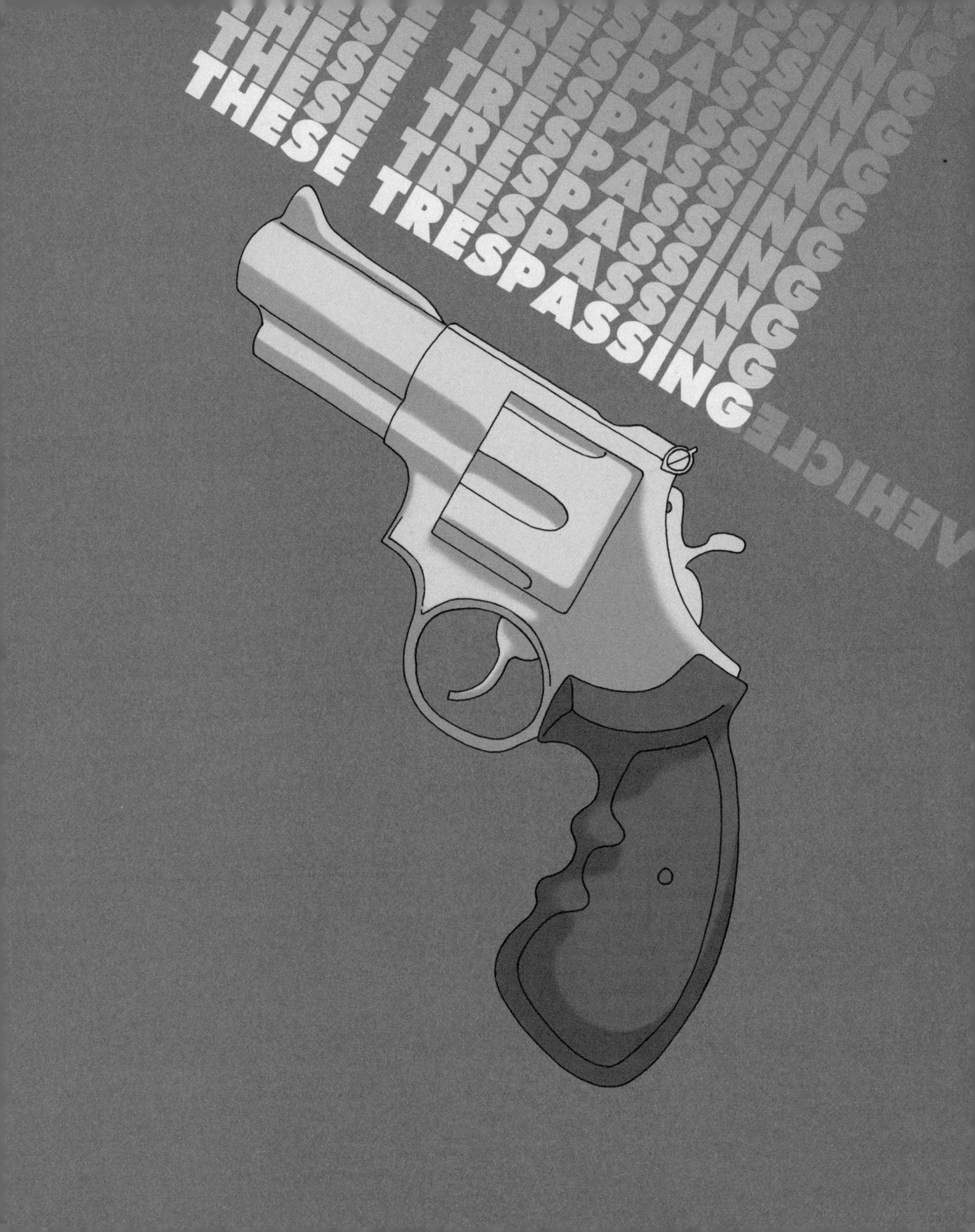
THESE TRESPASSING
VEHICLE

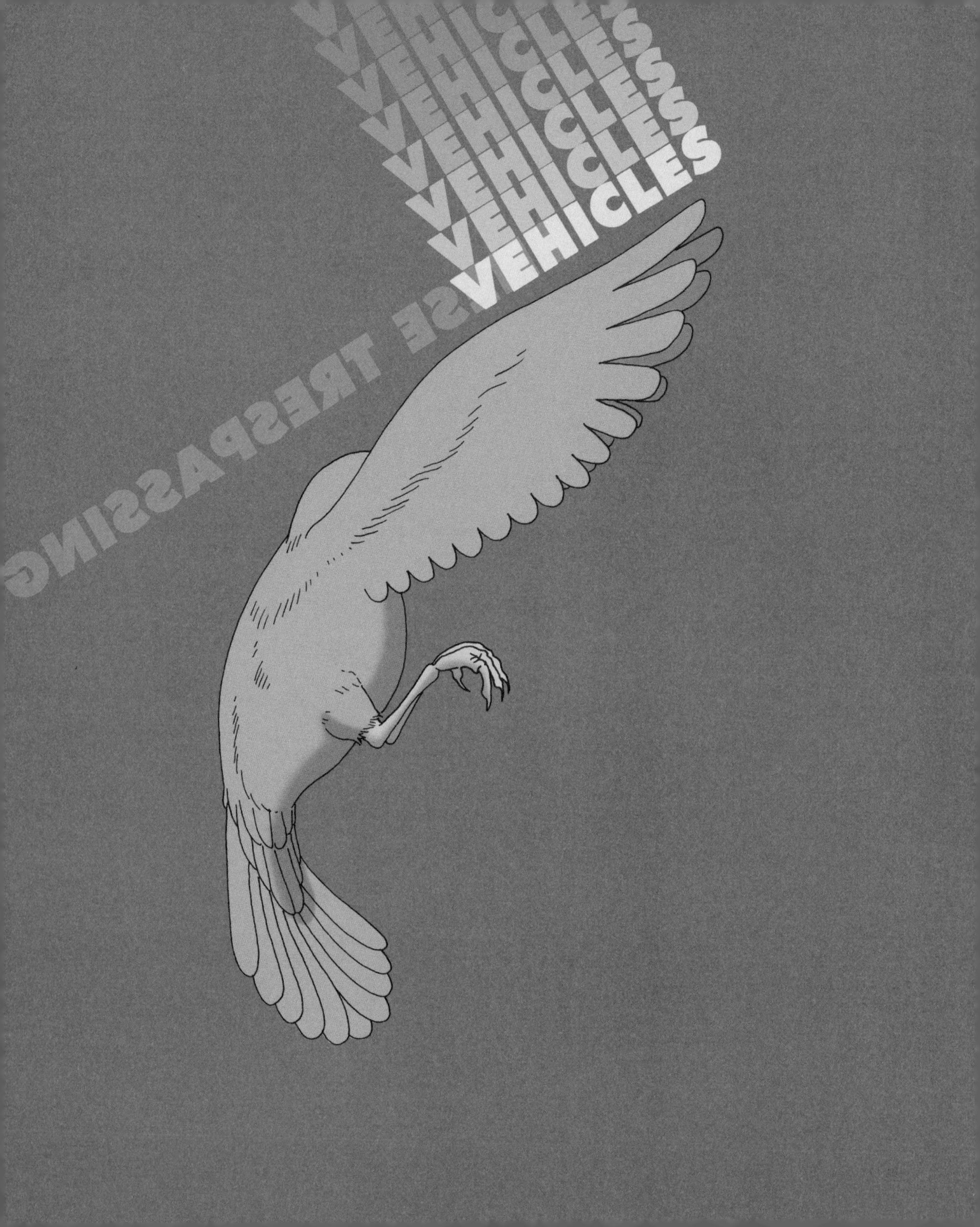
VEHICLES
TRESPASSING

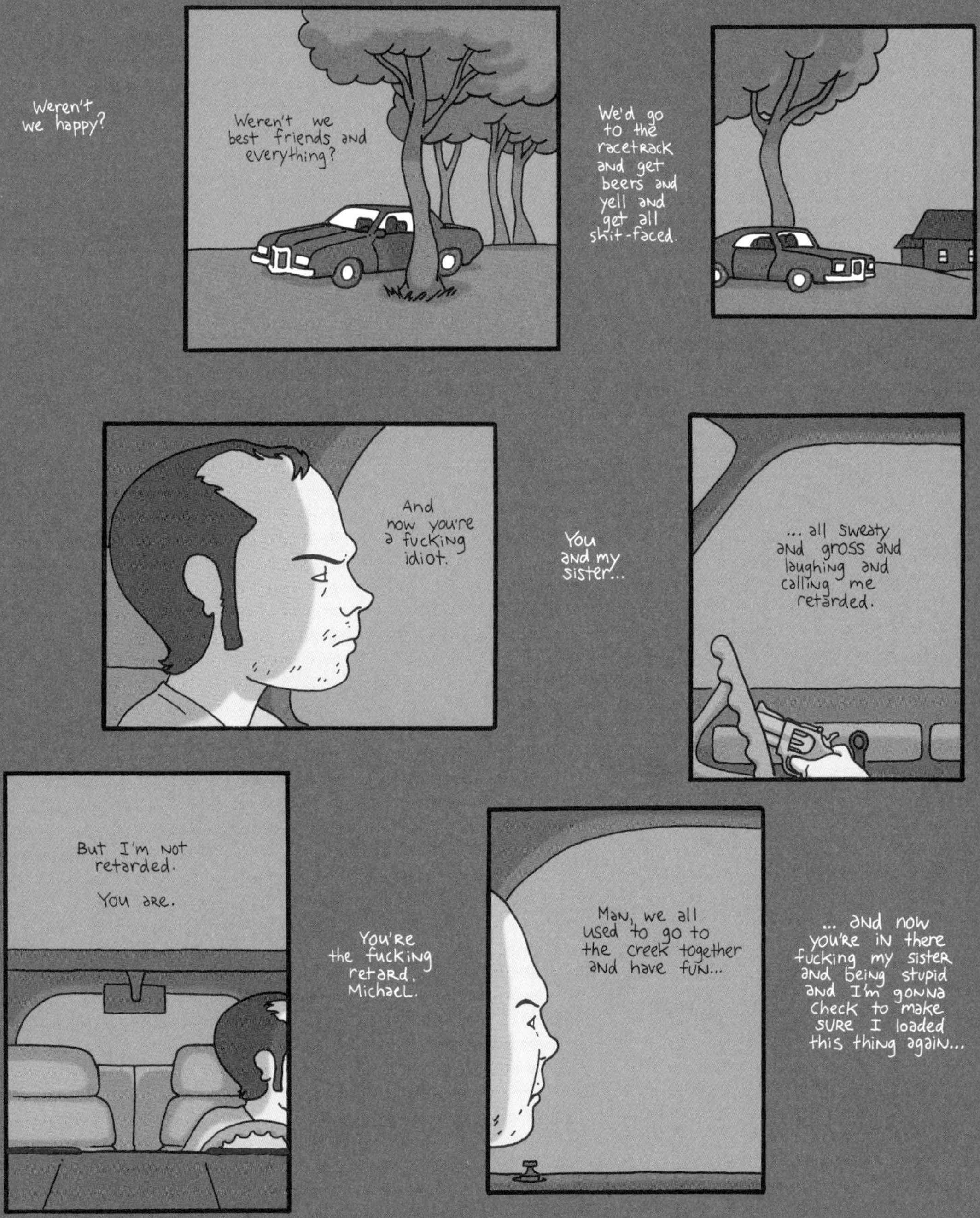
Weren't we happy?
Weren't we best friends and everything?
We'd go to the racetrack and get beers and yell and get all shit-faced.
And now you're a fucking idiot.
You and my sister...
... all sweaty and gross and laughing and calling me retarded.
But I'm not retarded.
You are.
You're the fucking retard, Michael.
Man, we all used to go to the creek together and have fun...
... and now you're in there fucking my sister and being stupid and I'm gonna check to make sure I loaded this thing again...

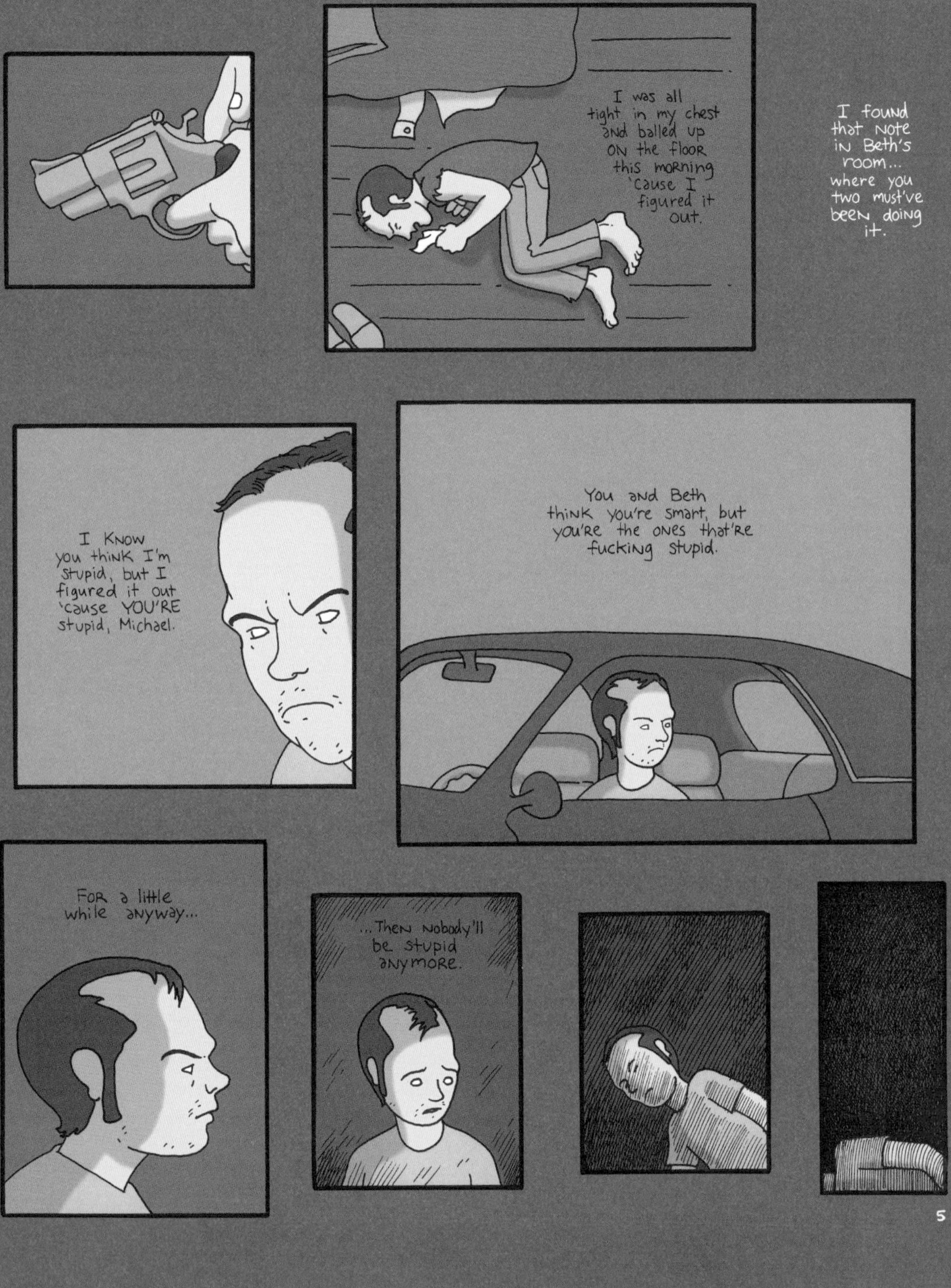
I was all tight in my chest and balled up on the floor this morning 'cause I figured it out.
I found that note in Beth's room... where you two must've been doing it.
I know you think I'm stupid, but I figured it out 'cause YOU'RE stupid, Michael.
You and Beth think you're smart, but you're the ones that're fucking stupid.
For a little while anyway...
...Then nobody'll be stupid anymore.

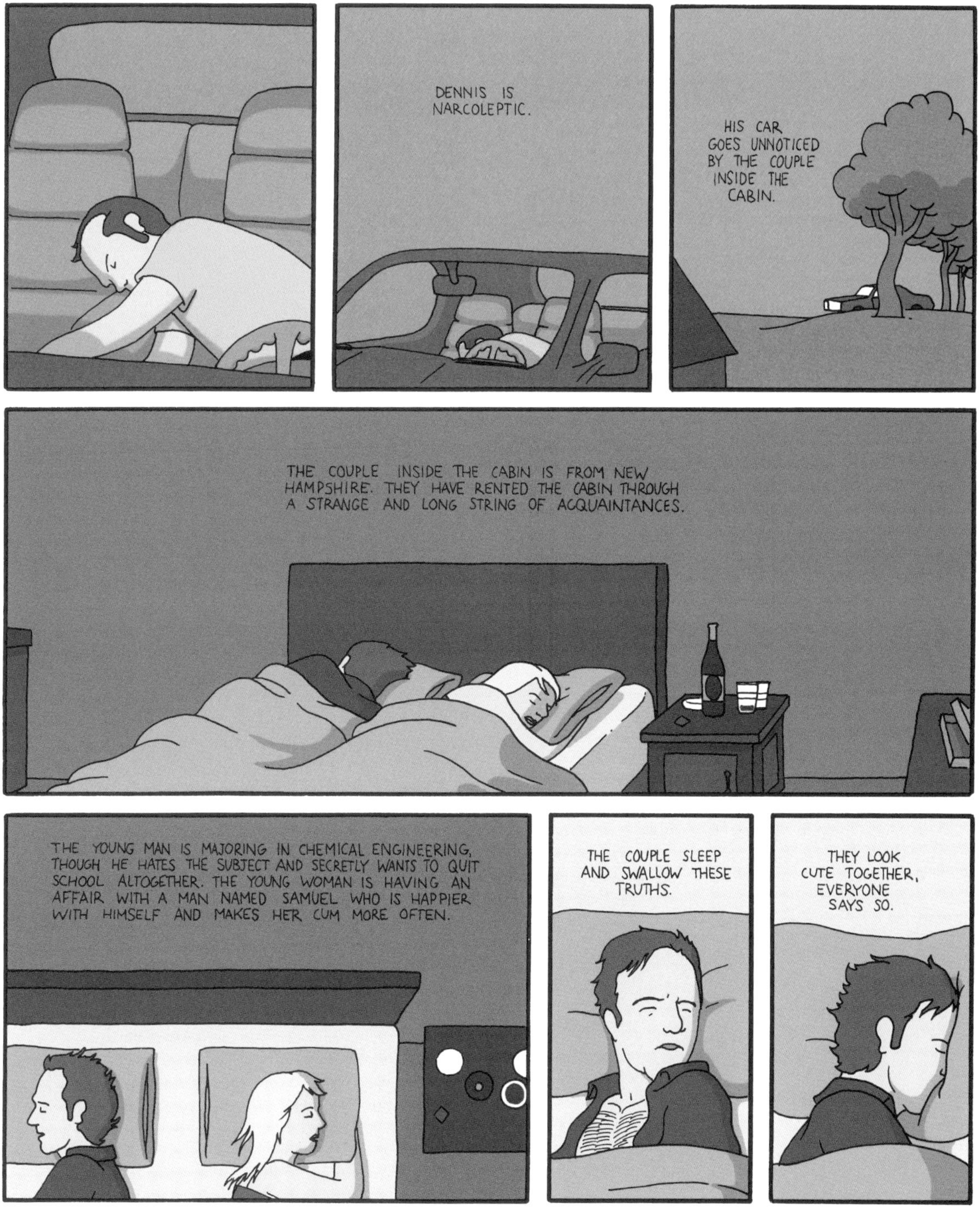
DENNIS IS NARCOLEPTIC.
HIS CAR GOES UNNOTICED BY THE COUPLE INSIDE THE CABIN.
THE COUPLE INSIDE THE CABIN IS FROM NEW HAMPSHIRE. THEY HAVE RENTED THE CABIN THROUGH A STRANGE AND LONG STRING OF ACQUAINTANCES.
THE YOUNG MAN IS MAJORING IN CHEMICAL ENGINEERING, THOUGH HE HATES THE SUBJECT AND SECRETLY WANTS TO QUIT SCHOOL ALTOGETHER. THE YOUNG WOMAN IS HAVING AN AFFAIR WITH A MAN NAMED SAMUEL WHO IS HAPPIER WITH HIMSELF AND MAKES HER CUM MORE OFTEN.
THE COUPLE SLEEP AND SWALLOW THESE TRUTHS.
THEY LOOK CUTE TOGETHER, EVERYONE SAYS SO.

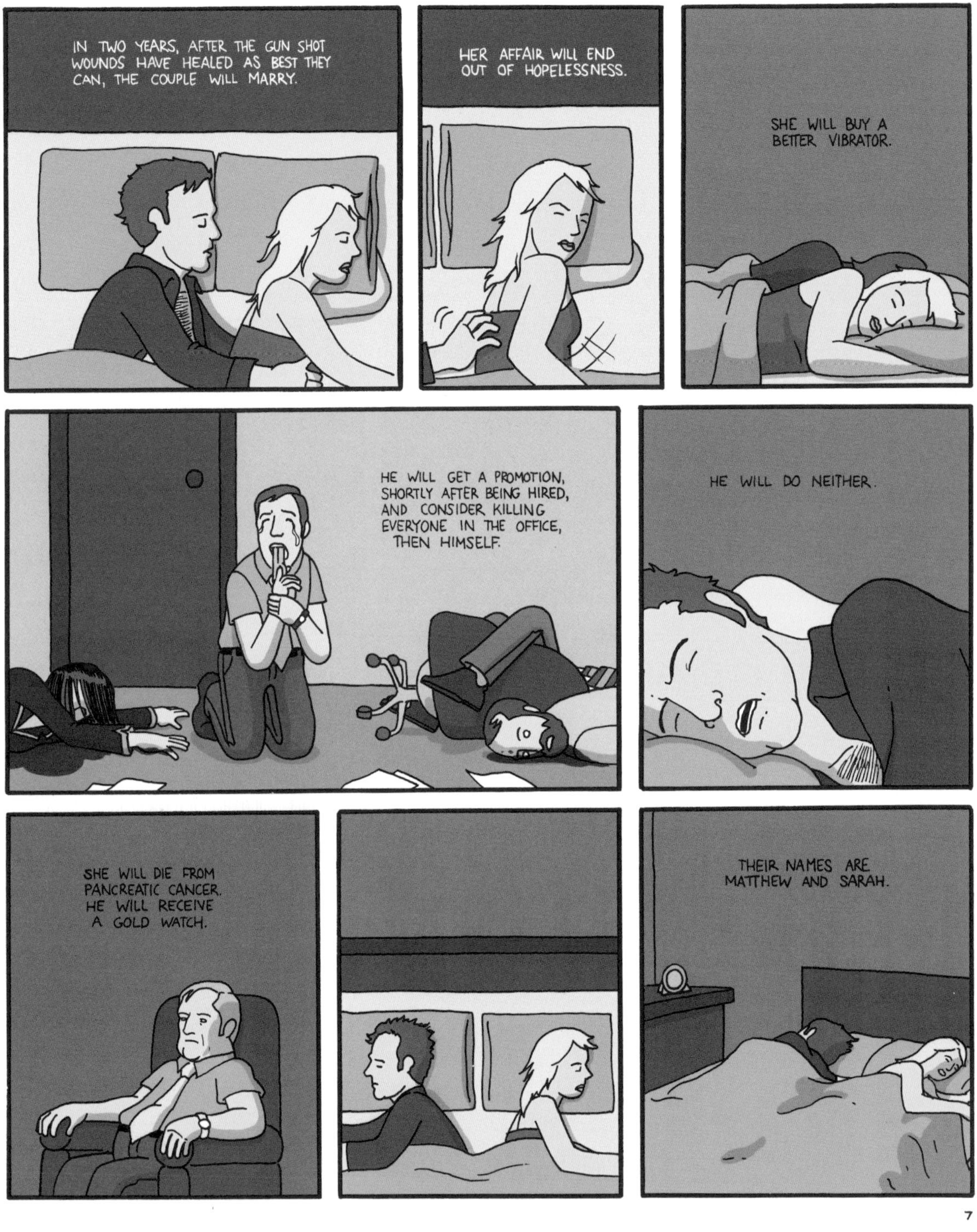
IN TWO YEARS, AFTER THE GUN SHOT WOUNDS HAVE HEALED AS BEST THEY CAN, THE COUPLE WILL MARRY.
HER AFFAIR WILL END OUT OF HOPELESSNESS.
SHE WILL BUY A BETTER VIBRATOR.
HE WILL GET A PROMOTION, SHORTLY AFTER BEING HIRED, AND CONSIDER KILLING EVERYONE IN THE OFFICE, THEN HIMSELF.
HE WILL DO NEITHER.
SHE WILL DIE FROM PANCREATIC CANCER. HE WILL RECEIVE A GOLD WATCH.
THEIR NAMES ARE MATTHEW AND SARAH.

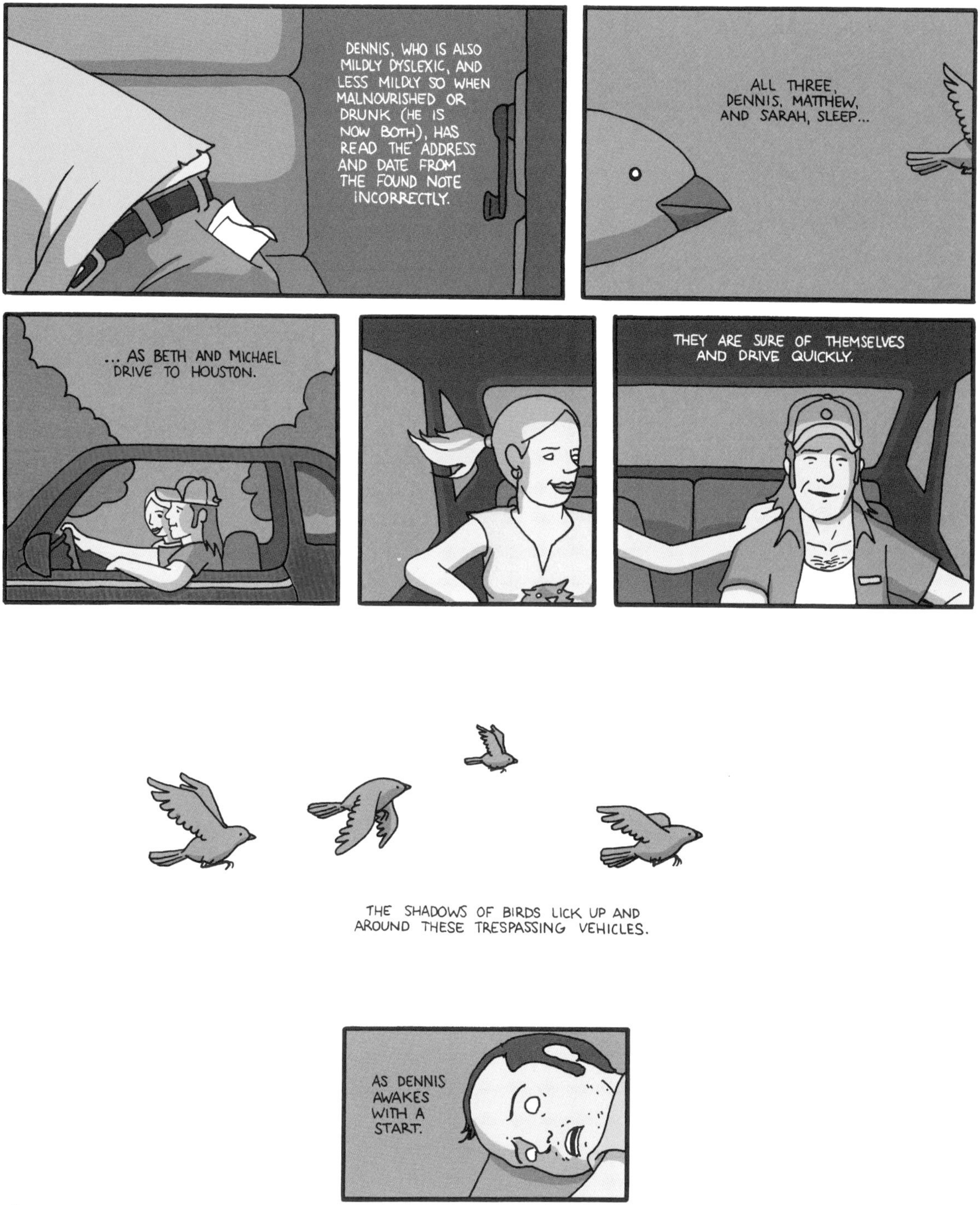
DENNIS, WHO IS ALSO MILDLY DYSLEXIC, AND LESS MILDLY SO WHEN MALNOURISHED OR DRUNK (HE IS NOW BOTH), HAS READ THE ADDRESS AND DATE FROM THE FOUND NOTE INCORRECTLY.
ALL THREE, DENNIS, MATTHEW, AND SARAH, SLEEP...
... AS BETH AND MICHAEL DRIVE TO HOUSTON.
THEY ARE SURE OF THEMSELVES AND DRIVE QUICKLY.
THE SHADOWS OF BIRDS LICK UP AND AROUND THESE TRESPASSING VEHICLES.
AS DENNIS AWAKES WITH A START.

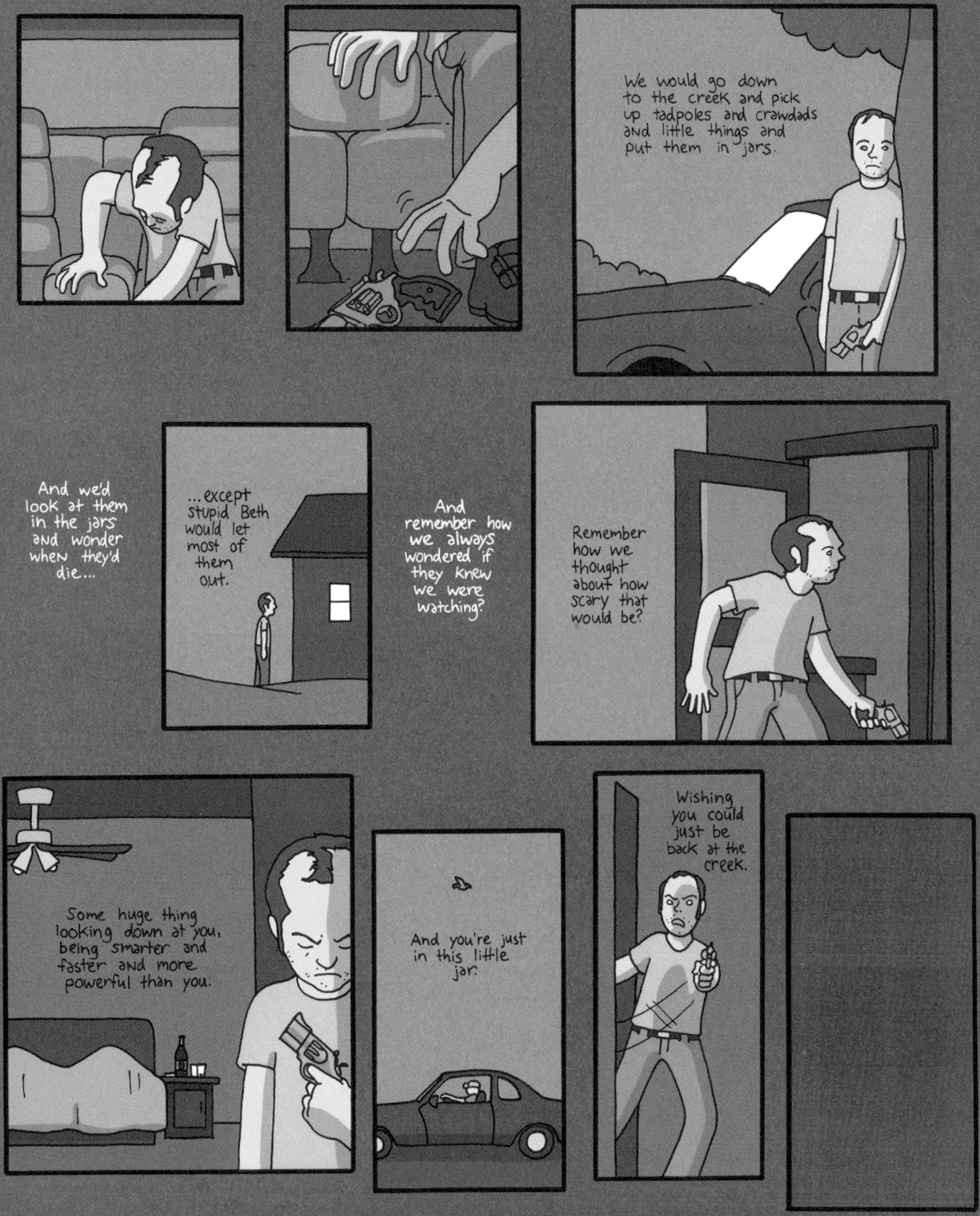
We would go down to the creek and pick up tadpoles and crawdads and little things and put them in jars.
And we'd look at them in the jars and wonder when they'd die...
...except stupid Beth would let most of them out.
And remember how we always wondered if they knew we were watching?
Remember how we thought about how scary that would be?
Some huge thing looking down at you, being smarter and faster and more powerful than you.
And you're just in this little jar.
Wishing you could just be back at the creek.

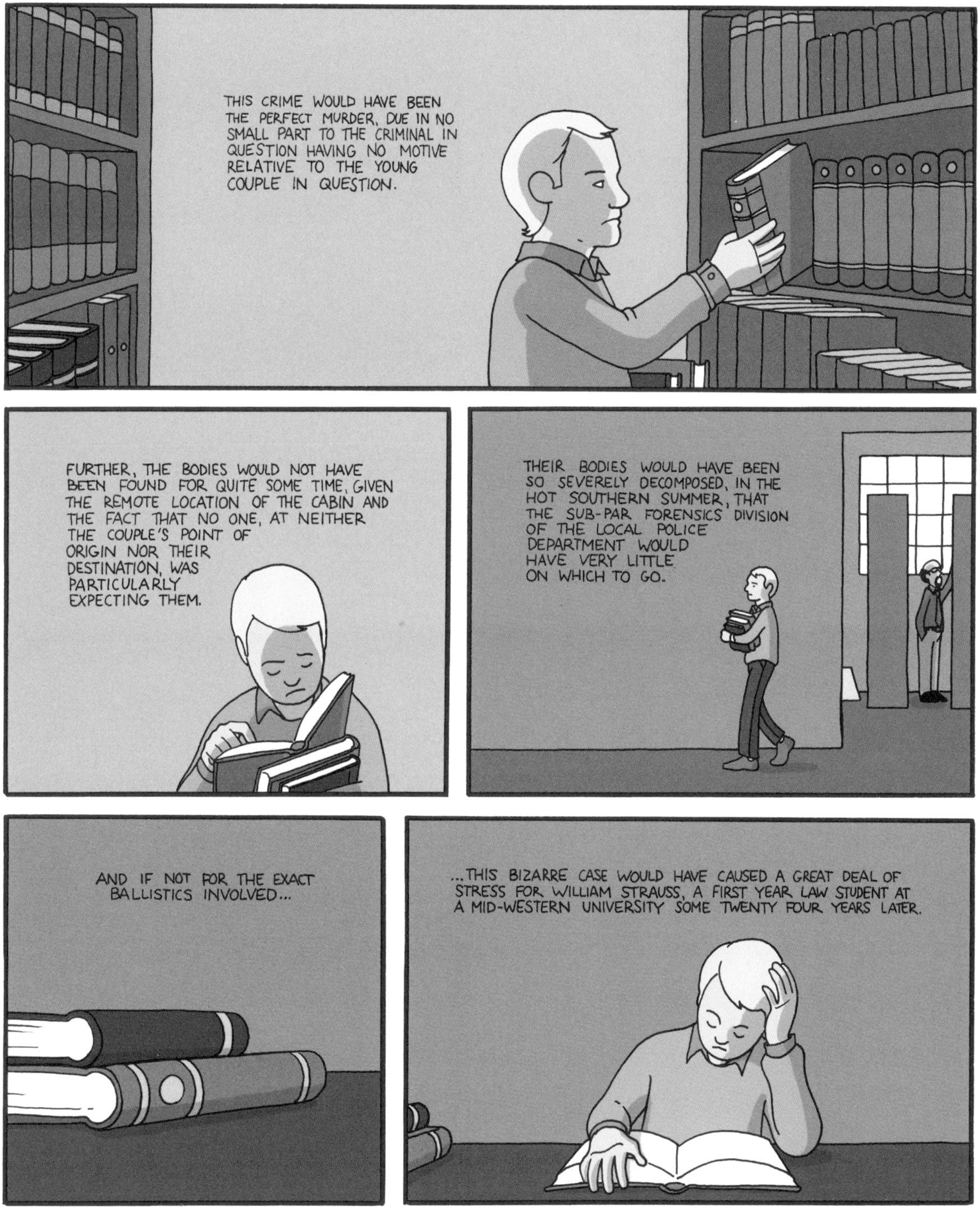
THIS CRIME WOULD HAVE BEEN THE PERFECT MURDER, DUE IN NO SMALL PART TO THE CRIMINAL IN QUESTION HAVING NO MOTIVE RELATIVE TO THE YOUNG COUPLE IN QUESTION.
FURTHER, THE BODIES WOULD NOT HAVE BEEN FOUND FOR QUITE SOME TIME, GIVEN THE REMOTE LOCATION OF THE CABIN AND THE FACT THAT NO ONE, AT NEITHER THE COUPLE'S POINT OF ORIGIN NOR THEIR DESTINATION, WAS PARTICULARLY EXPECTING THEM.
THEIR BODIES WOULD HAVE BEEN SO SEVERELY DECOMPOSED, IN THE HOT SOUTHERN SUMMER, THAT THE SUB-PAR FORENSICS DIVISION OF THE LOCAL POLICE DEPARTMENT WOULD HAVE VERY LITTLE ON WHICH TO GO.
AND IF NOT FOR THE EXACT BALLISTICS INVOLVED...
...THIS BIZARRE CASE WOULD HAVE CAUSED A GREAT DEAL OF STRESS FOR WILLIAM STRAUSS, A FIRST YEAR LAW STUDENT AT A MID-WESTERN UNIVERSITY SOME TWENTY FOUR YEARS LATER.

FOUR ROUNDS WERE FIRED FROM DENNIS' GUN. TWO OF THESE ROUNDS FOUND THEIR TARGET, FOR THE MOST PART, AT THE COUPLES' HEADS. THE THIRD ROUND PIERCED THE MID-SECTION OF SARAH, ON HER LEFT SIDE. THE FOURTH ROUND WAS FIRED AT THE MID-SECTION OF MATTHEW, IN THE EXACT CENTER OF HIS WAISTLINE.

THE ROUNDS FIRED AT THE COUPLE'S HEADS DID NOT FALL SQUARELY ON THE SKULLS, INSTEAD GRAZING THE JUST-WAKING MATTHEW AND SARAH.

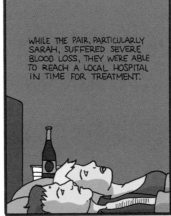

WHILE THE PAIR, PARTICULARLY SARAH, SUFFERED SEVERE BLOOD LOSS, THEY WERE ABLE TO REACH A LOCAL HOSPITAL IN TIME FOR TREATMENT.

THE FOURTH ROUND, FIRED AT MATTHEW'S MID-SECTION, FOUND HIS BELT BUCKLE, HAVING NEVER BEEN REMOVED FROM THE NIGHT PREVIOUS.

FROM MATTHEW'S BELT BUCKLE, THE SHOT RICOCHETED TO DENNIS, OR, MORE PRECISELY, TO DENNIS' NECK.

THUS BLEEDING HIM TO DEATH...

... AND IN TO CONNECTION WITH AN OTHERWISE UNTRACEABLE CRIME.

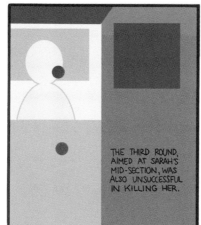

THE THIRD ROUND, AIMED AT SARAH'S MID-SECTION, WAS ALSO UNSUCCESSFUL IN KILLING HER.

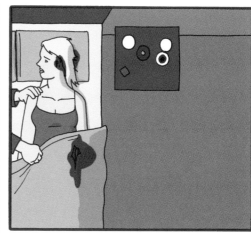

THOUGH IT DID SUCCESSFULLY WOUND HER TO SUCH AN EXTENT THAT SHE MISCARRIED.

SHE HAD NOT TOLD MATTHEW SHE WAS PREGNANT, DISCOVERING THIS FACT ONLY TWO DAYS BEFORE THEIR TRIP.

NOR DID SHE TELL THE CHILD'S FATHER:

SAMUEL STRAUSS.

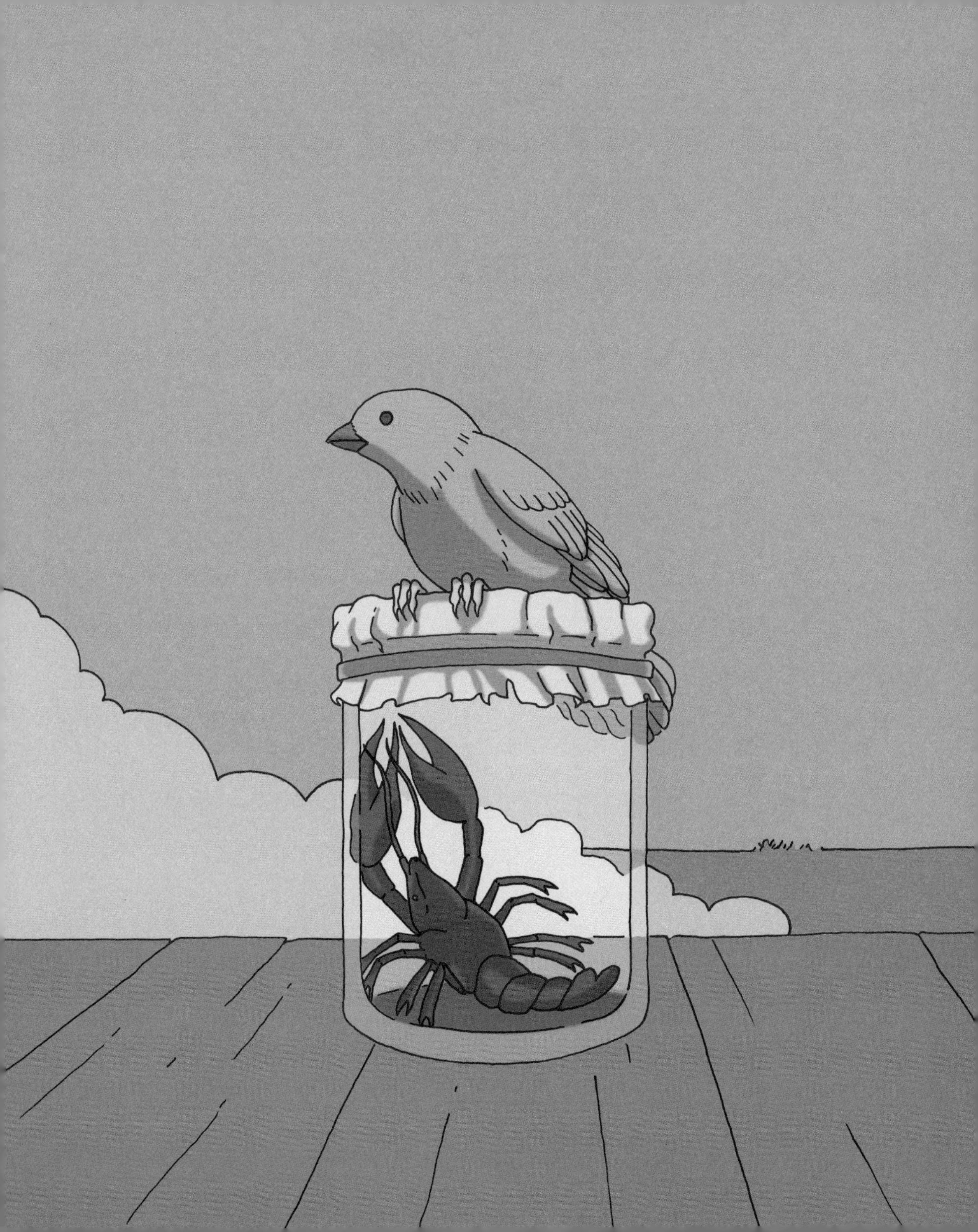

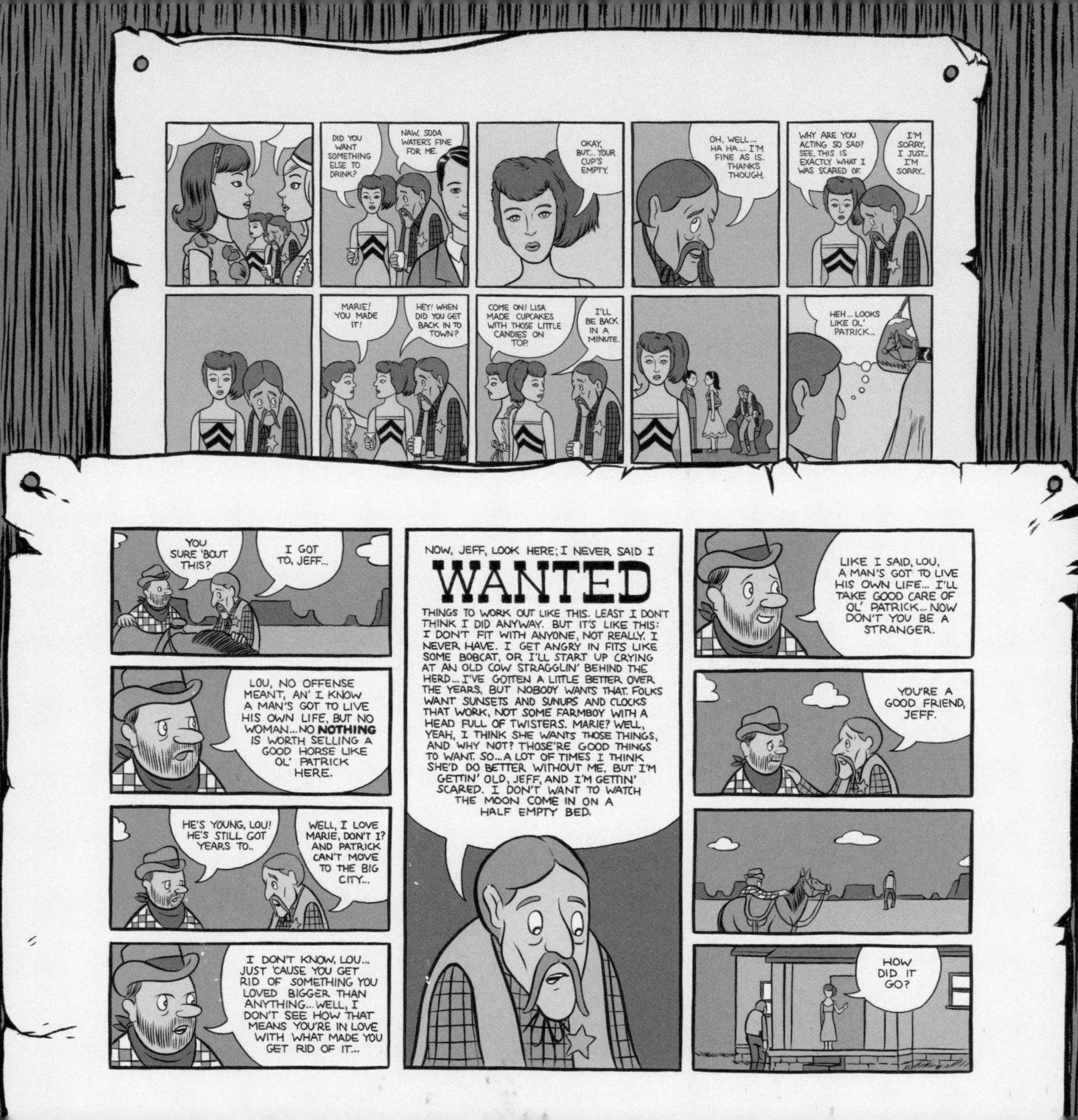
DID YOU WANT SOMETHING ELSE TO DRINK?
NAW, SODA WATER'S FINE FOR ME.
OKAY, BUT... YOUR CUP'S EMPTY.
OH, WELL... HA HA... I'M FINE AS IS. THANKS THOUGH.
WHY ARE YOU ACTING SO SAD? SEE, THIS IS EXACTLY WHAT I WAS SCARED OF.
I'M SORRY, I JUST... I'M SORRY...
MARIE! YOU MADE IT!
HEY! WHEN DID YOU GET BACK IN TO TOWN?
COME ON! LISA MADE CUPCAKES WITH THOSE LITTLE CANDIES ON TOP.
I'LL BE BACK IN A MINUTE.
HEH... LOOKS LIKE OL' PATRICK...
YOU SURE 'BOUT THIS?
I GOT TO, JEFF...
LOU, NO OFFENSE MEANT, AN' I KNOW A MAN'S GOT TO LIVE HIS OWN LIFE, BUT NO WOMAN... NO NOTHING IS WORTH SELLING A GOOD HORSE LIKE OL' PATRICK HERE.
HE'S YOUNG, LOU! HE'S STILL GOT YEARS TO..
WELL, I LOVE MARIE, DON'T I? AND PATRICK CAN'T MOVE TO THE BIG CITY...
I DON'T KNOW, LOU... JUST 'CAUSE YOU GET RID OF SOMETHING YOU LOVED BIGGER THAN ANYTHING... WELL, I DON'T SEE HOW THAT MEANS YOU'RE IN LOVE WITH WHAT MADE YOU GET RID OF IT...
NOW, JEFF, LOOK HERE; I NEVER SAID I
WANTED
THINGS TO WORK OUT LIKE THIS. LEAST I DON'T THINK I DID ANYWAY. BUT IT'S LIKE THIS: I DON'T FIT WITH ANYONE, NOT REALLY. I NEVER HAVE. I GET ANGRY IN FITS LIKE SOME BOBCAT, OR I'LL START UP CRYING AT AN OLD COW STRAGGLIN' BEHIND THE HERD... I'VE GOTTEN A LITTLE BETTER OVER THE YEARS, BUT NOBODY WANTS THAT. FOLKS WANT SUNSETS AND SUNUPS AND CLOCKS THAT WORK, NOT SOME FARMBOY WITH A HEAD FULL OF TWISTERS. MARIE? WELL, YEAH, I THINK SHE WANTS THOSE THINGS, AND WHY NOT? THOSE'RE GOOD THINGS TO WANT. SO... A LOT OF TIMES I THINK SHE'D DO BETTER WITHOUT ME, BUT I'M GETTIN' OLD, JEFF, AND I'M GETTIN' SCARED. I DON'T WANT TO WATCH THE MOON COME IN ON A HALF EMPTY BED.
LIKE I SAID, LOU, A MAN'S GOT TO LIVE HIS OWN LIFE... I'LL TAKE GOOD CARE OF OL' PATRICK... NOW DON'T YOU BE A STRANGER.
YOU'RE A GOOD FRIEND, JEFF.
HOW DID IT GO?

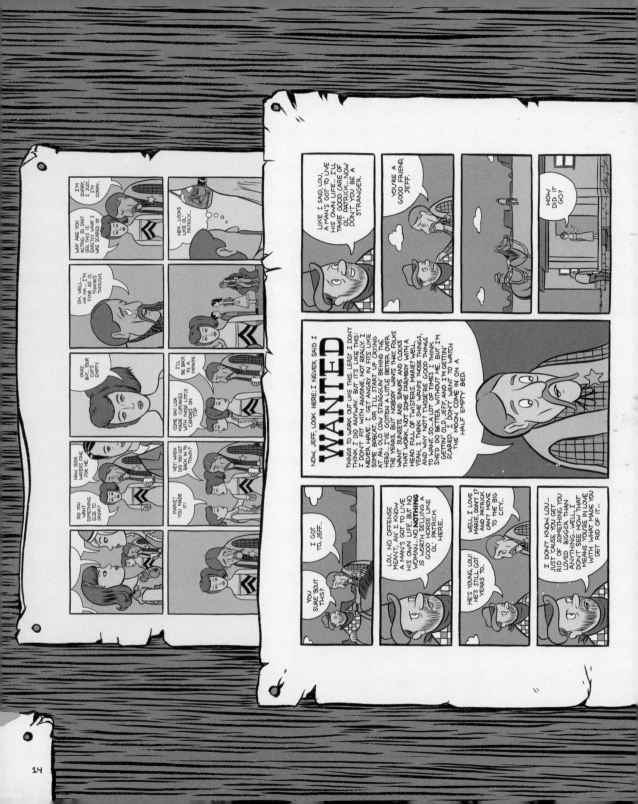

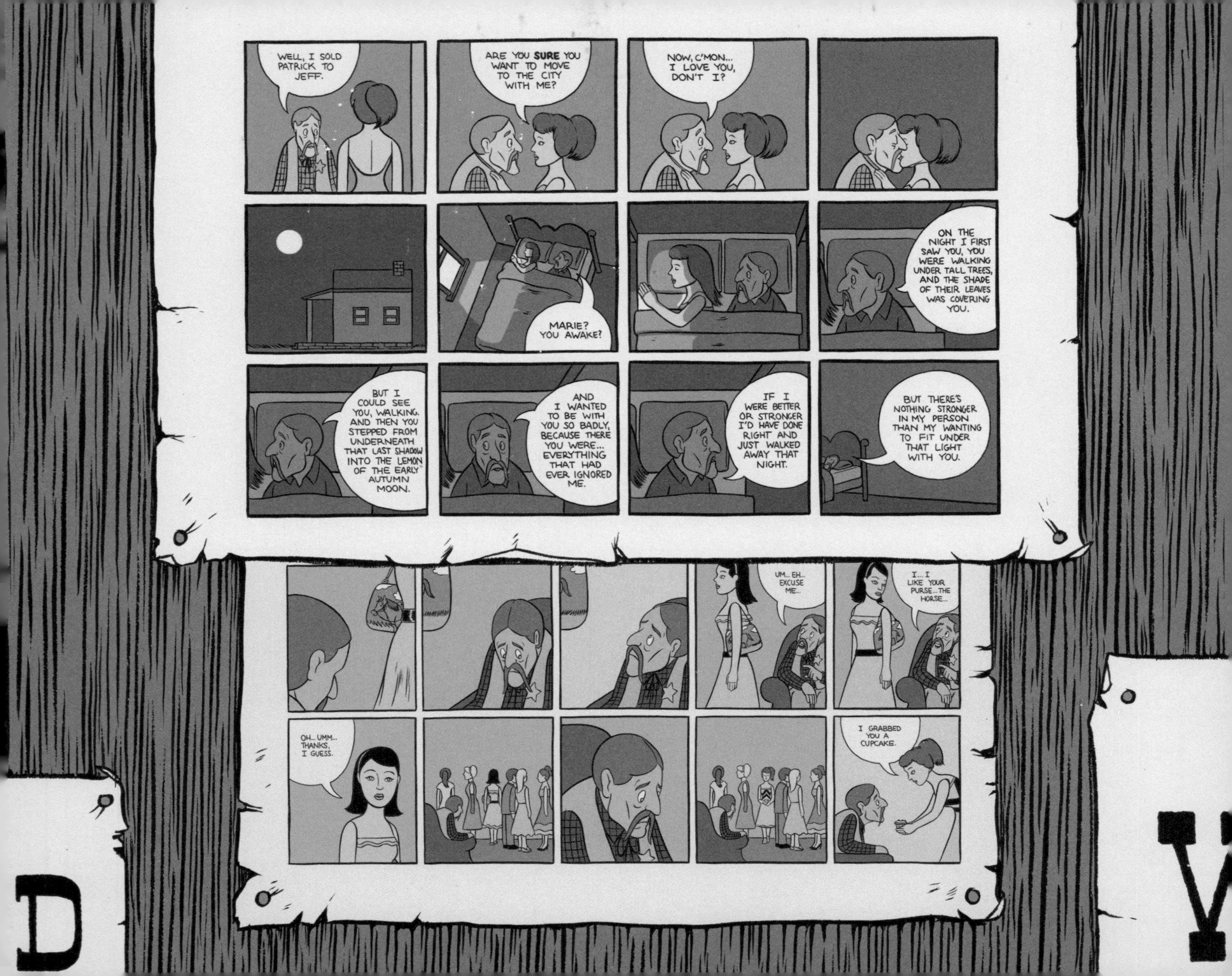
WELL, I SOLD PATRICK TO JEFF.
ARE YOU **SURE** YOU WANT TO MOVE TO THE CITY WITH ME?
NOW, C'MON... I LOVE YOU, DON'T I?
MARIE? YOU AWAKE?
ON THE NIGHT I FIRST SAW YOU, YOU WERE WALKING UNDER TALL TREES, AND THE SHADE OF THEIR LEAVES WAS COVERING YOU.
BUT I COULD SEE YOU, WALKING. AND THEN YOU STEPPED FROM UNDERNEATH THAT LAST SHADOW INTO THE LEMON OF THE EARLY AUTUMN MOON.
AND I WANTED TO BE WITH YOU SO BADLY, BECAUSE THERE YOU WERE... EVERYTHING THAT HAD EVER IGNORED ME.
IF I WERE BETTER OR STRONGER I'D HAVE DONE RIGHT AND JUST WALKED AWAY THAT NIGHT.
BUT THERE'S NOTHING STRONGER IN MY PERSON THAN MY WANTING TO FIT UNDER THAT LIGHT WITH YOU.
UM... EH... EXCUSE ME...
I... I LIKE YOUR PURSE... THE HORSE...
OH... UMM... THANKS, I GUESS.
I GRABBED YOU A CUPCAKE.

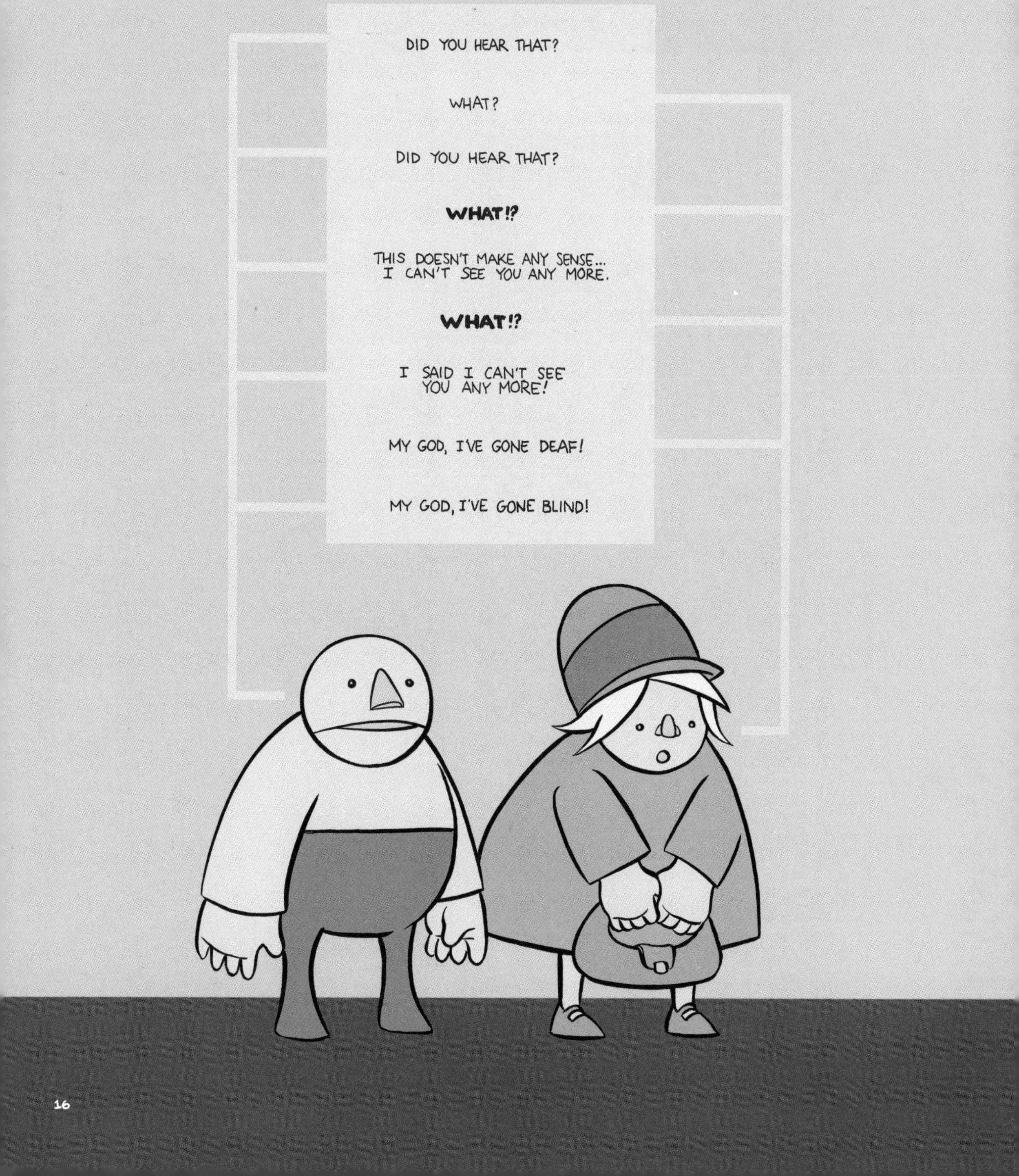
DID YOU HEAR THAT?
WHAT?
DID YOU HEAR THAT?
WHAT!?
THIS DOESN'T MAKE ANY SENSE... I CAN'T SEE YOU ANY MORE.
WHAT!?
I SAID I CAN'T SEE YOU ANY MORE!
MY GOD, I'VE GONE DEAF!
MY GOD, I'VE GONE BLIND!

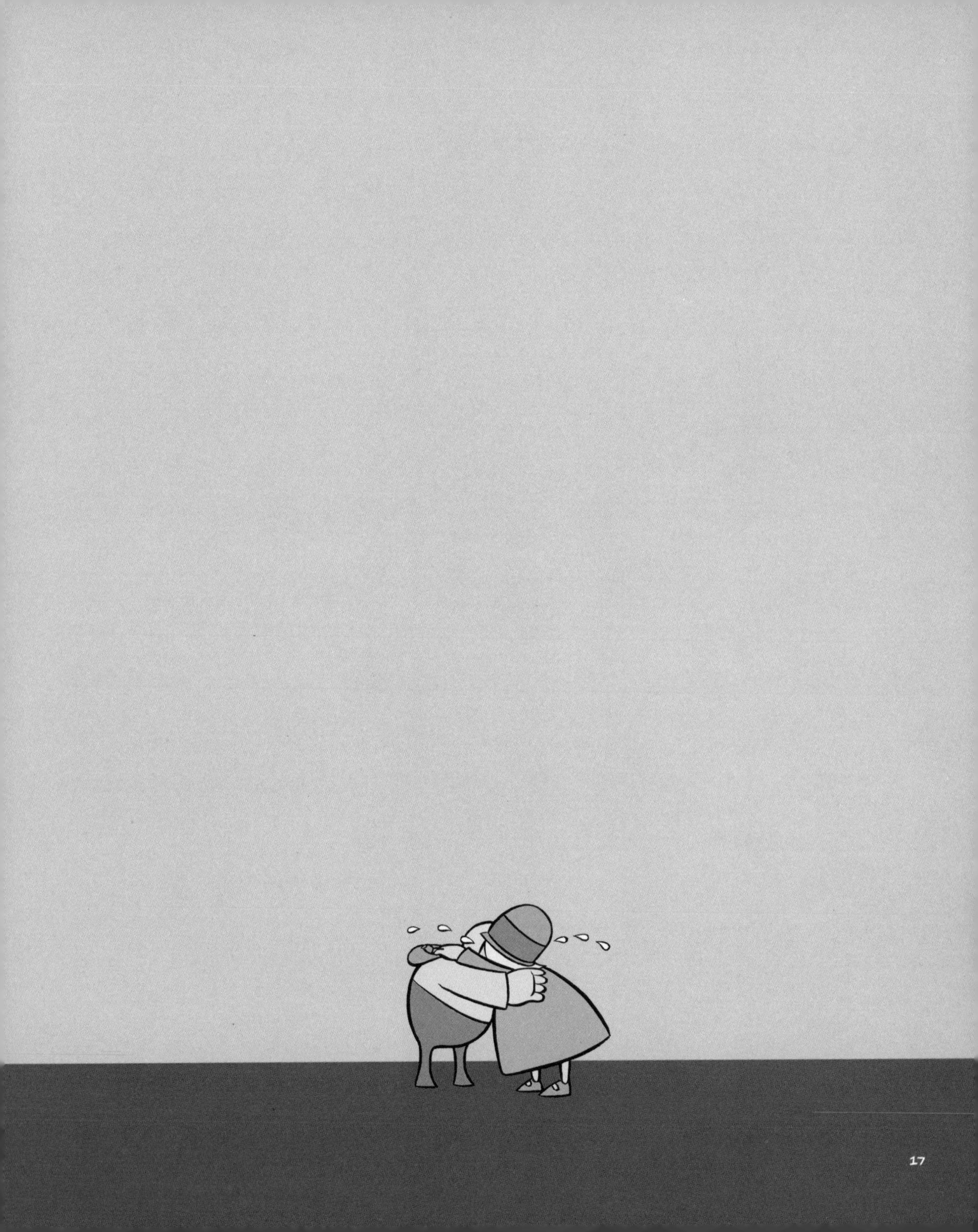

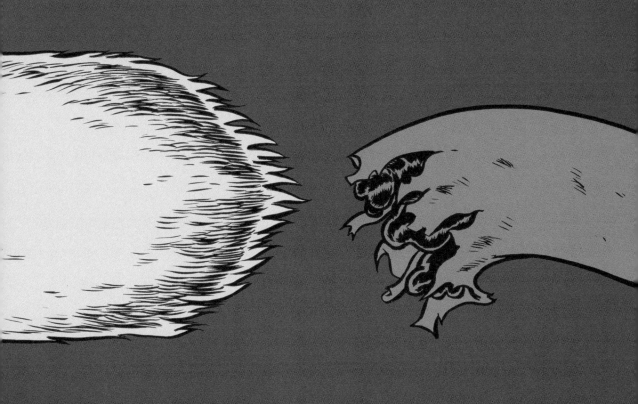

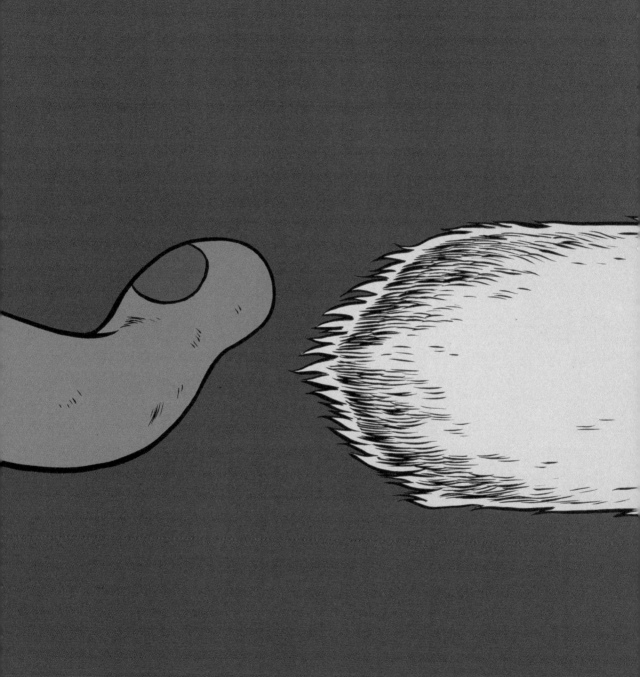

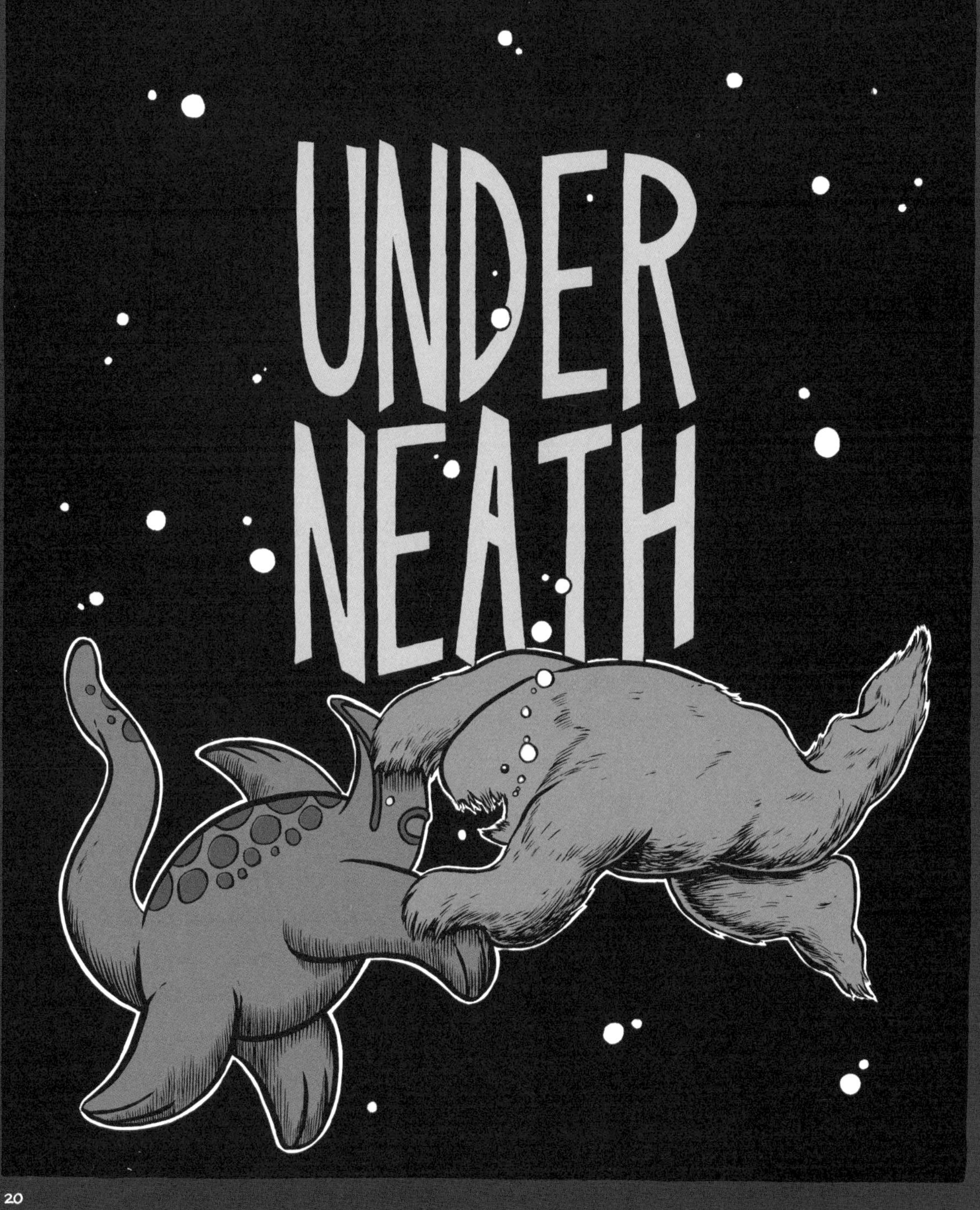
UNDER
NEATH

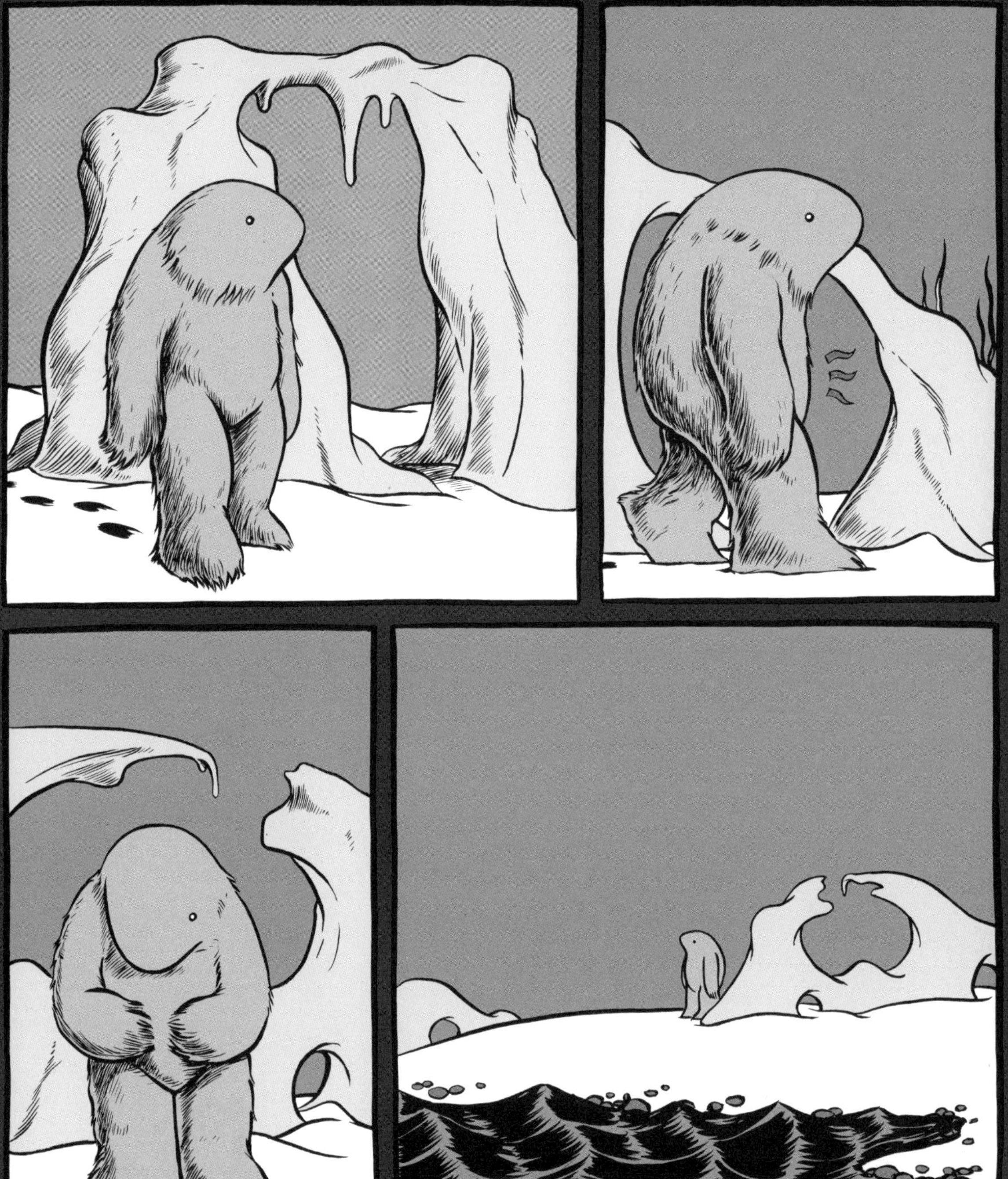

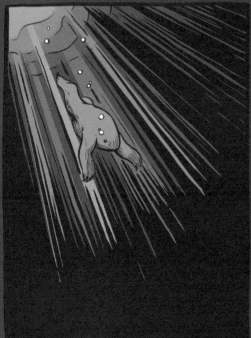

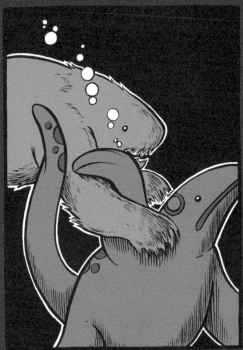

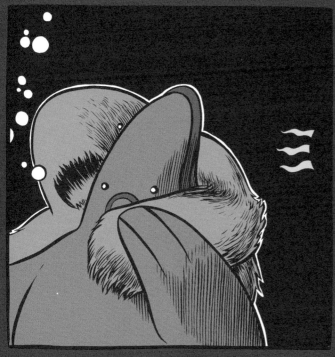

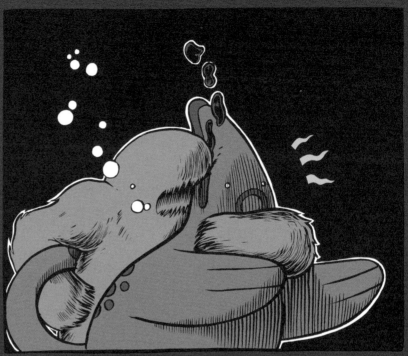

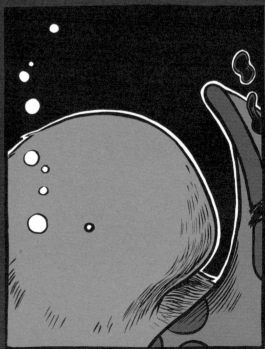

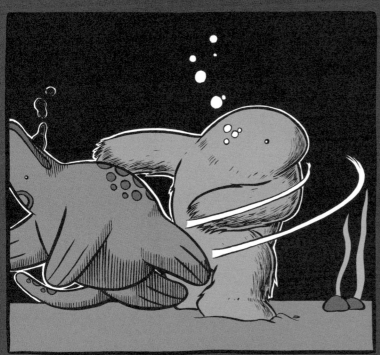

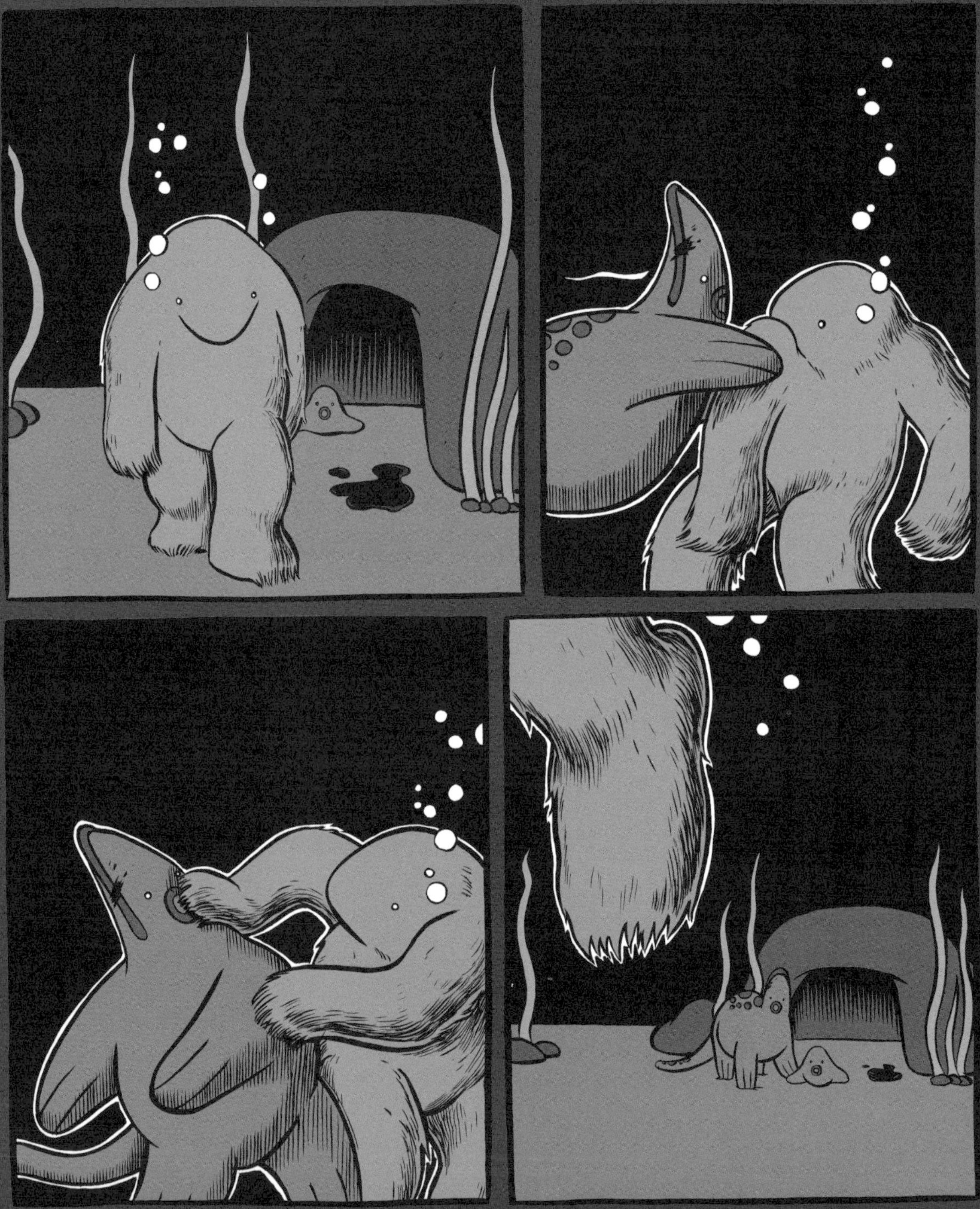

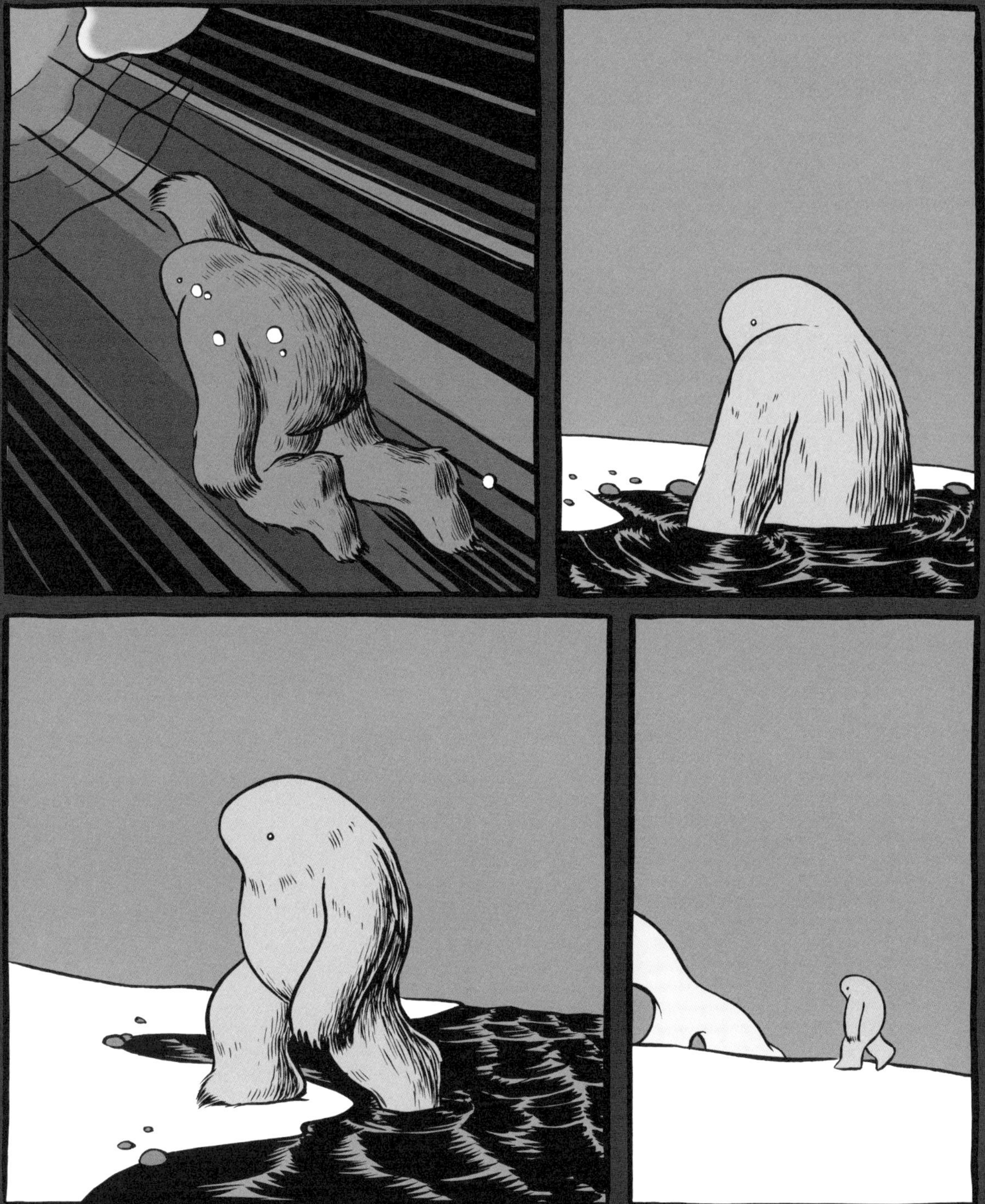

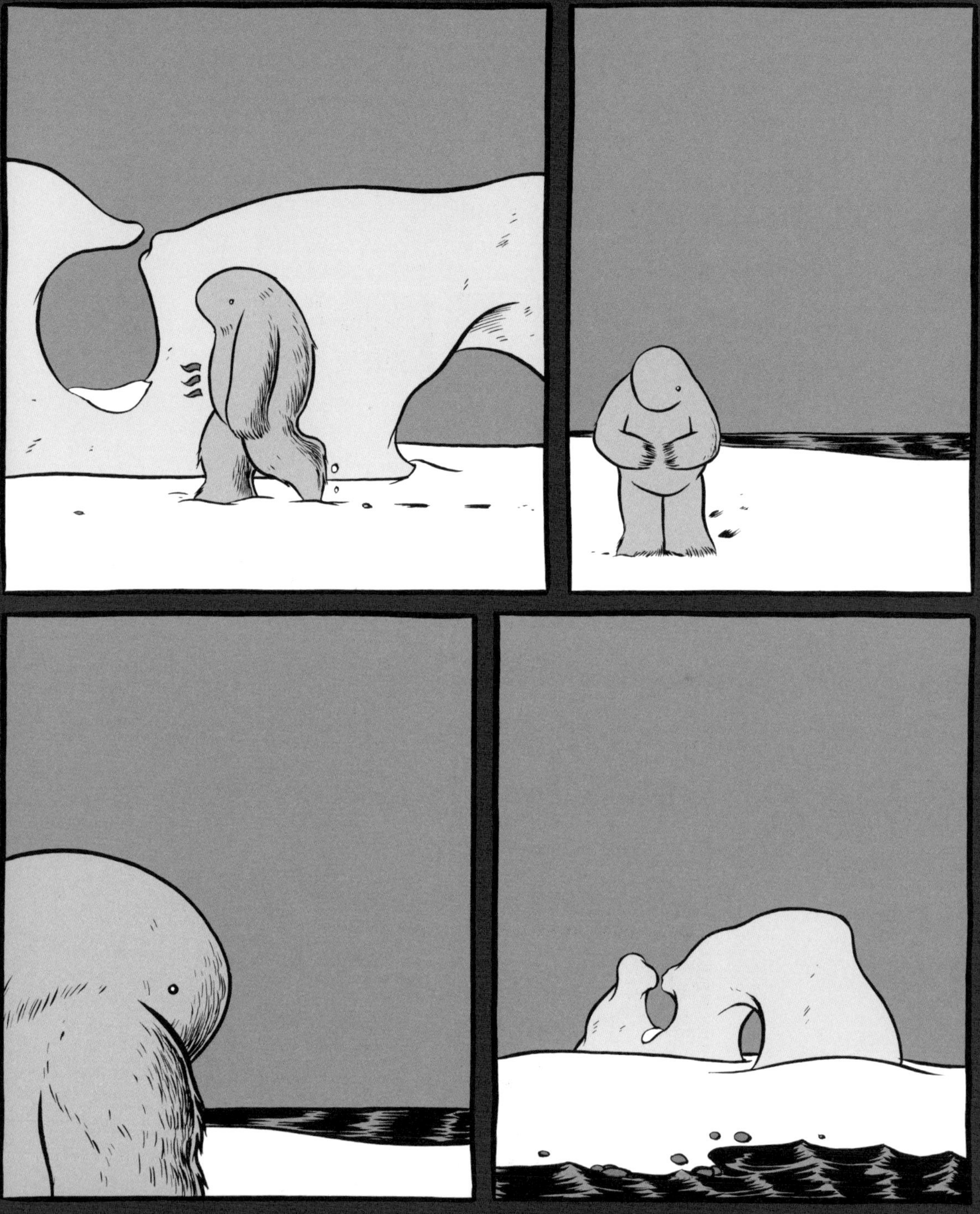

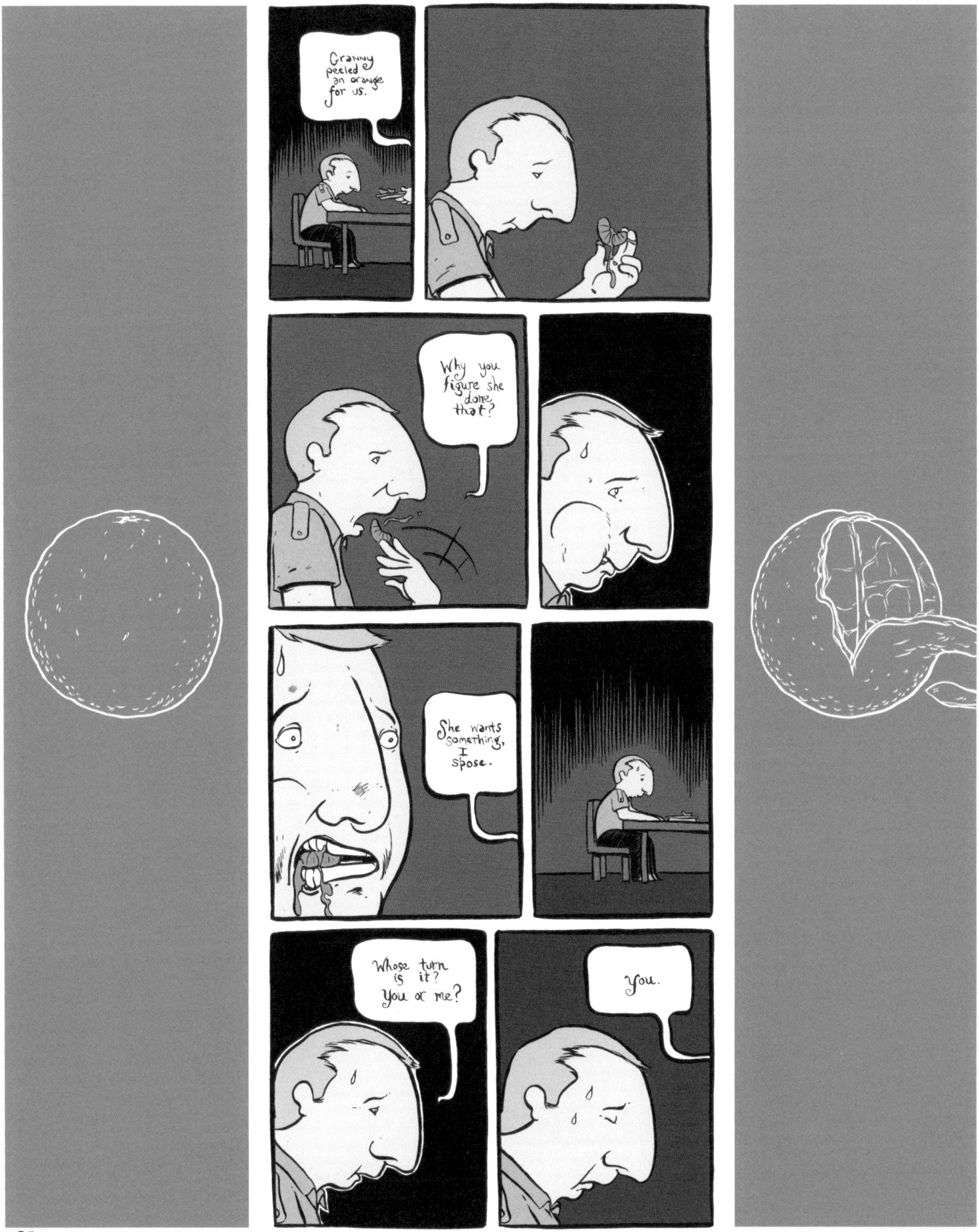
Granny peeled an orange for us.
Why you figure she done that?
She wants something, I spose.
Whose turn is it? You or me?
You.

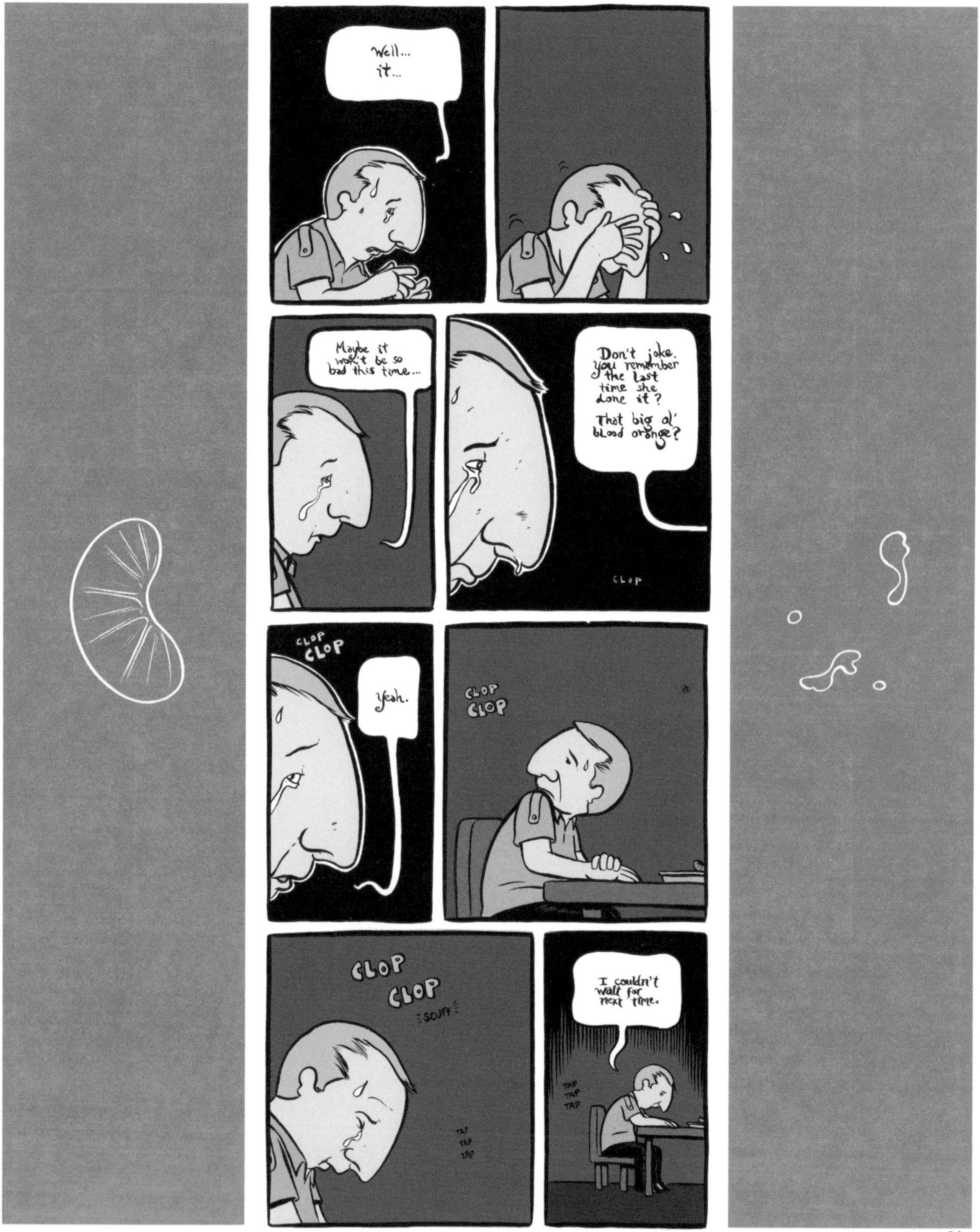
Well... it...
Maybe it won't be so bad this time...
Don't joke. you remember the last time she done it?
That big ol' blood orange?
CLOP
CLOP CLOP
Yeah.
CLOP CLOP
CLOP CLOP
SCUFF
TAP TAP TAP
I couldn't wait for next time.
TAP TAP TAP

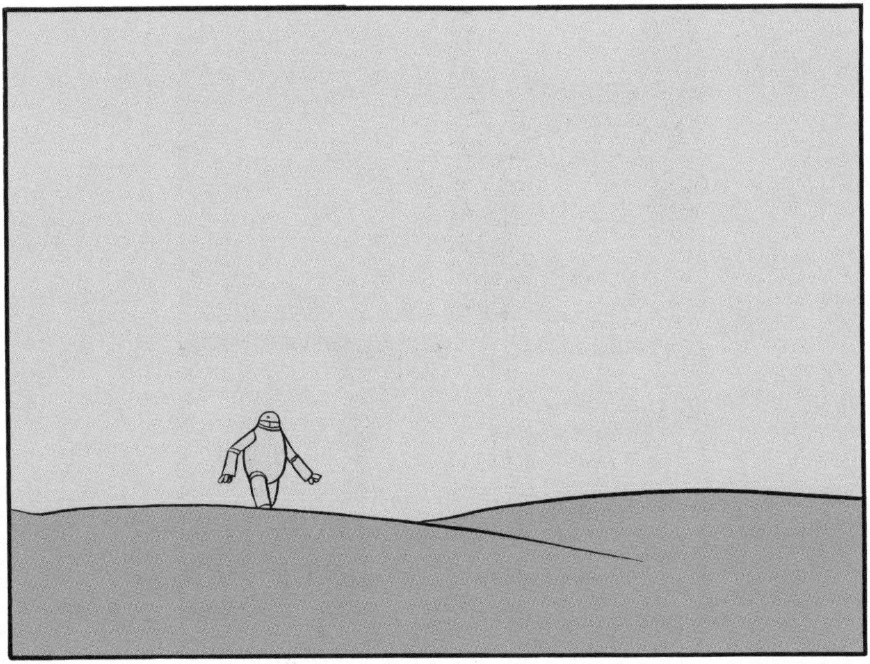

• WE WERE NOT MADE FOR THIS WORLD •

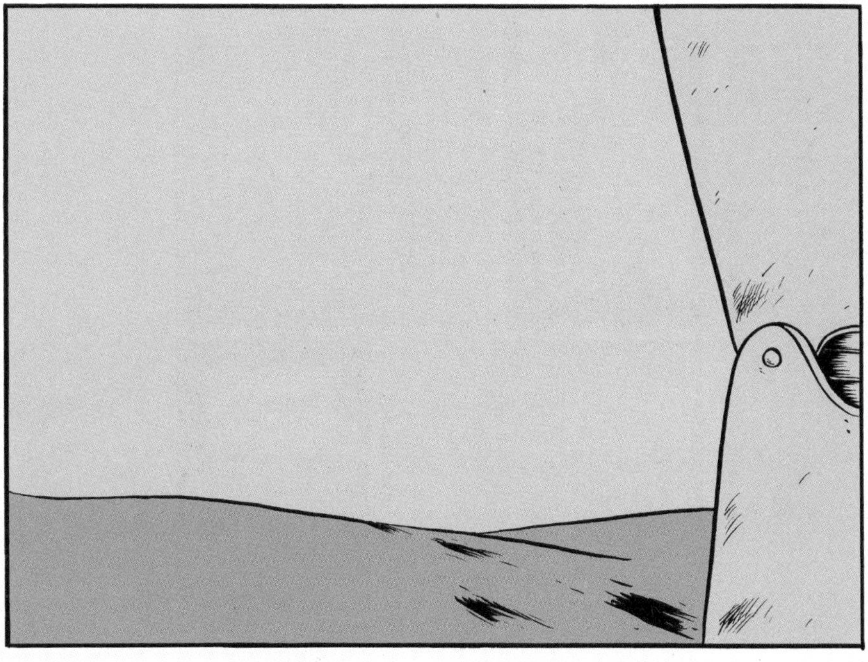

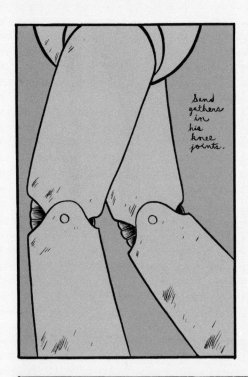

Sand gathers in his knee joints.

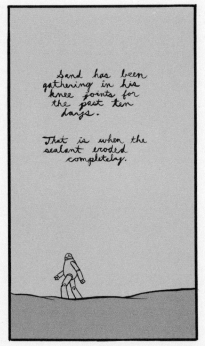

Sand has been gathering in his knee joints for the past ten days.

That is when the sealant eroded completely.

Sand gathers in his knee joints at sixteen to thirty-two granules per minute, depending on wind speed.

Eight to ten are forced out by the still functioning internal defenses...

...but clearly this leaves accumulation.

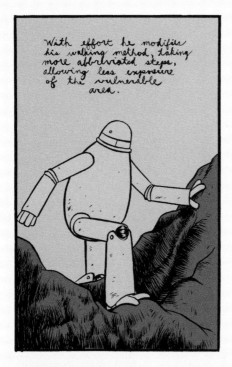

With effort he modifies his walking method, taking more abbreviated steps, allowing less exposure of the vulnerable area.

Now there is slightly less accumulation...

... but still ground is lost.

He is sharply aware he may not reach his destination.

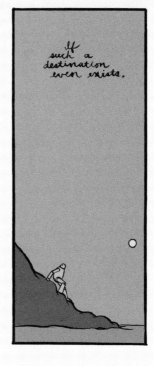

If such a destination even exists.

34

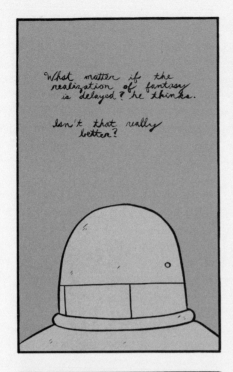

What matter if the realization of fantasy is delayed? he thinks.

Isn't that really better?

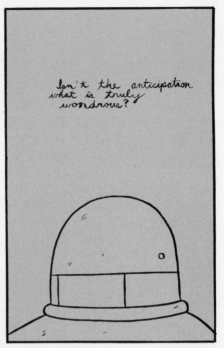

Isn't the anticipation what is truly wondrous?

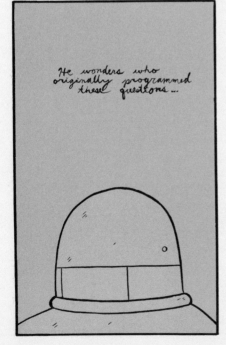

He wonders who originally programmed these questions...

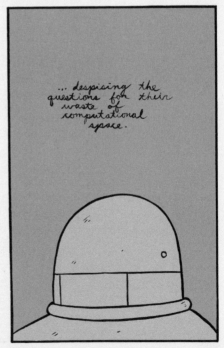

...despising the questions for their waste of computational space.

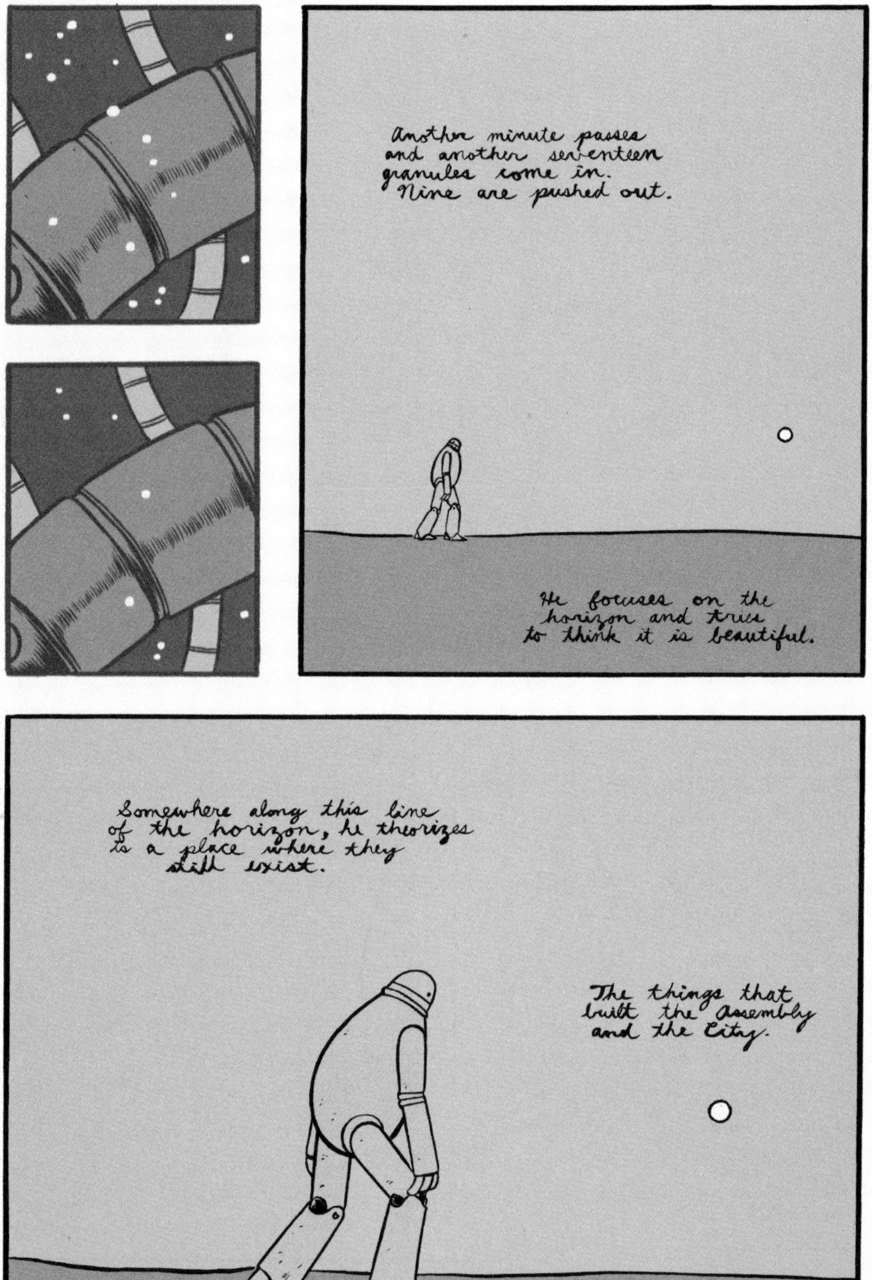
Another minute passes and another seventeen granules come in. Nine are pushed out.
He focuses on the horizon and tries to think it is beautiful.
Somewhere along this line of the horizon, he theorizes is a place where they still exist.
The things that built the Assembly and the City.

Series and series ago, somewhere something had to have built them, or so he reasoned.

And perhaps these things would explain why they built them.

And perhaps it would explain everything.

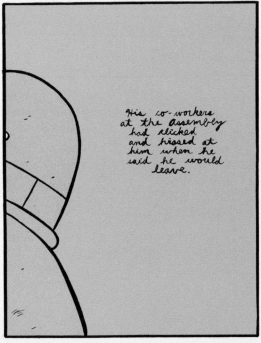

His co-workers at the Assembly had clicked and hissed at him when he said he would leave.

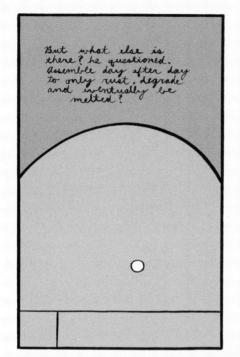

But what else is there? he questioned. Assemble day after day to only rust, degrade and eventually be melted?

Is that all there is?

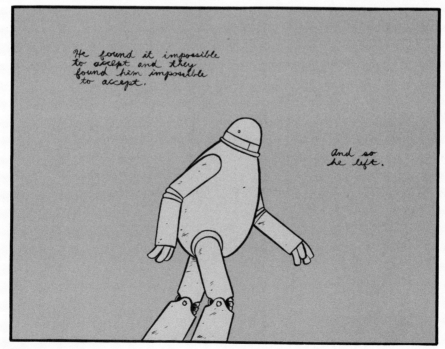

He found it impossible to accept and they found him impossible to accept.

And so he left.

Because of
the sand,
perhaps, he
cannot bring
up how long
ago that exchange
was. He estimates
thirty days.
Unknowingly,
he is correct
in his
estimation.

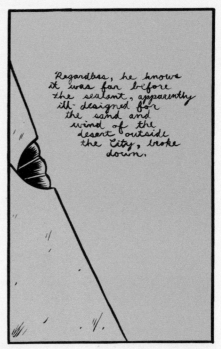

Regardless, he knows
it was far before
the sealant, apparently
ill-designed for
the sand and
wind of the
desert outside
the City, broke
down.

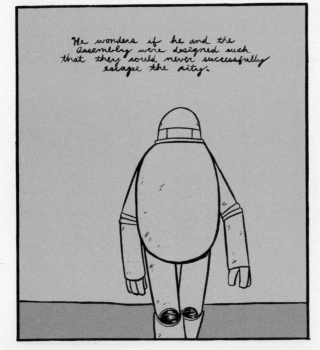

He wonders if he and the
assembly were designed such
that they would never successfully
escape the city.

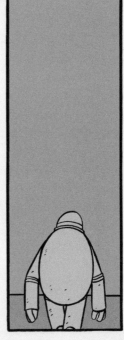

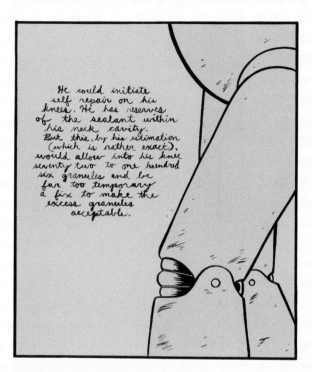

He could initiate self repair on his knees. He has reserves of the sealant within his neck cavity. But this, by his estimation (which is rather exact), would allow into his knee seventy two to one hundred six granules and be far too temporary a fix to make the excess granules acceptable.

He estimates he will not be able to walk within a week.

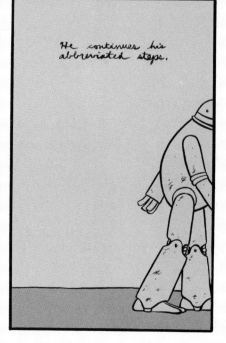

He continues his abbreviated steps.

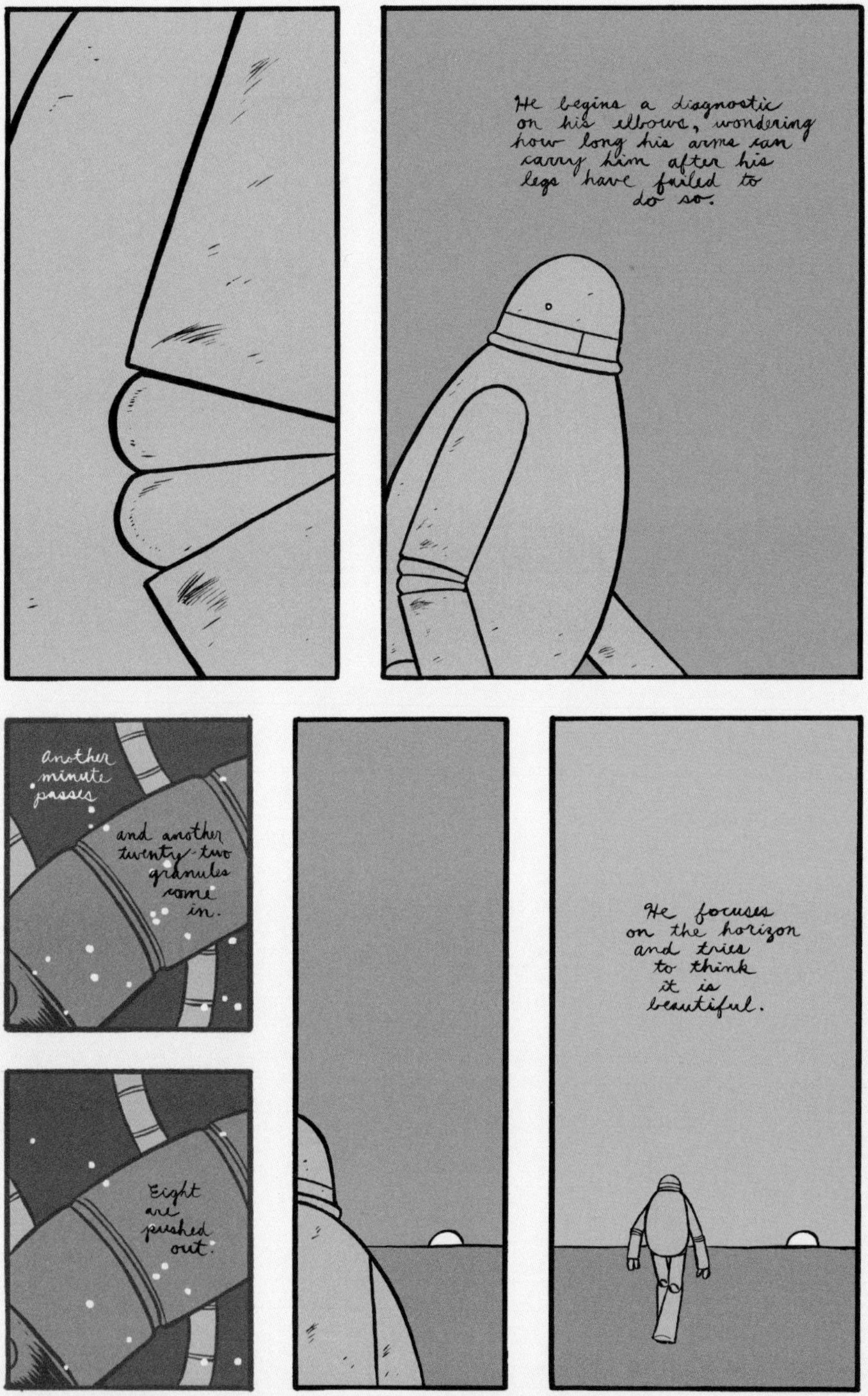
He begins a diagnostic on his elbows, wondering how long his arms can carry him after his legs have failed to do so.
another minute passes
and another twenty-two granules come in.
Eight are pushed out.
He focuses on the horizon and tries to think it is beautiful.

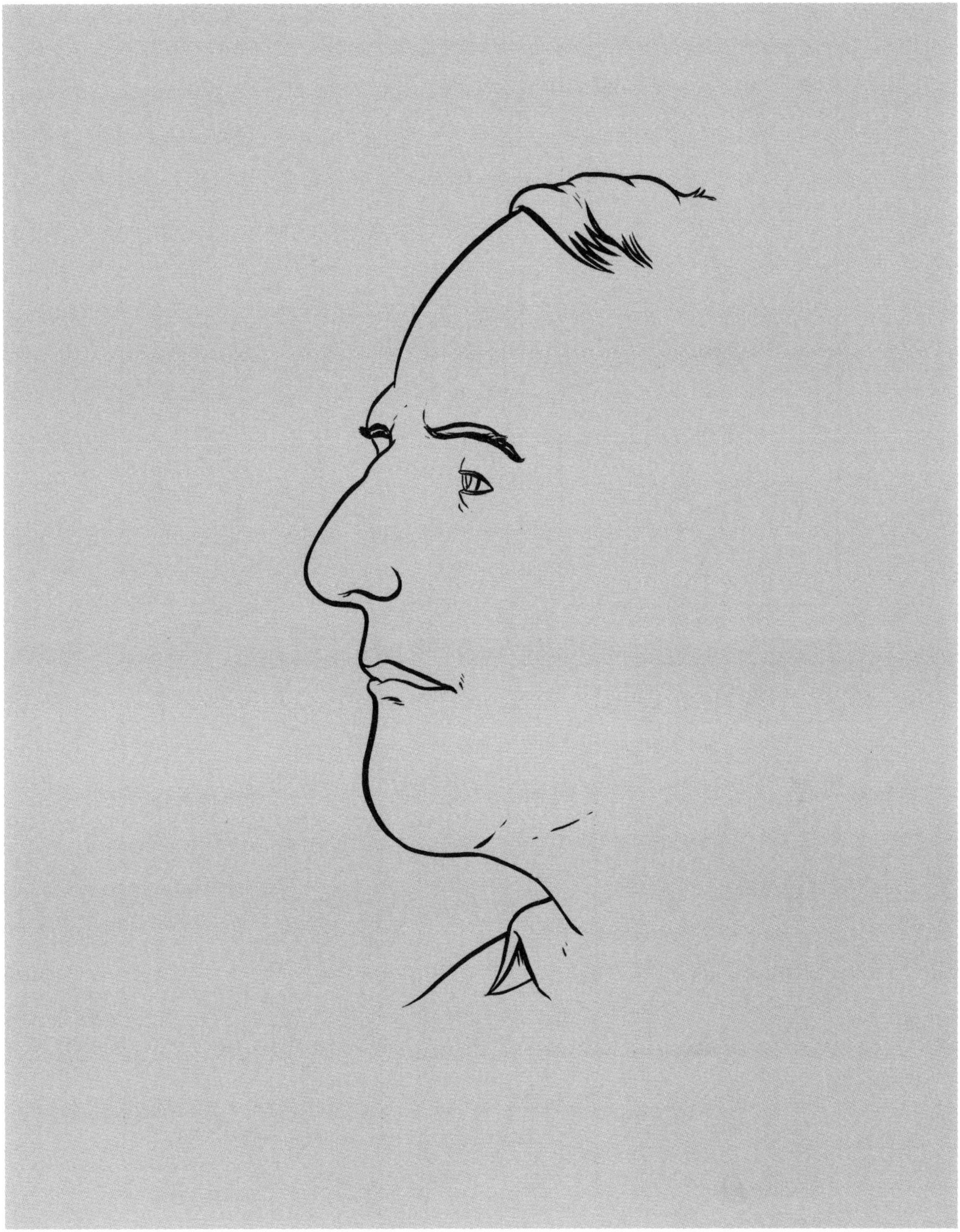

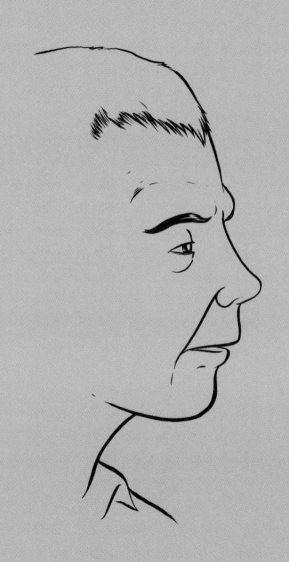

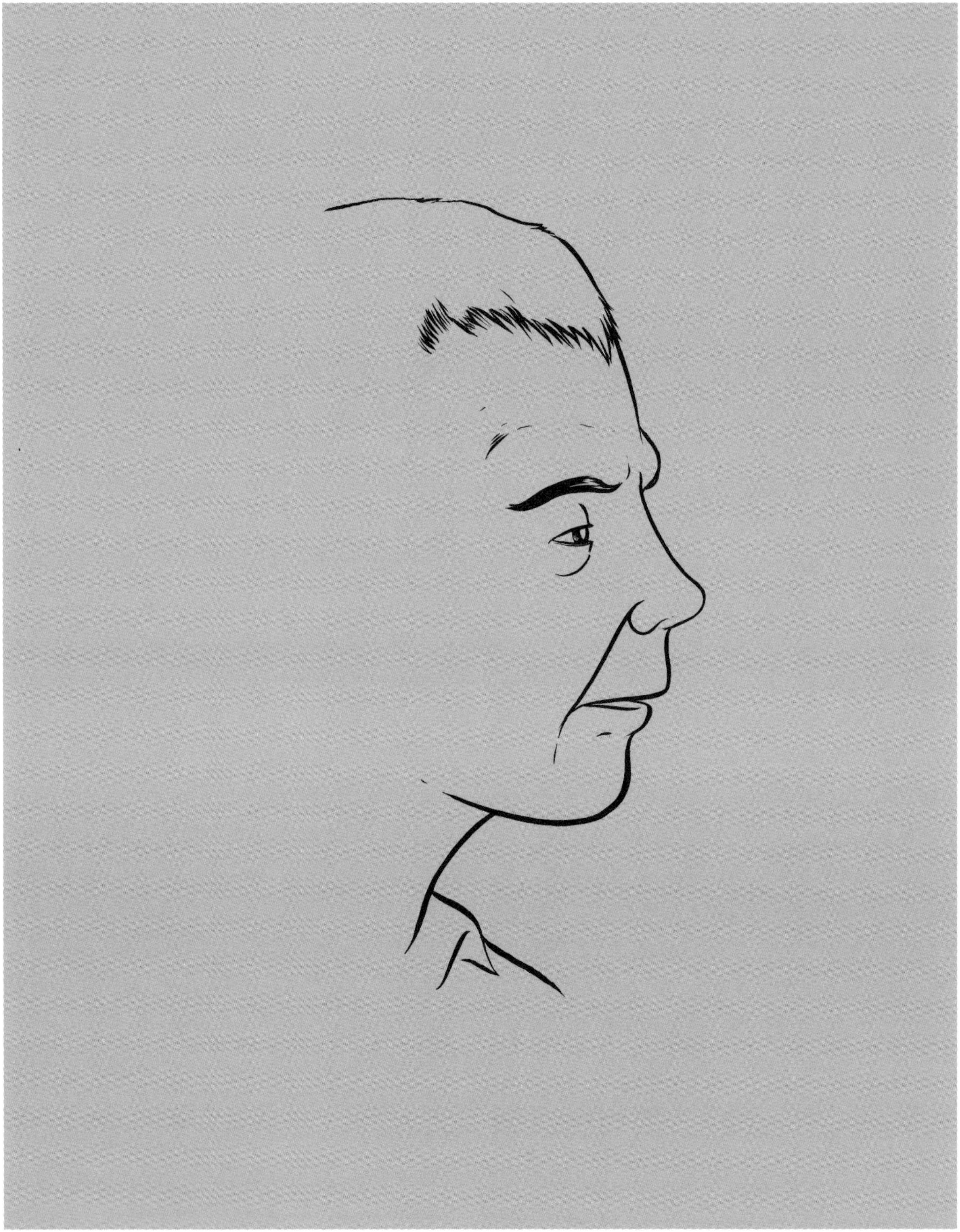

RETURN OF THE ELEPHANT

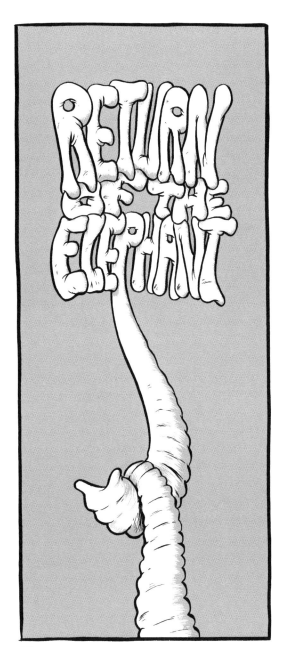

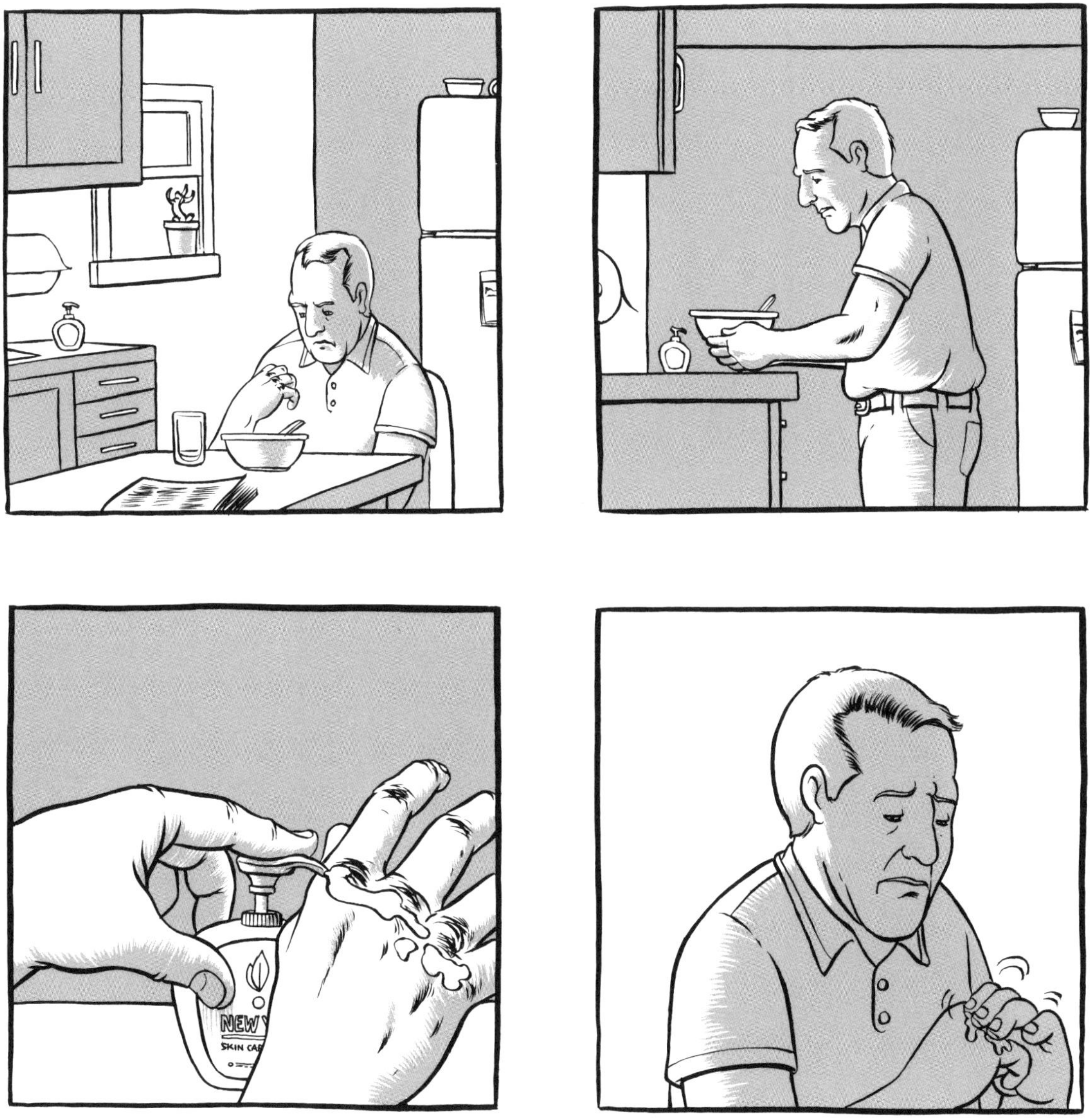
NEW
SKIN

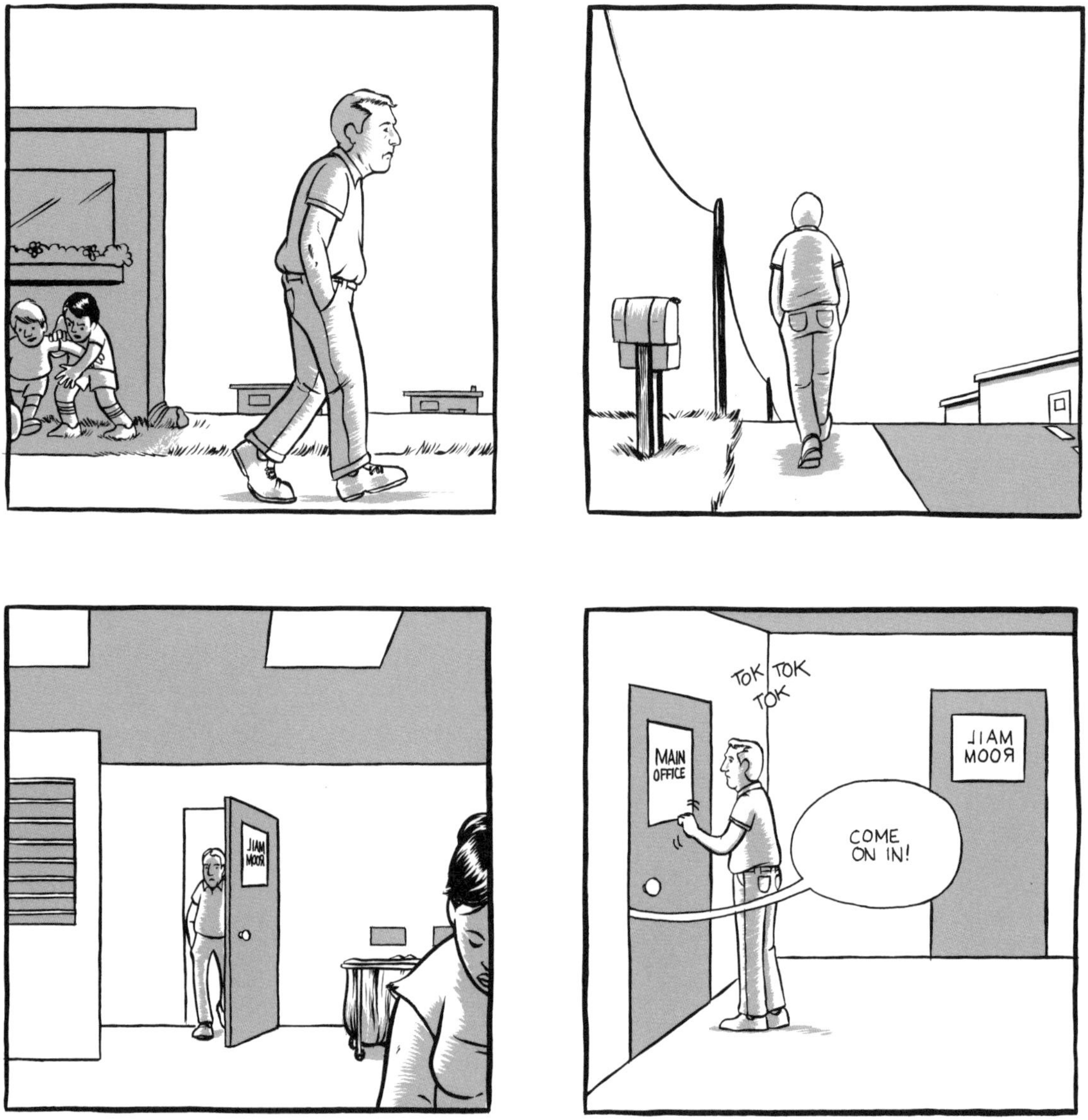
MAIL ROOM
TOK TOK TOK
MAIN OFFICE
MAIL ROOM
COME ON IN!

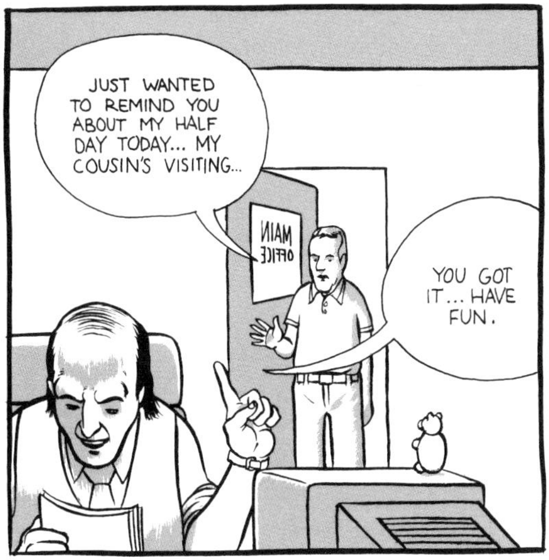
JUST WANTED TO REMIND YOU ABOUT MY HALF DAY TODAY... MY COUSIN'S VISITING...
MAIN OFFICE
YOU GOT IT... HAVE FUN.

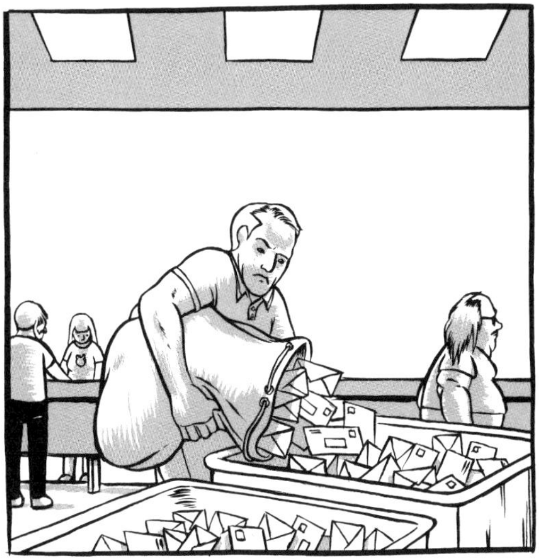

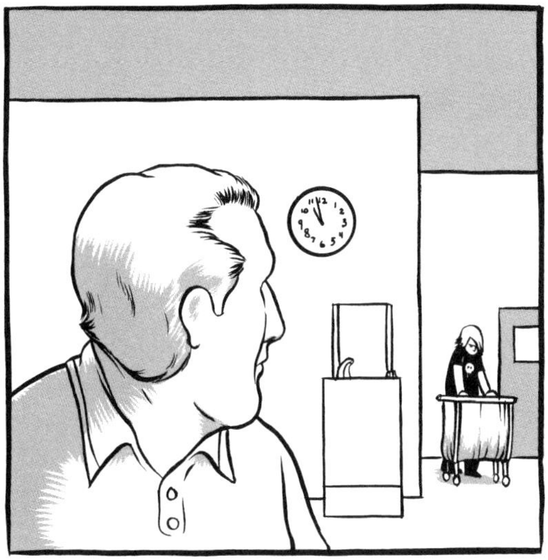

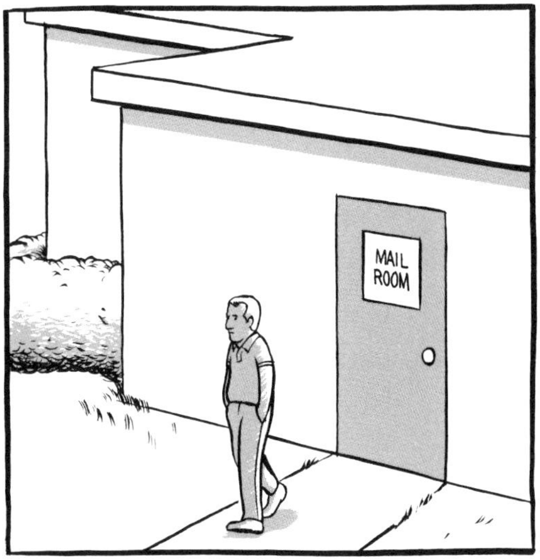
MAIL ROOM

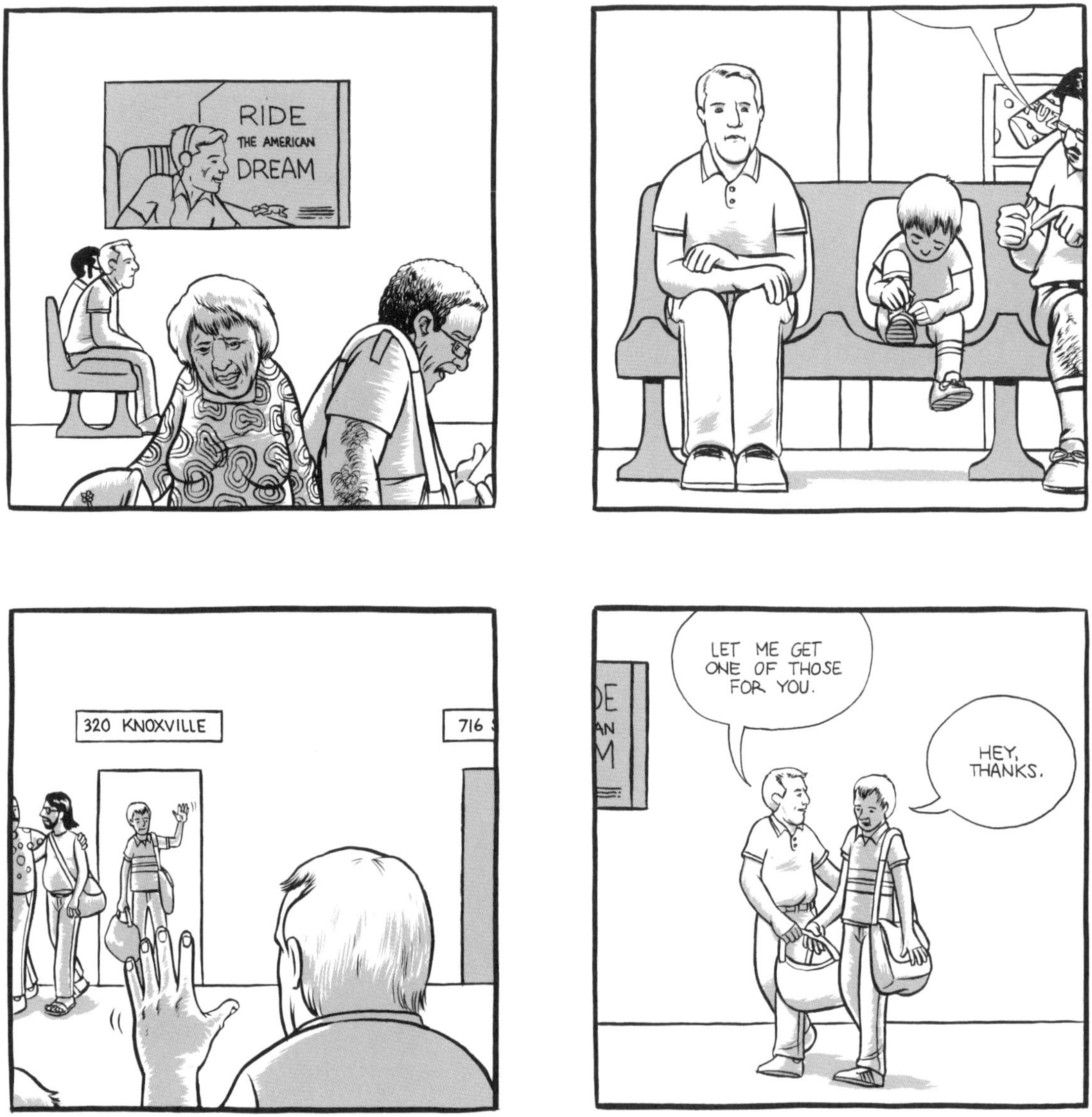
RIDE THE AMERICAN DREAM
320 KNOXVILLE
716
LET ME GET ONE OF THOSE FOR YOU.
HEY, THANKS.

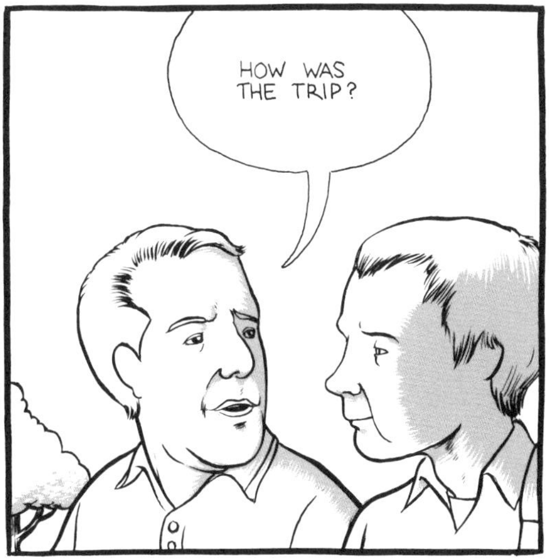
HOW WAS THE TRIP?

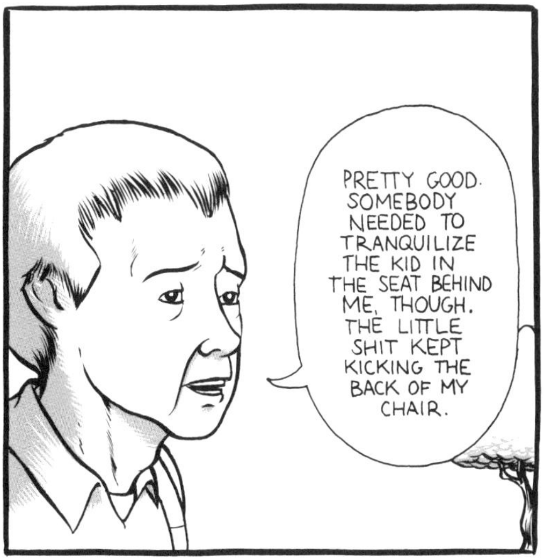
PRETTY GOOD. SOMEBODY NEEDED TO TRANQUILIZE THE KID IN THE SEAT BEHIND ME, THOUGH. THE LITTLE SHIT KEPT KICKING THE BACK OF MY CHAIR.

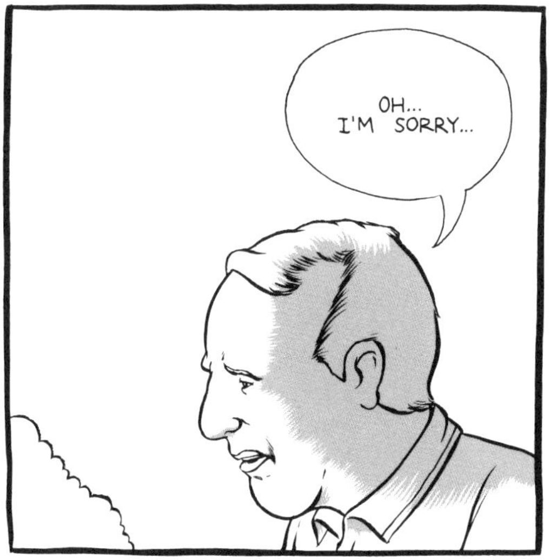
OH... I'M SORRY...

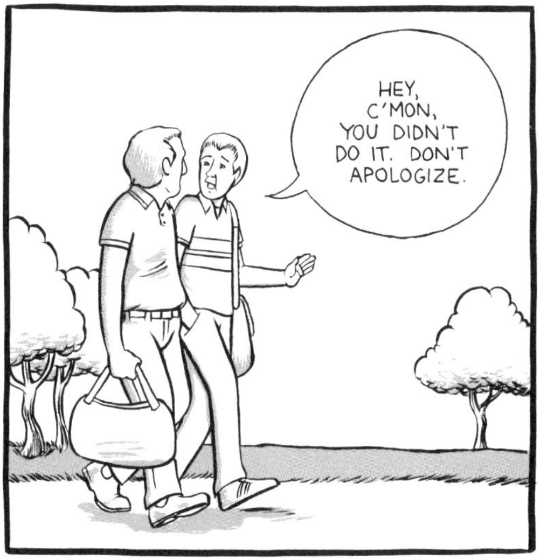
HEY, C'MON, YOU DIDN'T DO IT. DON'T APOLOGIZE.

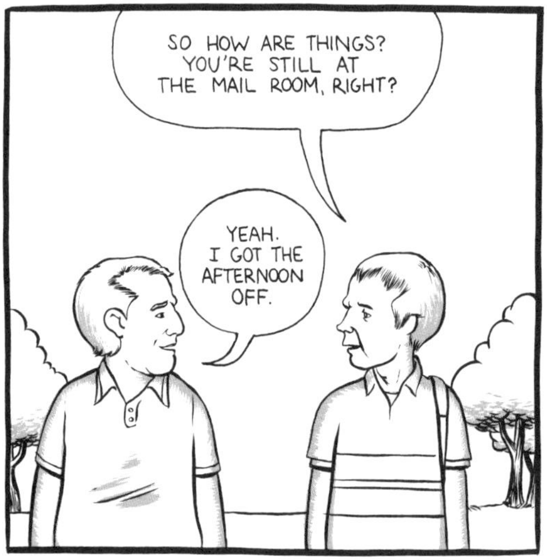
SO HOW ARE THINGS? YOU'RE STILL AT THE MAIL ROOM, RIGHT?
YEAH. I GOT THE AFTERNOON OFF.
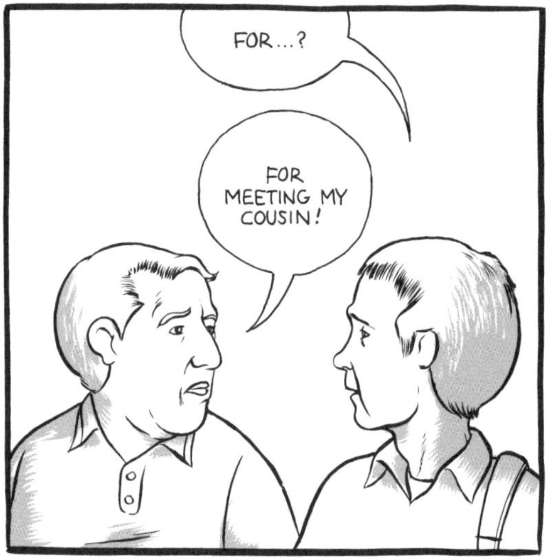
FOR...?
FOR MEETING MY COUSIN!
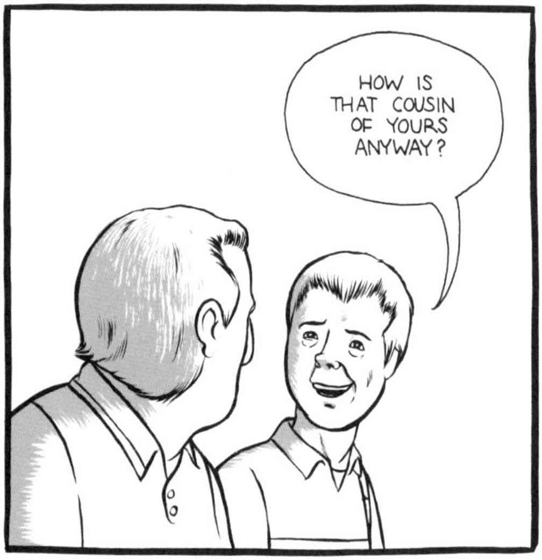
HOW IS THAT COUSIN OF YOURS ANYWAY?
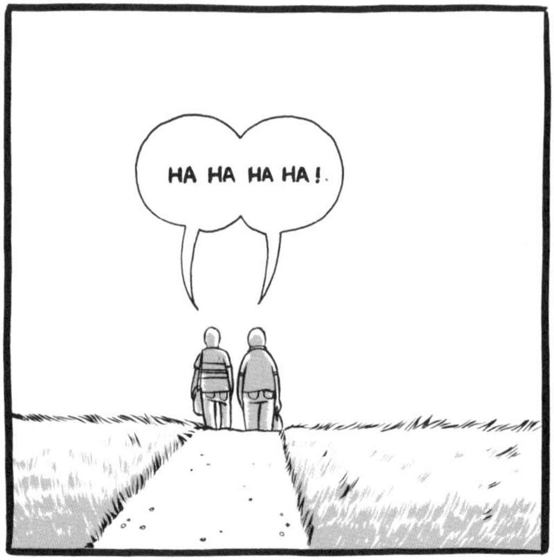
HA HA HA HA!

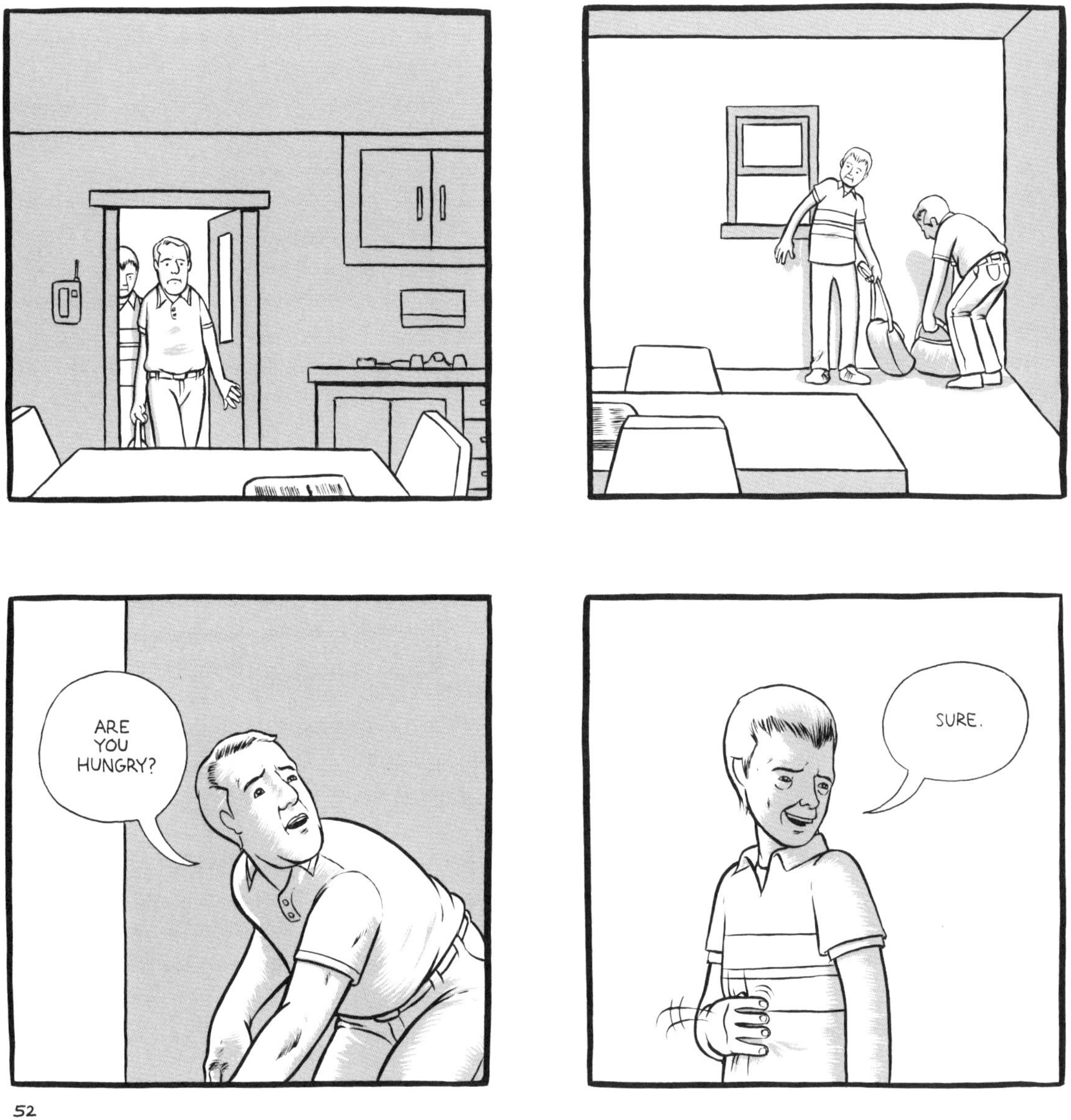
ARE YOU HUNGRY?
SURE.

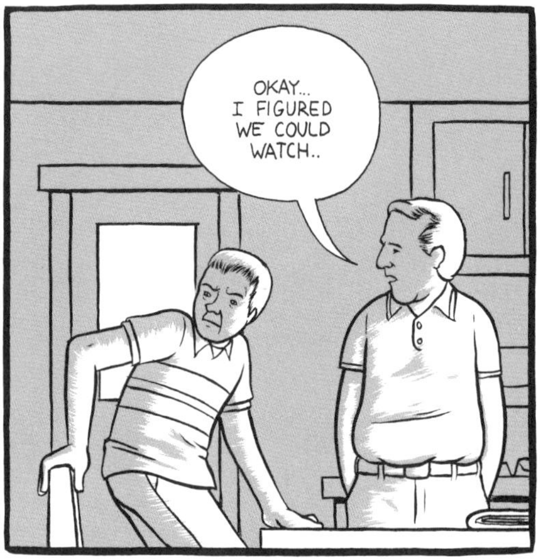
OKAY... I FIGURED WE COULD WATCH..
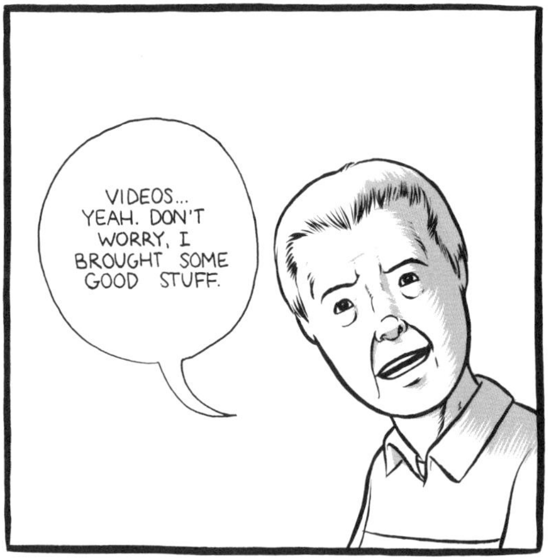
VIDEOS... YEAH. DON'T WORRY, I BROUGHT SOME GOOD STUFF.
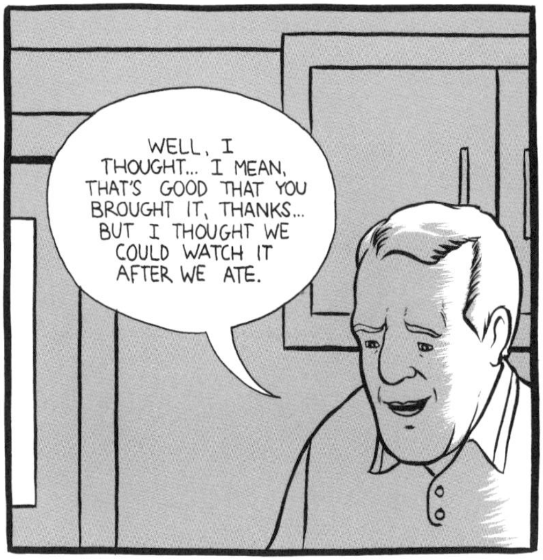
WELL, I THOUGHT... I MEAN, THAT'S GOOD THAT YOU BROUGHT IT, THANKS... BUT I THOUGHT WE COULD WATCH IT AFTER WE ATE.
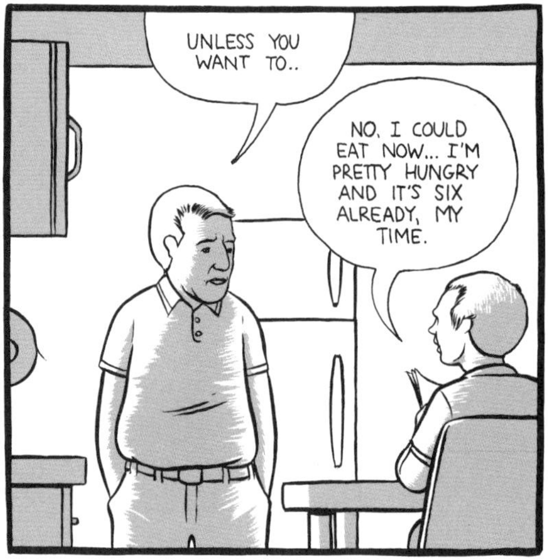
UNLESS YOU WANT TO..
NO, I COULD EAT NOW... I'M PRETTY HUNGRY AND IT'S SIX ALREADY, MY TIME.

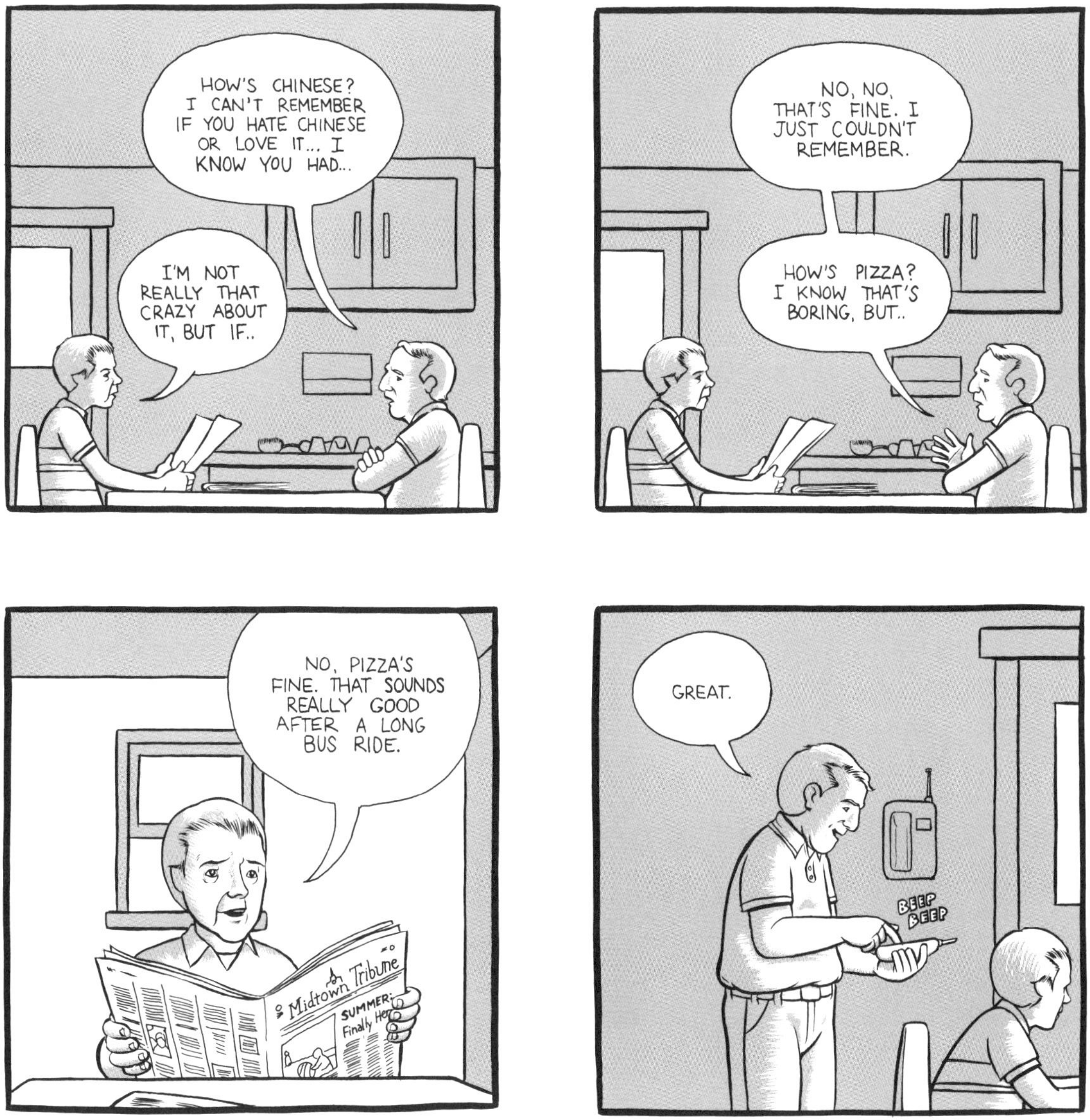
HOW'S CHINESE? I CAN'T REMEMBER IF YOU HATE CHINESE OR LOVE IT... I KNOW YOU HAD...
I'M NOT REALLY THAT CRAZY ABOUT IT, BUT IF..
NO, NO, THAT'S FINE. I JUST COULDN'T REMEMBER.
HOW'S PIZZA? I KNOW THAT'S BORING, BUT..
NO, PIZZA'S FINE. THAT SOUNDS REALLY GOOD AFTER A LONG BUS RIDE.
Midtown Tribune
SUMMER: Finally Here
GREAT.
BEEP BEEP

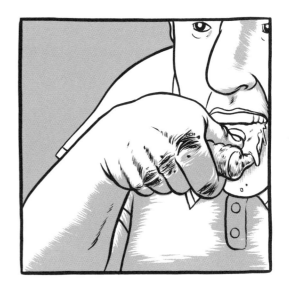

YOUR KNUCKLES ARE ALL CHAPPED AND DRIED OUT.

YEAH... EVERY WINTER... AND EACH YEAR IT TAKES LONGER TO HEAL.

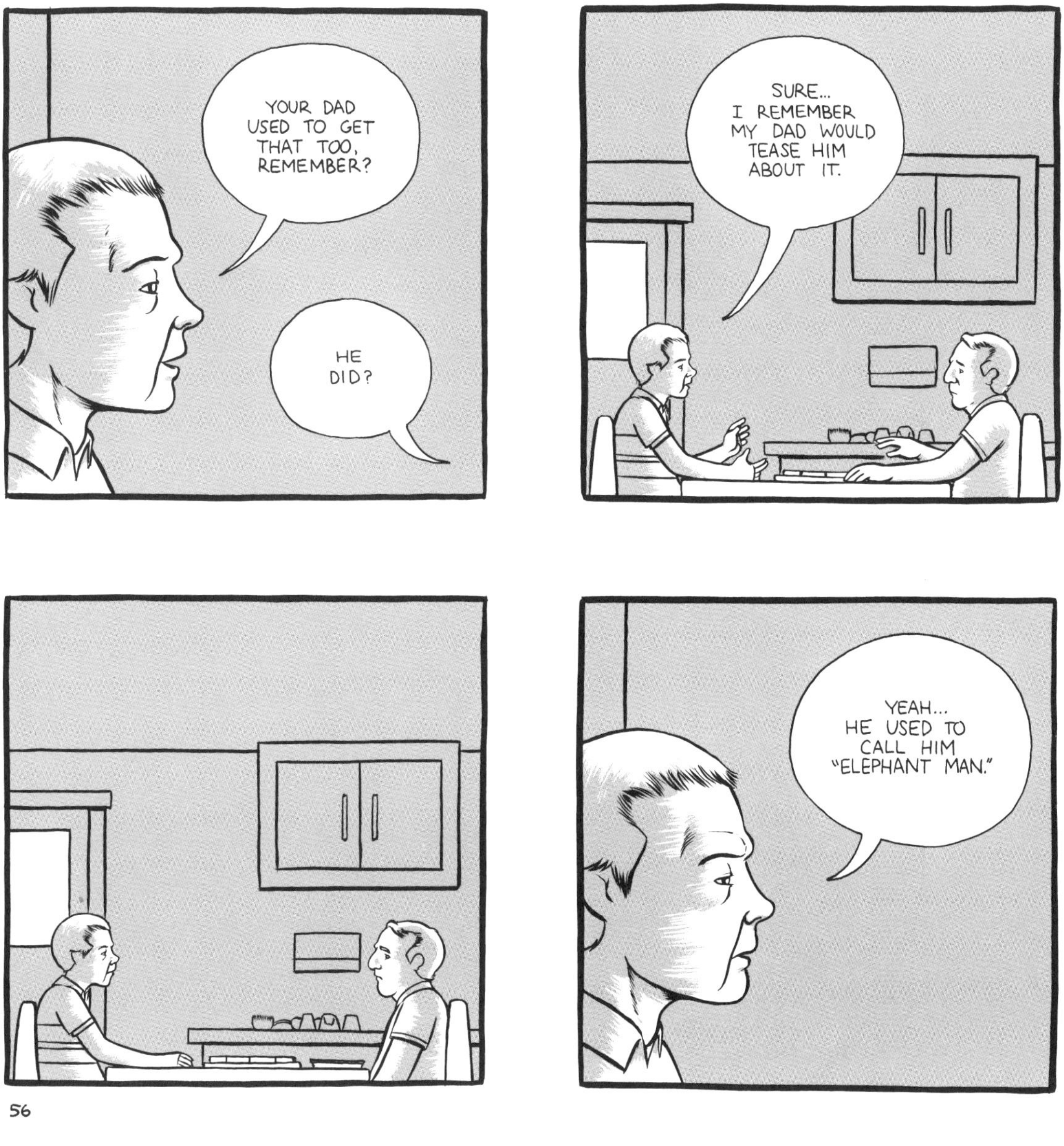
YOUR DAD USED TO GET THAT TOO, REMEMBER?
HE DID?
SURE... I REMEMBER MY DAD WOULD TEASE HIM ABOUT IT.
YEAH... HE USED TO CALL HIM "ELEPHANT MAN."

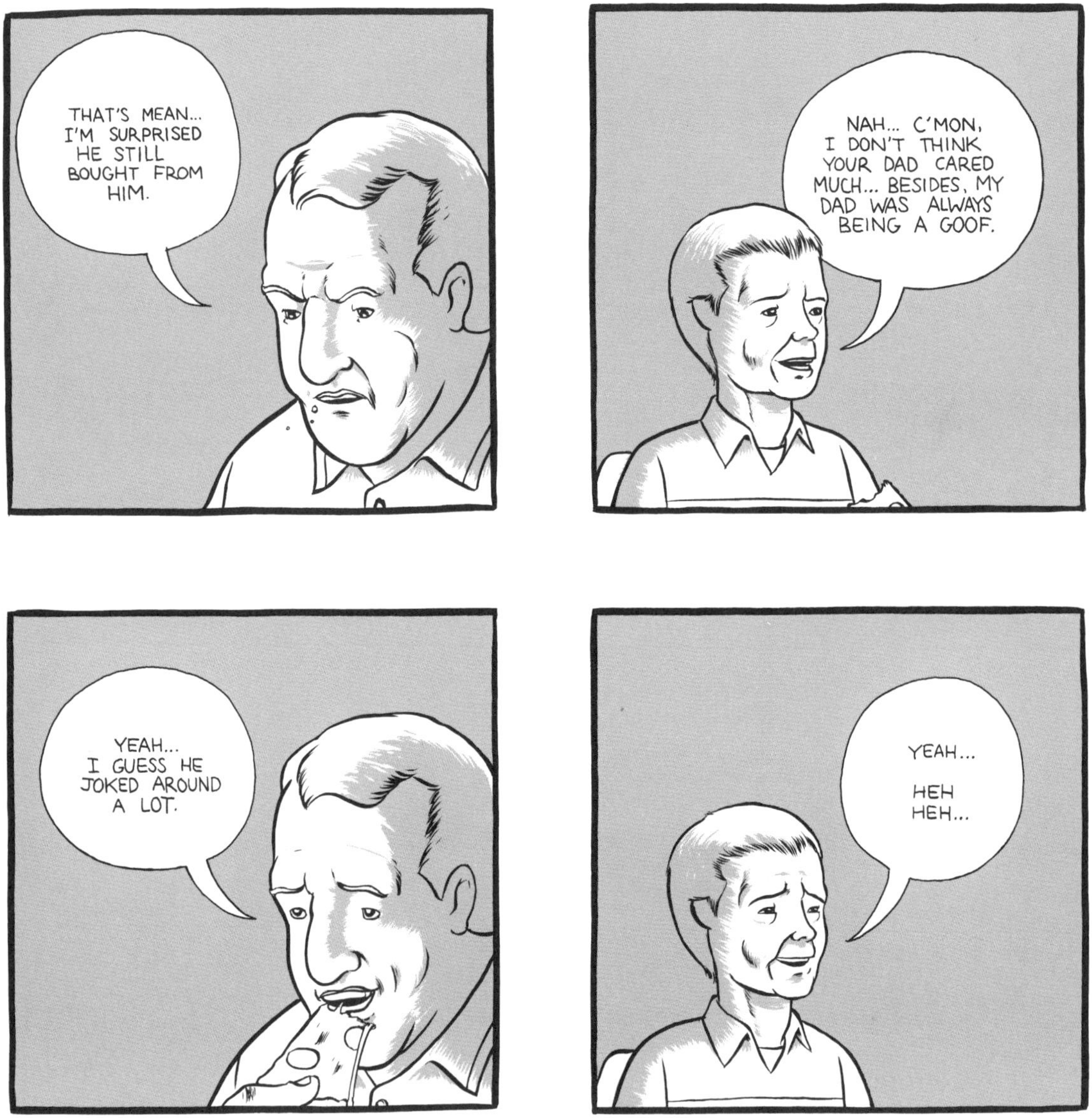
THAT'S MEAN... I'M SURPRISED HE STILL BOUGHT FROM HIM.
NAH... C'MON, I DON'T THINK YOUR DAD CARED MUCH... BESIDES, MY DAD WAS ALWAYS BEING A GOOF.
YEAH... I GUESS HE JOKED AROUND A LOT.
YEAH...
HEH HEH...

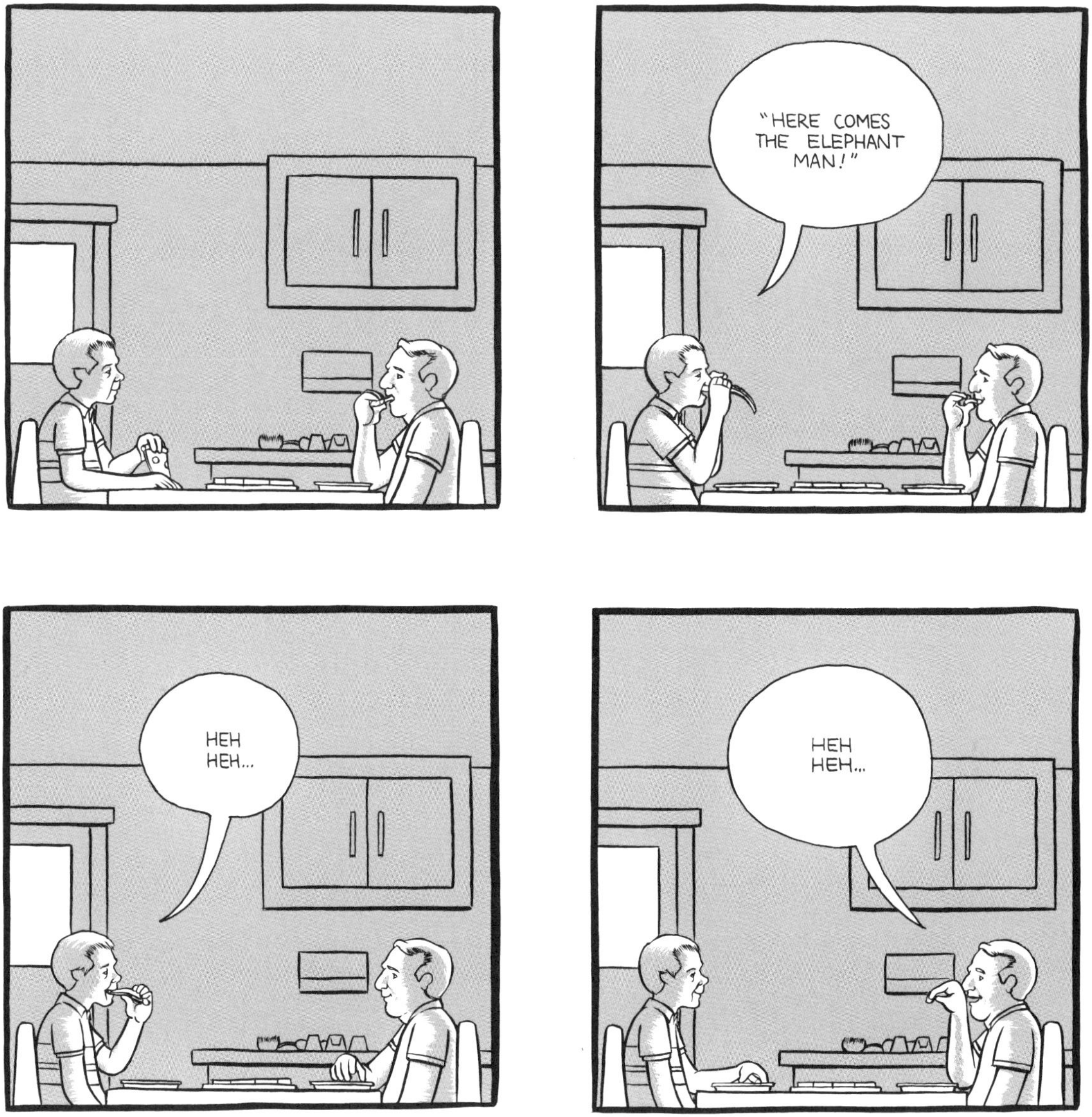
"HERE COMES THE ELEPHANT MAN!"
HEH HEH...
HEH HEH...

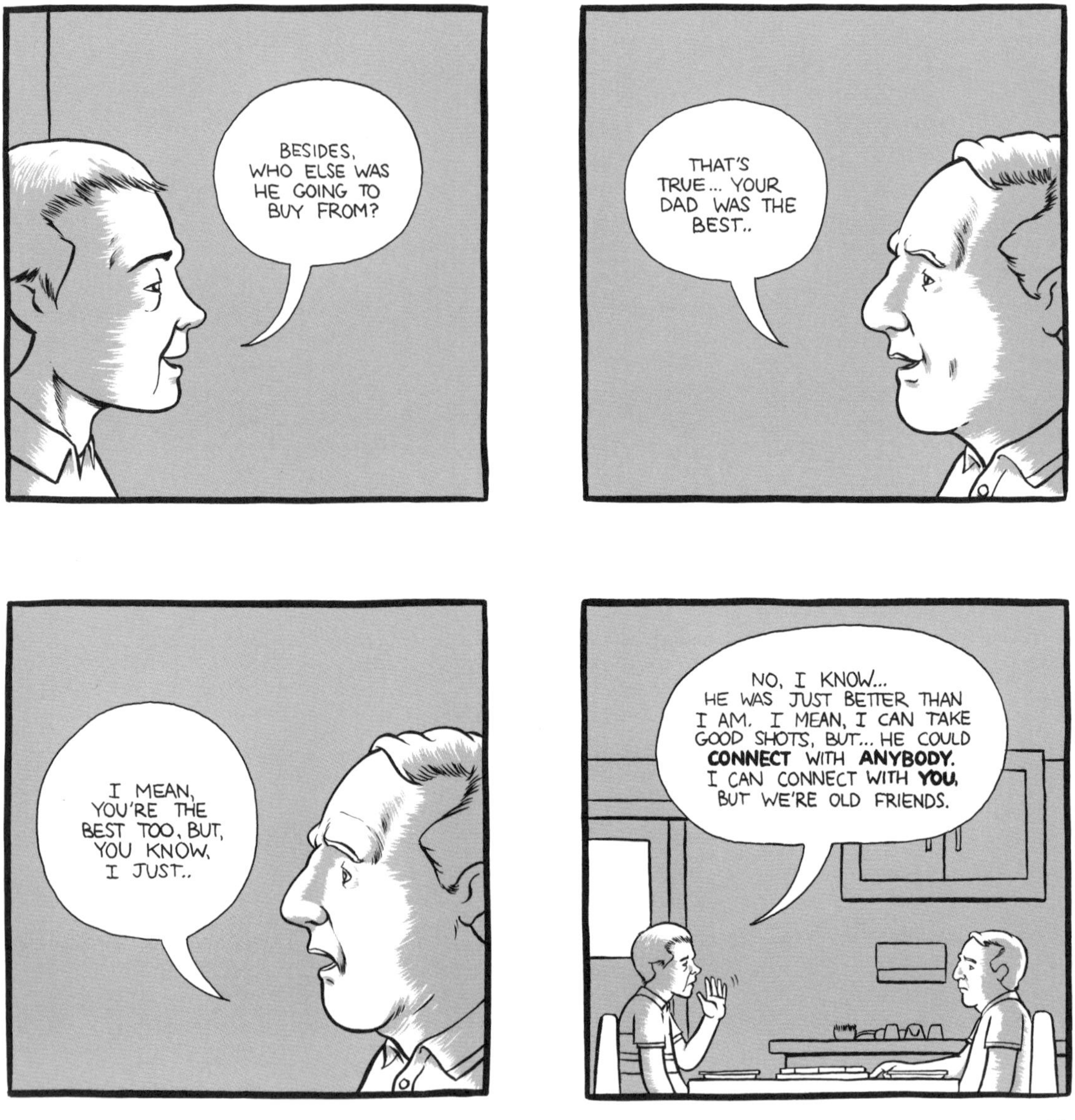
BESIDES, WHO ELSE WAS HE GOING TO BUY FROM?
THAT'S TRUE... YOUR DAD WAS THE BEST..
I MEAN, YOU'RE THE BEST TOO, BUT, YOU KNOW, I JUST..
NO, I KNOW... HE WAS JUST BETTER THAN I AM. I MEAN, I CAN TAKE GOOD SHOTS, BUT... HE COULD **CONNECT** WITH **ANYBODY.** I CAN CONNECT WITH **YOU,** BUT WE'RE OLD FRIENDS.

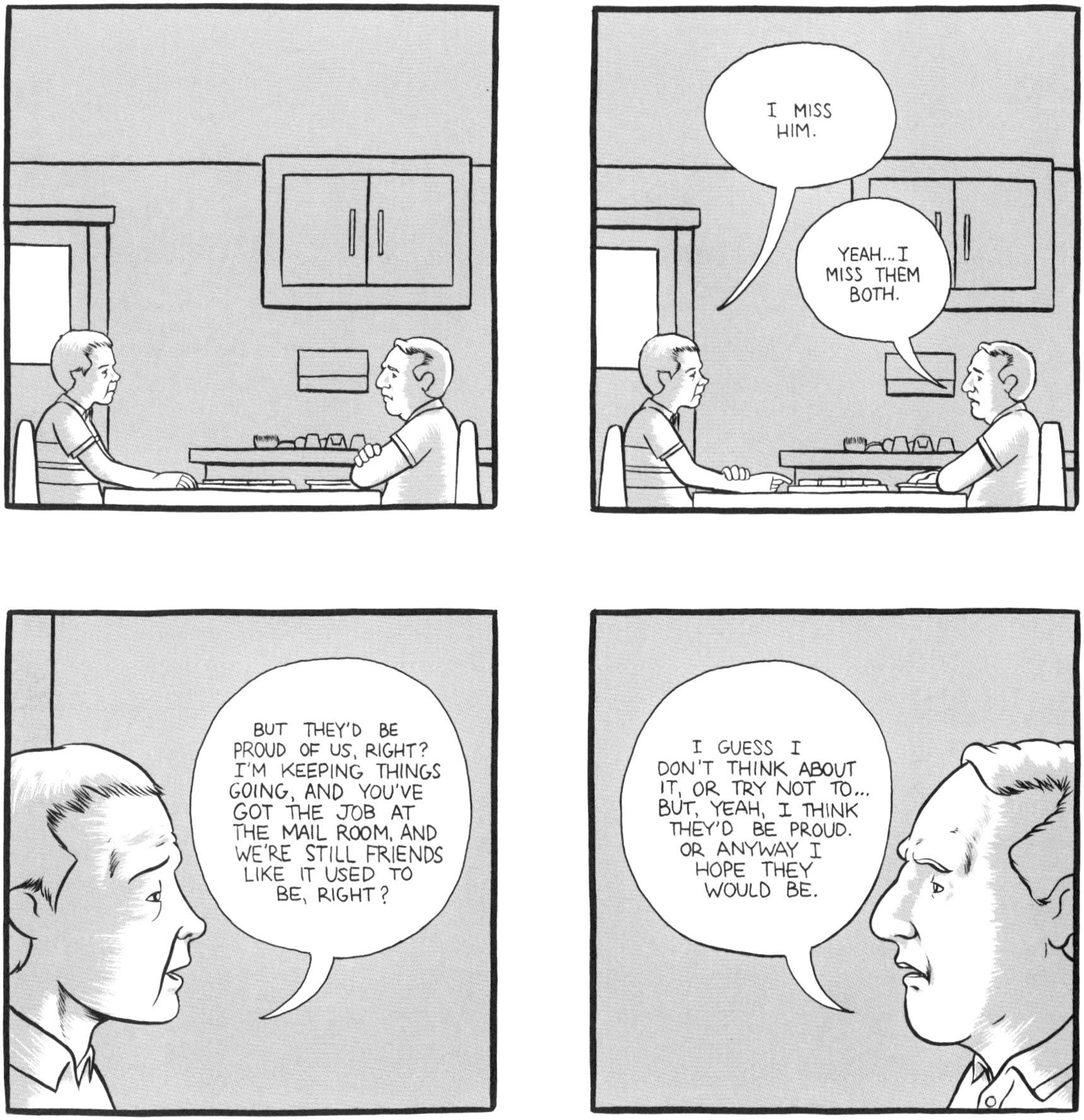
I MISS HIM.
YEAH... I MISS THEM BOTH.
BUT THEY'D BE PROUD OF US, RIGHT? I'M KEEPING THINGS GOING, AND YOU'VE GOT THE JOB AT THE MAIL ROOM, AND WE'RE STILL FRIENDS LIKE IT USED TO BE, RIGHT?
I GUESS I DON'T THINK ABOUT IT, OR TRY NOT TO... BUT, YEAH, I THINK THEY'D BE PROUD. OR ANYWAY I HOPE THEY WOULD BE.

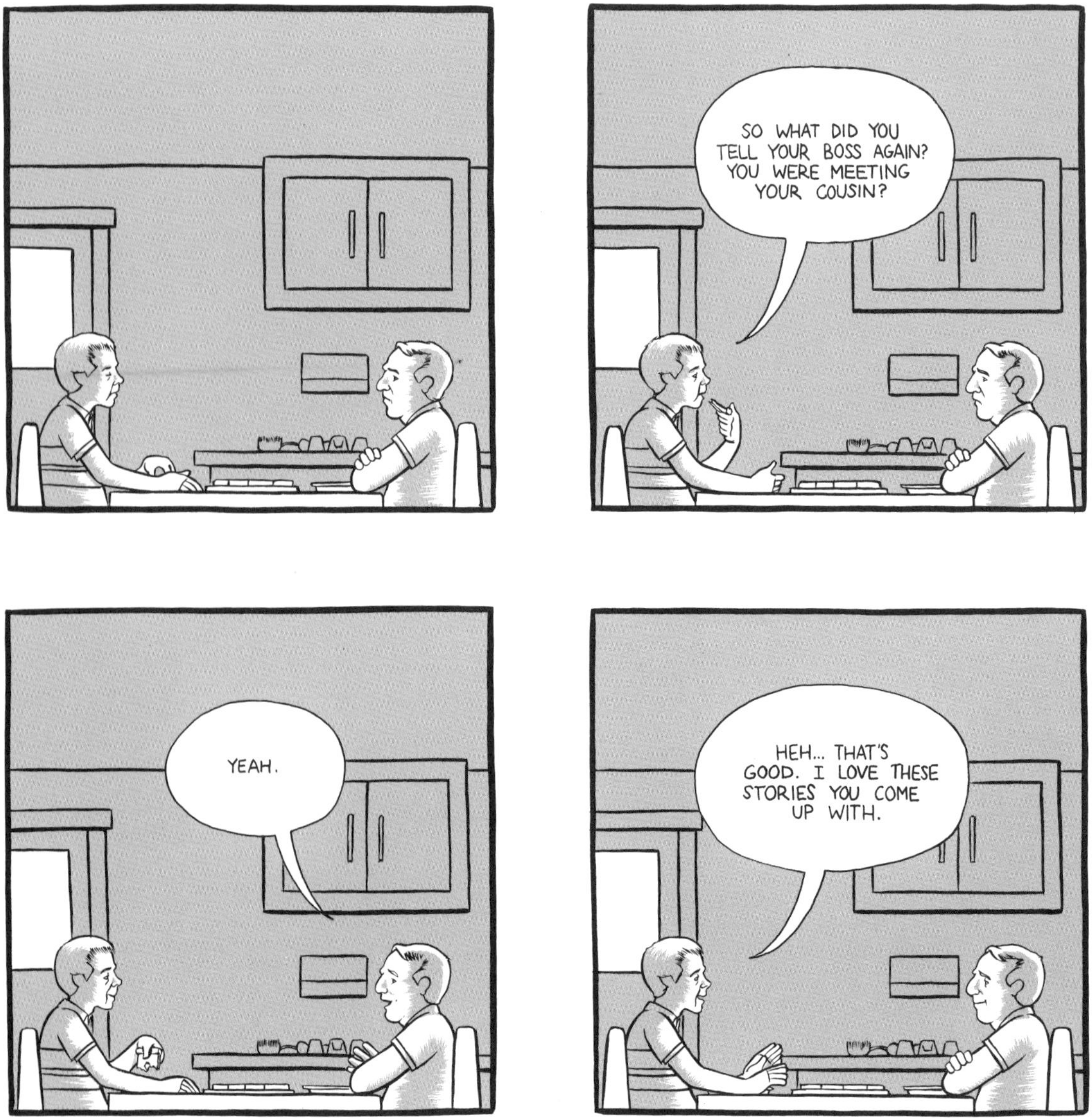
SO WHAT DID YOU TELL YOUR BOSS AGAIN? YOU WERE MEETING YOUR COUSIN?
YEAH.
HEH... THAT'S GOOD. I LOVE THESE STORIES YOU COME UP WITH.

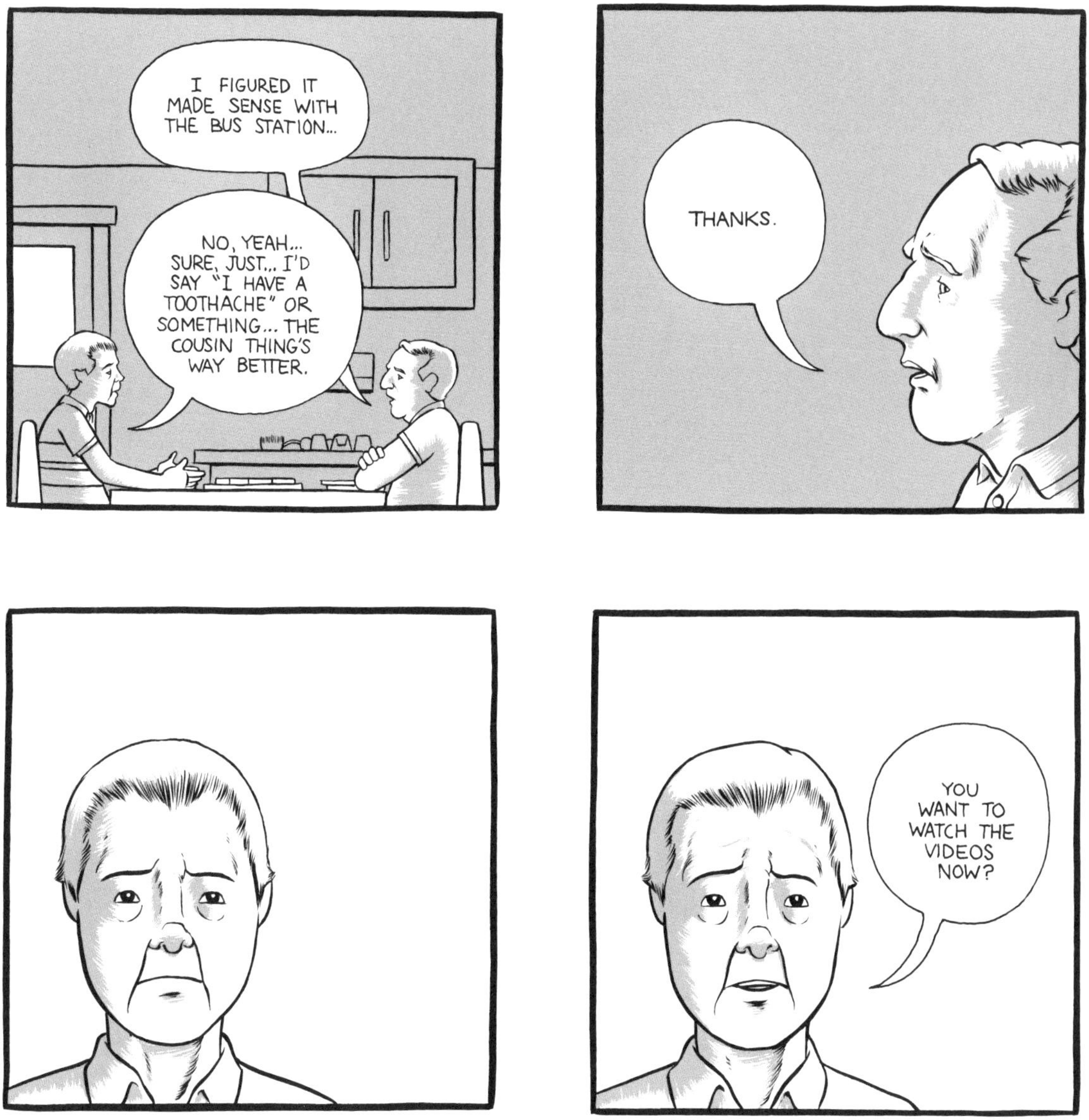
I FIGURED IT MADE SENSE WITH THE BUS STATION...
NO, YEAH... SURE, JUST... I'D SAY "I HAVE A TOOTHACHE" OR SOMETHING... THE COUSIN THING'S WAY BETTER.
THANKS.
YOU WANT TO WATCH THE VIDEOS NOW?

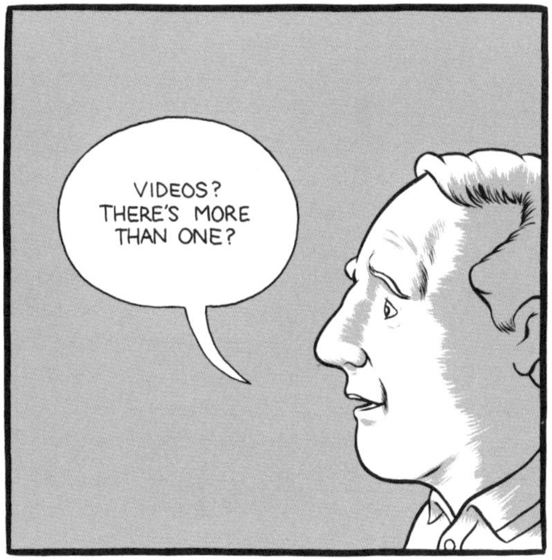
VIDEOS? THERE'S MORE THAN ONE?
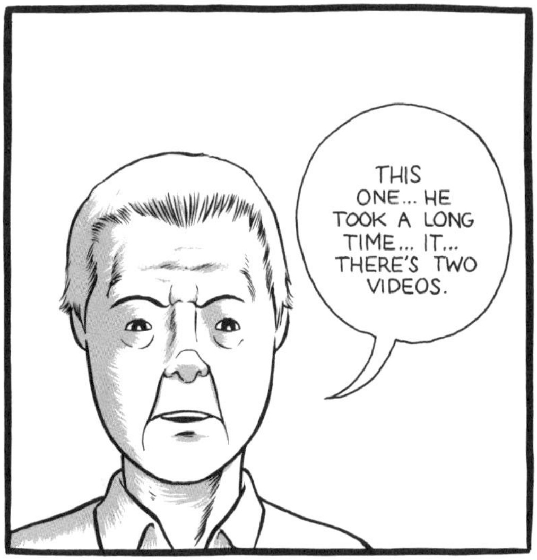
THIS ONE... HE TOOK A LONG TIME... IT... THERE'S TWO VIDEOS.
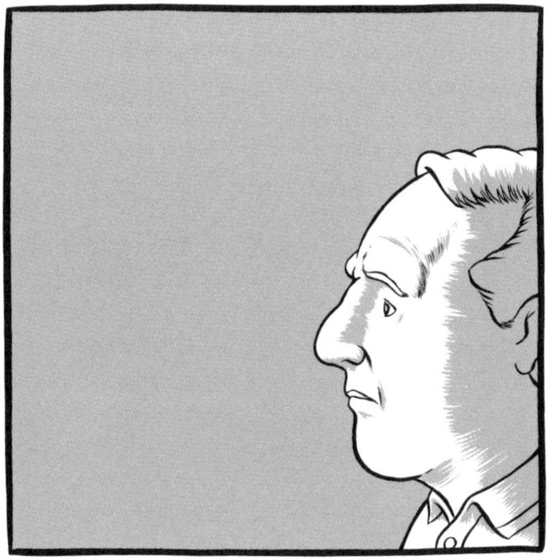
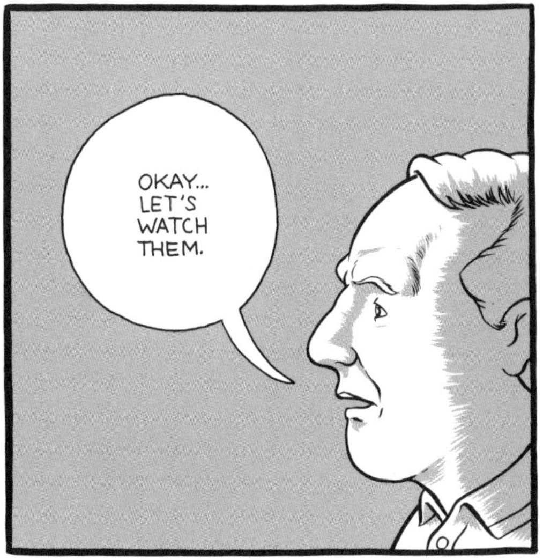
OKAY... LET'S WATCH THEM.

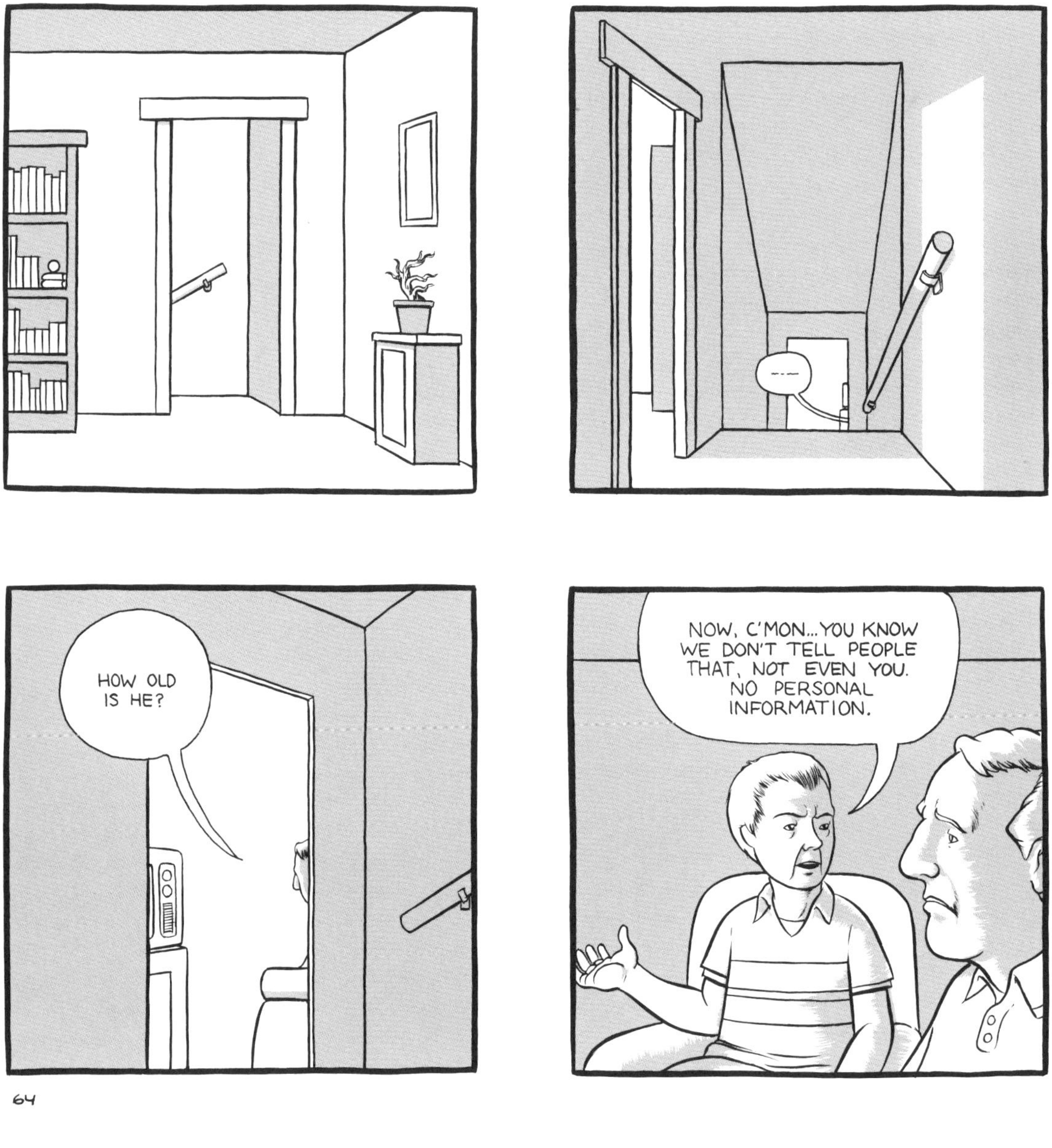
HOW OLD IS HE?
NOW, C'MON...YOU KNOW WE DON'T TELL PEOPLE THAT, NOT EVEN YOU. NO PERSONAL INFORMATION.

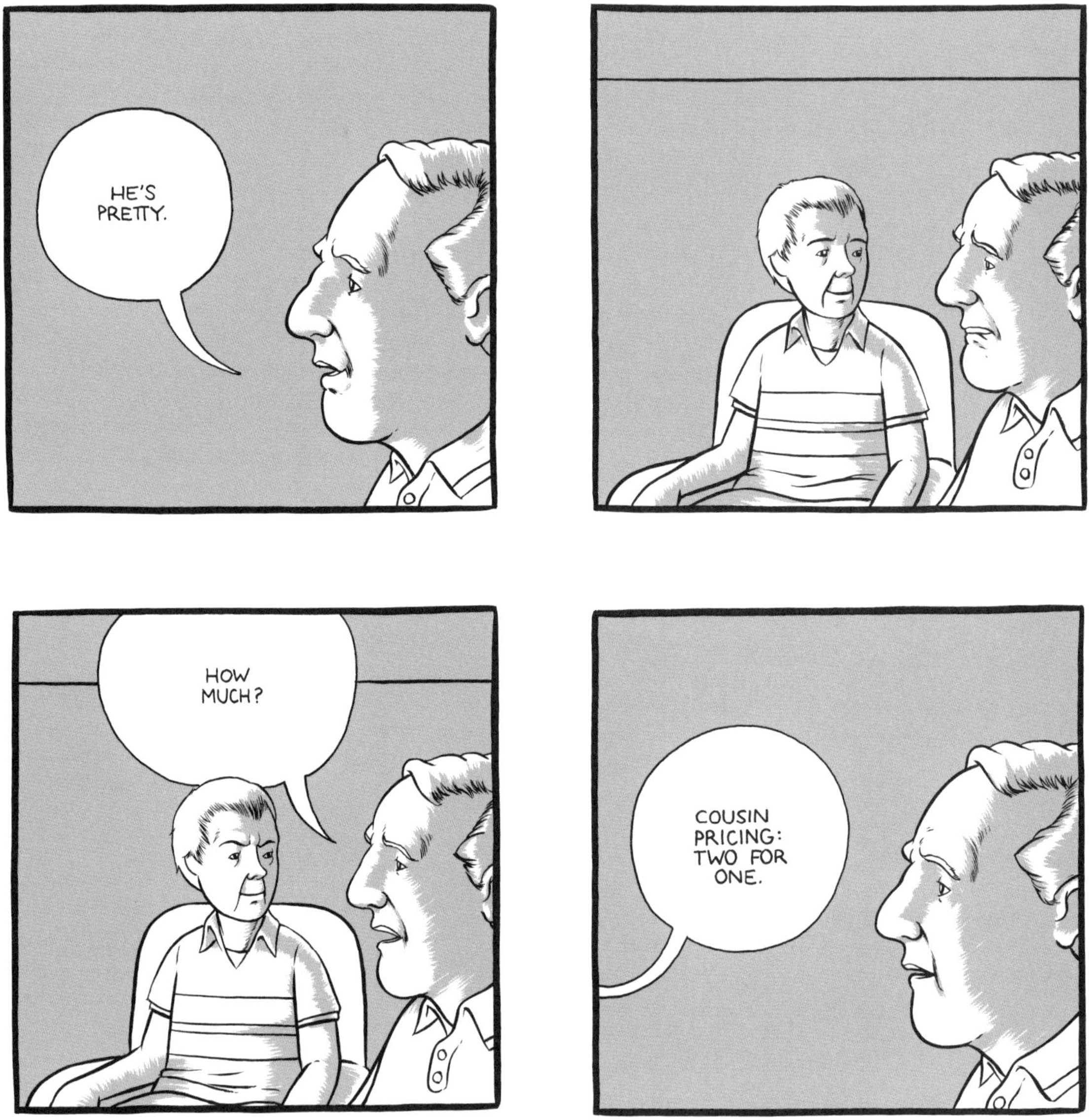
HE'S PRETTY.
HOW MUCH?
COUSIN PRICING: TWO FOR ONE.

THAAAAT'S IT...

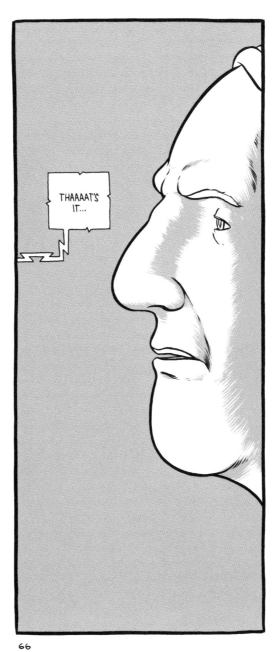

OKAY.

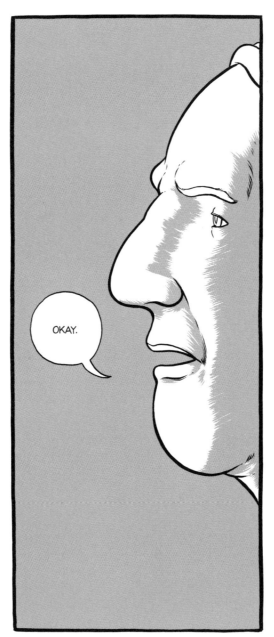

ABOUT
THE AUTHOR

PAUL HORNSCHEMEIER WAS BORN IN CINCINNATI IN THE FALL OF 1977. HE WAS REARED, ALONG WITH HIS TWO SISTERS, IN GEORGETOWN, A PREDOMINANTLY AGRICULTURE-BASED VILLAGE IN SOUTHERN OHIO. IN 1996, HE LEFT HIS HOMETOWN FOR COLLEGE IN COLUMBUS. THERE HE BEGAN HIS EXPERIMENTAL SERIES "SEQUENTIAL," WHICH RAN SEVEN ISSUES, EACH VOLUME LARGER THAN ITS PREDECESSOR. AFTER FOUR YEARS OF STUDY IN COGNITIVE PSYCHOLOGY AND PHILOSOPHY OF SCIENCE AND MIND, HE RECEIVED HIS DEGREE IN PHILOSOPHY. HE THEN MOVED TO CHICAGO WHERE HE CURRENTLY RESIDES AND WORKS ON HIS IGNATZ, HARVEY, AND EISNER AWARD NOMINATED BOOKS —GROUPED BENEATH THE BANNER "FORLORN FUNNIES"— ALONG WITH SUNDRY WRITING, MUSIC, AND ILLUSTRATION WORK.

OTHER BOOKS
BY PAUL HORNSCHEMEIER

MOTHER, COME HOME
DARK HORSE BOOKS

THE COLLECTED SEQUENTIAL
ADHOUSE BOOKS

THE THREE PARADOXES
FANTAGRAPHICS BOOKS

TO CONTACT

PLEASE VISIT

WWW.FORLORNFUNNIES.COM

OR E-MAIL
FEEDBACK@SEQUENTIALCOMICS.COM

ABOUT
THE AUTHOR

PAUL HORNSCHEMEIER WAS BORN IN CINCINNATI IN THE LATE SEVENTIES, A TIME OF UNNATURAL FABRICS AND BRIGHTLY STRIPED SOCKS. HE GREW UP IN GEORGETOWN, OHIO, A TOWN WHOSE SCHOOL MASCOT IS A "G-MAN," ORIGINALLY DEPICTED AS A DIRECT PLAGIARIZATION OF DICK TRACY, THEN LATER A VANILLA, BULBOUS IMP DUBBED "HUSTLING GEORGE" WITH THE LETTER "G" AS HIS BODY. IN 1996, AMID INCREASING MEMORY LOSS AND WONTON MISTREATMENT OF FRIENDS AND HYGIENE, HE ATTENDED COLLEGE, MANAGING TO EMERGE, CONFUSED, DEGREE IN HAND. SOMEWHERE IN THERE HE STARTED PUBLISHING COMICS THAT HAD SCADS OF INDECIPHERABLE RAMBLINGS AND ARTSY BOO-HOOERY. HE NOW LIVES IN CHICAGO WITH A CAT. HE STILL MAKES COMICS WHEN NOT DOING OTHER THINGS THAT DETRACT SIGNIFICANTLY FROM MAKING COMICS.

THANKS

TO GARY GROTH, KIM THOMPSON, AND ERIC REYNOLDS FOR ALL THEIR WORK ON THIS COLLECTION. TO ED IRVIN, CHRIS PITZER, DIANA SCHUTZ, DAVID YOUNGBLOOD, HENRY OWINGS, AND THE STAFF AT THE CHICAGO READER FOR PUBLISHING THESE AND OTHER CARTOONS PREVIOUSLY. TO JULIANE GRAF FOR UNERRING ENCOURAGEMENT. TO ALL FRIENDS AND FAMILY FOR THEIR PATIENCE AND SUPPORT.

ARTWORK

FROM THIS AND OTHER BOOKS IS AVAILABLE FOR PURCHASE AT:

WWW. COMICARTCOLLECTIVE.COM
WWW. BEGUILING. COM

VISIT

WWW. THEHOLYCONSUMPTION.COM

FOR CARTOONS BY THE AUTHOR, JEFFREY BROWN, ANDERS NILSEN, AND JOHN HANKIEWICZ.

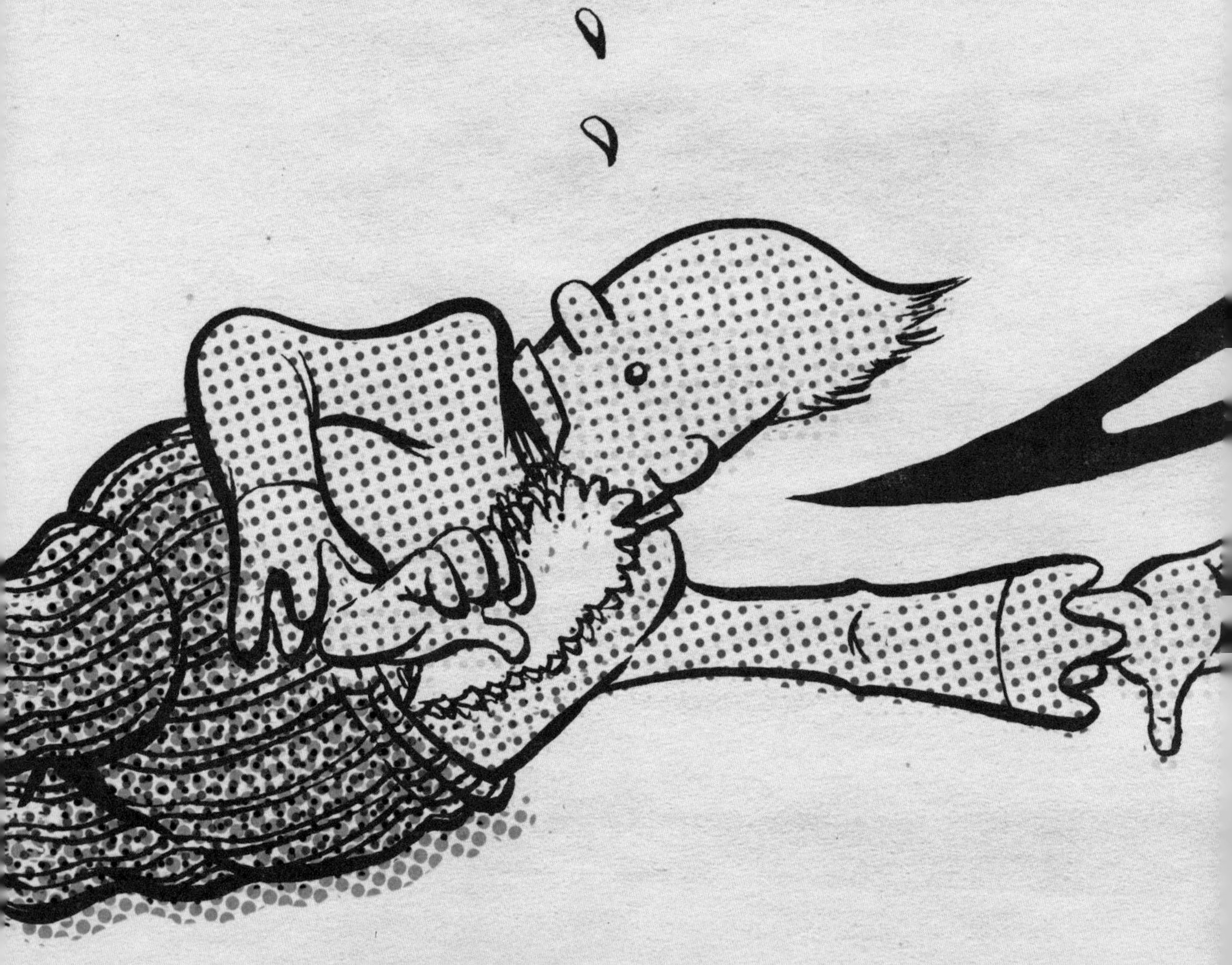